TASMAN SEA

SOUTH ISLAND

Tasman
Bay

D'Urville
Island

Nelson

Waiau

Christchurch

Ashburton

SOUTH PACIFIC

OCEAN

Otago Peninsula
Dunedin

Invercargill

STEWART ISLAND

NEW ZEALAND

NORTH
ISLAND

SOUTH
ISLAND

Chatham
Islands

Stewart
Island

The
Maori
Wars

The Maori Wars

THE BRITISH ARMY
IN NEW ZEALAND
1840 - 1872

by
TOM GIBSON

LEO COOPER · LONDON

First published in Great Britain 1974
by LEO COOPER LTD
196 Shaftesbury Avenue, London WC2H 8JL

Copyright © 1974 by Tom Gibson

ISBN 0 85052 133 5

Printed in Great Britain by
Clarke, Doble & Brendon Ltd.
Plymouth

CONTENTS

CONTENTS

ILLUSTRATIONS

*The illustrations are reproduced by kind permission of the following:
The Hocken library, University of Otago, Dunedin, Nos. 1, 2, 3, 6, 8,
10, 13, 16, 20, 21, and 22; The Auckland Institute and Museum, Nos.
4, 5, 9, 14, 15, and 17; The Mansell Collection, Nos. 7, 11, 12 and 18;
and the National Portrait Gallery, No. 19.*

ACKNOWLEDGEMENTS

The Author and Publishers wish to express their gratitude to Colonel B. M. Poananga OBE, New Zealand Army, who kindly read the whole typescript and made many valuable comments, especially about Maori lore; to Mr D. W. King OBE, FLA, Chief Librarian of the Ministry of Defence Library (Central and Army) and his Staff who were very patient and helpful with prolonged loans of books and provision of photostated material to a Regular soldier-author then serving outside the United Kingdom; to Miss Rose B. Coombs, Head of the Printed Book Section, Imperial War Museum, Mr R. A. Barber, Defence Librarian, and Captain (Retd.) G. T. Stagg, both of the Ministry of Defence, Wellington, for their full and informative assistance concerning Victoria Cross and New Zealand Cross awards during the Maori Wars; to Lieutenant-Colonel R. E. Cole-Mackintosh, Intelligence Corps, an authority on medals who also supplied particular material about the rare New Zealand Cross; to Major David Jenkinson R.A. and 94 (New Zealand) Medium Battery, Royal Artillery, for use of the Battery historical records; and also to others who kindly contributed with material: Doctor M. J. McNamara, Second Secretary, New Zealand Embassy, Bonn, Major P. G. E. Hill, Regimental Headquarters, The Queen's Regiment (Queen's Surreys Office), Kingston-on-Thames, and James E. R. Macmillan F.S.S. Scotland, Curator, The Black Watch Museum, Perth, Scotland.

MAPS

The Maps are based on those in the Encyclopaedia of New Zealand, Volume II; the author and publishers are grateful to the Government Printer and the Department of Lands and Survey, New Zealand, for permission to copy them. The endpapers and tribal map were drawn by Patrick Leeson.

The campaign against Hone Heke
and Kawiti, Bay of Islands, 1845–46

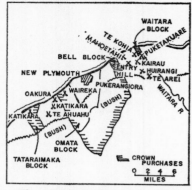

The Tataraimaka and Waitara
Blocks, 1860

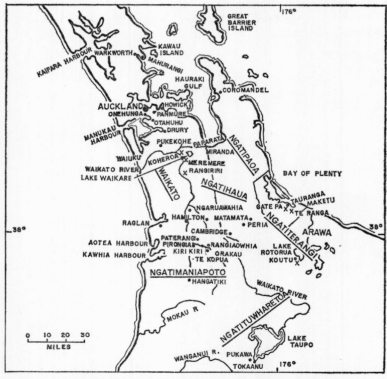

The Waikato and Tauranga Campaigns, 1863–64

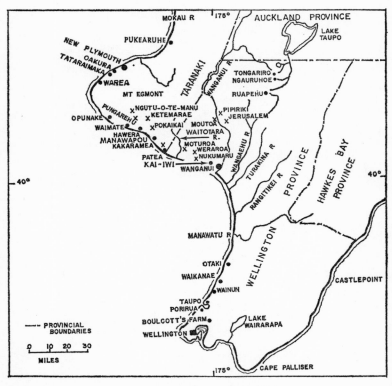

Wanganui and Taranaki, 1865–66

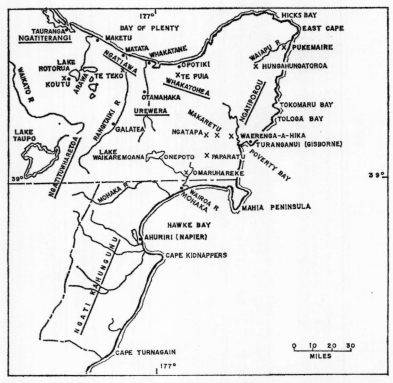

The campaign against the Hauhaus and Te Kooti on the east coast, 1865–70

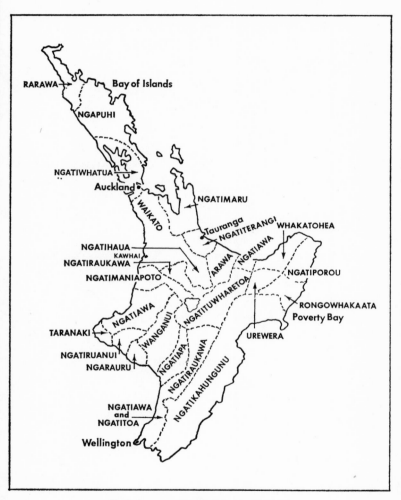

Tribal areas, North Island, 1845–70

GLOSSARY OF COMMON MAORI TERMS

Haka: dance.
Hapu: sub-tribe.
Kainga: unfortified or open village.
Korero: discussion, speech-making.
Kumara: sweet potato.
Kupapa: friendly Maori enlisted by the Government.
Mana: prestige, power, authority.
Mere: a fashioned flat stone club weapon.
Nga: plural of the definite article.
Ngati: prefix denoting the tribe.
Ope: a large war party or army.
Pa: fort.
Pakeha: a European (literally, a stranger or foreigner).
Rangatira: Chief or noble.
Taiaha: long handled war club or quarter staff.
Tapu: declared sacred or under divine protection.
Taua: war party.
Te: singular form of the definite article.
Tohunga: native priest.
Utu: revenge.
Whare: house.

CHAPTER 1

The Land of the Long White Cloud

As the renowned chief of the Ngapuhi tribe, Hongi Hika, lay dying at Hokianga in 1828, he delivered a fateful last message: 'Children, and you, my old comrades, be brave and strong in your country's cause. Let not the land of your ancestors pass into the hands of the *Pakeha*. Behold! I have spoken.'

The old warrior then drew his mat across his face 'and passed through the gates of Ruakipouri—the gates that inexorably open only one way.' Before those final, sombre words, he had been exhorting the weeping assemblage to help the missionaries and even be friendly to the settlers, but to resist the soldiers, 'the men who wear red garments, the men who neither reap nor sow'.

Hongi's warning was to be only too visionary. His death marked the end of an epoch, the transition from the old, wild, free-and-easy way of life, where the writ of tribal warlords and the commercial dealings of European freebooters were the sole arbiters of local society, to an era when Government authority appeared and began inserting the many tentacles of its regulations.

Twelve years later, when Captain William Hobson RN landed at the settlement of Kororareka, in the Bay of Islands, North Island, on 30 January, 1840, amid a salute of eleven guns from HMS *Herald*, the spectre of the old chieftain's fear was shaping into reality. Hobson, as Lieutenant-Governor designate of the prospective colony of New Zealand under the tutelage of distant New South Wales, was charged with negotiating a treaty with the Maori chiefs for the cession of their authority to Queen Victoria. But it was an unenthusiastic Government of Her Majesty that acquiesced, under some pressure, to making this ambiguous offer, for Britain was suffering from a surfeit of overseas acquisitions and the prospect of yet another colony to administer, finance and protect raised little exhilaration in most Whitehall breasts. It was the vitality and determination of the seafarer, the merchant adventurer, the pioneer settler and the missionary who pulled along timid Imperial power to decision.

The early stimulus in England for colonization of the new discovery in the South-West Pacific came from the publication in 1777 of Captain James Cook's Journal after his second voyage in 1773. The great seaman and navigator reported that the land was fair for settlement as European-type crops would flourish, with timber and flax as obvious native exports, and he added that the indigenous people, though warlike, were intelligent and quick to learn. James Cook had previously circumnavigated both North and South Islands in 1769 and 1770. The first European to sight the shores had been the Dutchman, Abel Tasman, in late 1642. Tasman charted the rough, inhospitable west coasts but the experience of his two ships at Murderers' Bay caused him to sail off into the Pacific, contributing only a handful of place names and the title of Staten Landt, which his own countrymen promptly changed to Nieuw Zeeland, and his own name to the rolling billows that surged to the Australian continent.

Cook, with British naval thoroughness, took possession in the name of King George III but little interest followed from a succession of dilatory British Governments. However, ships bearing tough and able adventurers attracted mainly by the excellent base that the Bay of Islands made for lucrative whaling and sealing operations arrived from Europe and the United States and began disgorging the *Pakeha* into makeshift, straggling settlements. Belatedly, in 1833, a British Resident, Mr James Busby, was appointed to the growing community of Kororareka, partly because several French expeditions had reached New Zealand after 1820, but he was an official figurehead without any vestiges of power. The diffidence of the Imperial Government over seventy years is quite remarkable, for not until 1840 did the first shipload of proper colonists reach New Zealand.

The impetus for these colonists came, inevitably, not from laggard officialdom but from a private venture, the New Zealand Company. Founded in 1837 as the New Zealand Association but forced by legal reasons to become a limited company in 1839, the New Zealand Company was the brain-child of a fertile intellectual and pamphleteer, Edward Gibbon Wakefield. As he had spent three years in Newgate Prison (1826–29) for abducting an heiress, Wakefield clearly had much time to think and he evolved a theory of planned colonization with balanced proportions from all walks of life—small farmers, artisans, professional men—so that a mirror of English society emerged in the chosen colony. Not for Wakefield were the degrading convict settlements of Australia and the haphazard arrival of a few free men who may choose to set up as merchants or craftsmen or go on the land.

Wakefield had much ready material at hand for his great idea. England was emerging from the long depression after the Napoleonic Wars into the new miseries of the Industrial Revolution, with overcrowding in the cities and towns and depopulation of the countryside. Many men were keen to take up the challenge of a new life in a favourably-reported colony of temperate climate, albeit thousands of miles away in the Pacific, and so in the early 1840s, the Company established settlements at New Plymouth, Wanganui, Wellington and Nelson, all broadly in the vicinity of Cook Strait. But it was the bustling land dealings of the Company's agents with local Maori chiefs that were soon to become the bane of colonial life. It is typical of the confusion of those days that William Hobson had landed at Kororareka with letters patent that not only gave him Her Majesty's authority over all British subjects in the embryo colony but, ominously for the New Zealand Company, also with an edict that all settlers' titles to the ownership of land were invalid unless derived from the Crown.

Hobson, meanwhile, was expeditious in discharging his task. In early February, 1840, a large concourse of Maoris gathered at the Bay of Islands to hear the draft treaty propounded and, as every Maori loved rhetoric, the debate was long and stormy as chief after chief spoke. Te Kemara, of the Ngatikawa, made a violent opposing speech that more or less echoed the dead Hongi Hika: 'Government go home and leave us to the missionaries.' A certain Hone Heke Pokai, of the Ngapuhi, came down soberly for the treaty. But probably the most influential and impressive address came from another Ngapuhi, Tamati Waaka Nene, of Hokianga, who spoke bitterly of the futile Maori history of bloody civil wars and urged abandonment of the old turbulent ways for peace and order under the White Queen. Both Hone Heke and Waaka Nene were to play leading, and opposing, parts in the clash soon to come.

On 6 February, 1840, forty-five chiefs signed the Treaty of Waitangi, to the booming of twenty-one guns from HMS *Herald*. The Lieutenant-Governor and his emissaries, mainly Protestant missionaries, then set off to gather more chiefly signatures throughout the country, but New Zealand had now been born, if belatedly, as a British colony. The Treaty of Waitangi, however, was meant to be an honourable transaction with the Maori peoples. For the Maoris' recognition of her sovereignty, the Queen promised her Royal protection and the rights and privileges of British subjects, and even more succinctly: 'the lands, forests, fisheries and food places of the natives should remain inviolate, but the right of pre-emptive purchase of their lands should rest in the Crown.' This latter phrase sounds sinister, but its intention was to protect the natives from speculators. To give certain conscientious and hard-working officials their due, every endeavour was made to enforce this crucial clause but local colonist pressure was to be considerable.

After the Treaty was signed, Nopera Panakareao, a chief of the Rarawa, growled consolingly: 'The shadow of the land belongs to the Queen, but the substance remains with us.'

To the colonist recruited by the New Zealand Company and embarking with his young family at Tilbury or Plymouth, to the clergyman about to leave the placid, ordered surrounds of his rural English parish for the call of the mission field among pagan savages, to the soldier in Sydney garrison under orders to sail to the new colony across the Tasman Sea, the character and reputation of the Maori can only have loomed largely in their minds.

In 1840, about 100,000 Maoris inhabited New Zealand, almost all in the North Island, while Europeans numbered a mere 1,000. A well-built, handsome and hardy race of Polynesian stock, their legends told of an epic voyage from Tahiti in about the 10th century, of Kupe, whose wife unwittingly reported an eventual landfall by calling out that she saw a long white cloud on the horizon—giving rise to the Maori name Aotearoa. The tribe, with its *hapus* or sub-tribes, was the summit of their political and cultural structure and the lack of an overall leader, together with their self-destructive predilection for internecine strife, was to prove a fatal weakness in the coming struggle with the *Pakeha*. Their tactics evolved from hand-to-hand fighting and stoutly-constructed stockades, or *pas*, and they were a curious and fascinating amalgam of barbarity and chivalry, of savagery alleviated by a pronounced sense of humour. Two key Maori words, pointedly, were *mana*, the chief's authority or prestige, and *utu*, revenge. Inevitably, most inter-tribal fighting was about land disputes and real or imagined insults to the chief or tribe.

The advent of the white man, the *Pakeha*, to New Zealand brought decidedly mixed benefits to this proud, virile people. In the 1790s, P. G. King, Lt-Governor of Norfolk Island, greatly improved their pastoral well-being with gifts of pig and potato, and particularly in the deeply-indented, island-studded Bay of Islands in the Ngapuhi country, a thriving barter trade with pork and fresh vegetables sprang up with the whaling ships and soon the shanty town of Kororareka arose on the sandy shore. But what the Maoris wanted from the barter were muskets, rum and axeheads. Soon every second shack in Kororareka was a grog shop, with native girls also supplied to the ships. In 1814, that stern Scot, Major-General Lachlan Macquarie, late 73rd Foot and then Governor of New South Wales, was forced to inveigh heavily against the traffic in arms to the Maoris, and, for good measure, despatched missionaries from Sydney to the lawless Bay of Islands.

But muskets, ball ammunition and powder meant power in war

and this was quite irresistible to the Maori. Significantly, Hongi Hika was the first chief to secure muskets in appreciable quantity, through a voyage to England he undertook as a guest of the missionary, William Kendall, ostensibly to assist a Cambridge professor to compile a Maori dictionary and grammar. During this visit he met King George IV, saying as he shook hands: 'How do you do, Mister King George.' The King was equal to the occasion and replied: 'How do you do, Mister King Hongi.' Gifts were showered on the noble savage, including a suit of armour from the Tower, but when he reached Sydney on the return voyage, Hongi promptly sold all the gifts, except the prized armour, for muskets. On arriving home he set about slaughtering other tribes, gaining much plunder, captives and *mana*.

Hongi inevitably had his avid imitators and, as the gun traffic literally boomed, the powerful Waikato tribe of the central region drove the less numerous, though equally fierce, Ngatitoa from Kawhia and went on to invade the Taranaki littoral. The displaced Ngatitoa, under Te Rauparaha, moved south to Cook Strait and ejected the tribes on both its coastlines, terrorising the whalers at Kapiti Island as a side issue. But whereas Hongi was only after loot and *mana*, the forays of the others had a far more disruptive and lasting effect as land changed hands, and memories tended to be long and bitter about lost tribal territory.

Meanwhile, the Protestant missionaries who had come from Sydney or England to wrestle for the soul of the fierce Maori warrior had been making commendable inroads within the rude tribal societies and gaining many converts. Hongi and several other important incorrigibles embraced the Christian religion, becoming, from their study of the Bible, masters of the neat biblical turn of phrase to colour their much-enjoyed speech-making; in the future days of strife with the *Pakeha*, the plight of the Maori people was given a favourite analogy of the oppression of the Children of Israel by the Egyptians. Cannibalism gradually ceased (the flesh of the white man was never really in demand as it was considered too salty) and through the missionaries, some elementary education spread.

It was a suspect balance sheet that derived from the appearance of the white man in New Zealand; on the debit side, firearms, rum, his infectious diseases and some prostitution; on the credit, improved agriculture, a civilizing religion and education. The imponderable question was: could both races live harmoniously together in this attractive archipelago when more immigrant ships, full of hopeful *Pakeha* families seeking homesteads in good arable or pastoral land, were bearing down on its shores?

CHAPTER 2

Tinder Fires in the Fern

On 16 April, 1840, the Government storeship *Buffalo* sailed into the Bay of Islands with a company of the 80th Regiment under Major Thomas Bunbury. 'The men who wear red garments' had arrived in New Zealand in support of the Treaty of Waitangi. Though 2,500 troops under a Major-General were stationed on the Australian mainland and Van Diemen's Land, belonging to regiments who assembled there from convict escort duty, the Governor of New South Wales, Sir George Gipps, was expressly instructed by the Imperial Government, already operationally committed to China and Afghanistan and fearful of further involvement, to detach no more than a garrison of one hundred men to his new responsibility.

While the soldiers settled in at Kororareka, Bunbury was despatched almost immediately in *Herald* to South Island to gather the signatures of its chiefs to the Treaty. The presence of the 80th Company soon began to exercise some fascination for the Maoris about the Bay of Islands. When they first heard the military bugle and saw the soldiers obeying its calls, they asked wonderingly: 'What is this they have that speaks at so great a distance?'

In September, a second detachment of the 80th came from Australia and mostly went to the New Zealand Company's chief settlement at Wellington where concern had arisen about nearby Maori unrest. A month later Hobson selected Auckland for his capital but though he had the satisfaction of events moving well, for New Zealand became an independent colony with himself as Governor in May 1841, he died after chronic ill-health in September, 1842. He left the colony in an indifferent condition, as trade was stagnant because development was frustrated by the Crown's rights of pre-emptive land purchase and the Maoris were restless and uneasy.

Meanwhile, in 1841, the Grenadier Company of the 96th Regiment had arrived at Wellington from Hobart. When more reports of Maori tension reached him, the Governor of Van Diemen's Land, Sir Eardley Wilmot, had reacted like a true Victorian governor in distant parts dependent on intelligence brought by sailing ship. The 80th detachment at Wellington consequently rejoined Bunbury at Auckland and when Hobson died, Bunbury reported to the Acting Governor that his force consisted of 2 captains, 1 subaltern, 1 assistant surgeon, 5 sergeants, 2 drummers and 96 rank and file 'including the sick in hospital and the men employed by the Ordnance Department'. When asked what he required to meet the contingency of a native uprising, he calmly stated 200 bayonets and that the whole force should be concentrated at Auckland. Captain Eyton's company of the 96th was duly withdrawn from Wellington and joined the 80th at Auckland.

This modest garrison was soon to be more than merely decorative. In 1842, Bunbury took fifty soldiers to Tauranga, Bay of Plenty, on the East Coast to quell an imminent war between the Ngaiterangi and Arawa tribes which he did by the cool, if risky, British expedient of camping his red-coated soldiers between the two hostile factions. The following year brought the first *Pakeha*-Maori clash over land, the first spark of a conflagration that was to bring tragedy and terror to the North Island for the next thirty years. Curiously enough, the initial conflict occurred in South Island.

In his foray across Cook Strait, the Ngatitoa chief, Te Rauparaha, had overrun the fertile Wairau valley and in 1843 the colonists at the Company's settlement of Nelson coveted this excellent land, especially as they considered that the Company owned the valley. The disputed ownership of Wairau was a classic forerunner of similar tortuous land arguments to come. In 1830, John Blenkinsopp, master of the whaling schooner *Caroline*, had decided to settle in the valley, and had purchased it by the simple transaction of bartering his ship's 6-pounder gun. He had a proper deed drawn up, married the daughter of Te Rauparaha's uncle, and set off to Sydney to recruit some settlers. However, he was drowned off the Australian coast and eventually the New Zealand Company, hearing of the deed for Wairau, bought it from his widow for £300. But while Te Rauparaha was happy to have his *Pakeha* cousin-by-marriage settle in Wairau, the New Zealand Company was quite another matter and he showed this plainly by burning down their surveyors' huts and uprooting the survey poles.

The New Zealand Company became righteously bellicose from this harrying and the Nelson magistrate issued a warrant for Te Rauparaha's arrest. On 15 June, 1843, a Government brig landed at Cloudy Bay Captain Arthur Wakefield, the younger brother of Edward, and H. H. Thompson, a magistrate, with an impromptu posse of about fifty colonists, and next day they came on the old war chief and his ferocious nephew, Te Rangihaeata, by a stream in Wairau territory with about eighty armed tribesmen and their women and children. Te Rauparaha was initially quite reasonable, refusing to accompany the magistrate but quite willing to discuss the land dispute with the Government Land Commissioner. It seems that Thompson then became rather excited and began brandishing handcuffs. At this *moment critique* when tempers were being lost, a nervous settler accidentally discharged his firearm. This was the signal for a ragged exchange of shots and a running fight ensued with the raw Nelson men outnumbered and too inexperienced to fight together. Many escaped, but Wakefield and a small group were forced to surrender. Just when passions were cooling, word came that one of Te Rangihaeata's wives had been killed in the fight and he flew into a murderous fury, killing, with his uncle's acquiescence, every one of the captives with his own hand. Nineteen Englishmen, including the hotheaded Thompson, were slaughtered on that fateful day at Wairau, and four Ngatitoa died. Blood had now been spilt between the Maori and *Pakeha* and sensible men of both races, aware of the mounting friction, wondered where it would all end.

The news of the Wairau affray shocked England and the stock of the New Zealand Company fell. In New Zealand, Bunbury's insistence on concentrating his troops at Auckland drew fresh fury on the local Government from the colonists, though the 96th detachment was hurriedly embarked for Port Nicholson to placate nerves. In contrast, the citizens of Nelson composed a glowing memorial to the indefatigable Sir Eardley Wilmot who, again hearing of trouble, despatched a company of soldiers in the *Emerald Isle* but as his orders were not to disembark unless the settlers were in active danger, they returned soon after arrival to Hobart Town.

In the distant north, at the Bay of Islands, Hone Heke also heard the news of the Wairau incident. Some months later he was to say: 'Is Te Rauparaha to have the honour of killing all the *pakehas*?'

With the coming of William Hobson and Government, all that the dying Hongi Hika had predicted seemed to be mirrored in the rapid decline of Kororareka, once the thriving haven of the whaling fleet and consequently, the source of much prosperity to the Maoris about the Bay of Islands. But the hoped-for increased trade and growth of the township never occurred, as Hobson had selected Auckland as his capital and, even harder for the local chiefs to endure, the Crown's imposition of Customs dues and the suppression of smuggling had a crippling effect. The good old days were vanishing with alarming haste.

The seeming injustice of the new régime burned deeply into the mercurial, intelligent mind of Hone Heke. In a real sense he suffered financially as the Government usurped a lucrative £5 anchor duty from the whaling ships that he had formerly shared with his chiefly cousin, Pomare. He also sourly observed that his people were no longer smoking American tobacco but makeshift weeds, and wearing dilapidated old blankets instead of their dignified native cloaks. As a nephew of Hongi and also his son-in-law, as he had married the old warrior's handsome daughter as his second wife, he was present at the impressionable deathbed scene. 'Rash, impetuous and imperious, he was intolerant of all authority save his own,' is one description of Hone Heke, while a missionary, the Rev R. Davis, commented: 'Heke is a strange character and, I believe, not always sane.'

In the perennial tribal wars he had established a reputation as a bold and fearless leader. As a leading and proved chief of the Ngapuhi, related to the great Hongi, his bloodline was impeccable, with a consequent wide influence in the North. He was also a Christian. Moody and unpredictable, he was an excellent example, for all his known faults, of the old Maori chivalry leavened by Christian influence.

In November, 1841, he became very angry when, against his impassioned argument, other chiefs of the Ngapuhi surrendered to the Government a well-connected young Maori, Maketu, to be hanged for the brutal murder of an isolated European widow, Mrs Robertson, and her family. Heke was all for punishing Maketu but by Maoris under Maori law. His antagonism to the Government had a slow but steady incubation. Breaking point came in early 1844 when two American whalers at the Bay of Islands were heavily fined for smuggling, which caused ships to move their patronage to other harbours where Government officials were not so active. It was at this delicate stage that the acting American Consul at the Bay of Islands, Captain William Mayhew, drew the rum-soaked attention of the principal trading chief, Pomare, to the insidious power exerted by the British flag flying on the flagstaff at Maiki Hill, behind Kororareka: this signified, despite the Treaty of Waitangi, that the Maori was now a slave and no longer counted in his own land. Pomare pondered heavily on these words and passed them on to his fellow chiefs, of whom none was more recipient than Hone Heke.

This fateful flagstaff was a piece of stalwart kauri timber grown on Heke's own land which he had presented to James Busby to erect outside his house at Waitangi. Later, when William Hobson arrived, it was taken down and set up on the other side of the harbour at Maiki Hill, where it was used both as a signal halyard for ships entering the harbour and to fly the Queen's flag. The fact that his very own gift was now the symbol of the oppression of his people rankled deeply with Hone Heke.

His excuse for a trial of strength with authority at Kororareka came on 5 July, 1844. A slave girl named Kotiro was living with a European butcher named Lord, and Heke, her tribal chief, took it upon himself to order her to leave her *Pakeha* mate. Kotiro received his men scornfully and, turning and pointing to one of the fat hogs that hung in the shop, with a flash of her dark eyes, exclaimed: 'That is Heke!' Lord was equally truculent and refused to hand over placatory gifts of tobacco to salve the wound of this gross insult. The tribesmen repaired to the beach where they danced a furious *haka* and made inflammatory speeches about war. After some overbearing behaviour and pilfering in the township, where they swaggered about for several days, they were cooled down by hastily-summoned missionaries. However, the fact that their unruly domination of Kororareka went unchecked cleared the scene for Heke's real move. At daybreak on 8 July, his men felled the flagstaff on Maiki Hill.

While Hone Heke returned exultant to the hills, the news of the toppled emblem of British rule caused a furore in Auckland. Robert FitzRoy, another naval captain who had arrived as the new Governor only the previous December and who had already antagonized the European community by condemning the peremptory action that led to the Wairau incident, immediately despatched an officer and thirty soldiers of the 96th Regiment to the Bay Islands. The flagstaff was re-erected and by September Heke was alleged to be sufficiently contrite. However, it is clear that the sharp reaction to his assault on the flagstaff and a distinct lack of sympathy from many of his fellow chiefs induced a show of penitence. For in mid-August, the barque *Sydney* landed another one hundred and sixty troops of the 96th, who had relieved the 80th in New Zealand in March, under the command of Brevet-Lieutenant-Colonel William Hulme, and on 24 August the Governor himself arrived in HMS *Hazard* with another detachment of the 96th in the Government brig, *Victoria*. Some 250 soldiers were now encamped about Kororareka.

The Governor, anxious to ward off a native war, went inland to Waimate, the main mission station in the far north, with Bishop Selwyn, other clergymen and Hulme, to hear the deputations of the well-disposed chiefs, led by Waaka Nene, on this affront to the Government and Her Majesty. In his opening speech, FitzRoy tactfully abolished the hated Customs duties and his chiefly audience responded enthusiastically. Waaka's words were simple and reassuring: 'Governor, if the flagstaff is cut down again we will fight for it. We will fight for it, all of us. We are of one tribe and we will fight for the staff and our Governor. I am sorry this trouble has occurred, but you may return the soldiers. We, the old folks, are well disposed, and we will make the young ones so, also.'

But, noticeably, the *enfant terrible*, the recalcitrant Hone Heke, was not at this august gathering. Instead, he sent a rather barbed letter:

'Friend Governor: This is my speech to you. My disobedience and rudeness is no new thing. I inherit it from my parents—from my ancestors. Do not imagine it is a new feature of my character; but I am thinking of leaving off my rude conduct to Europeans. Now I say I will prepare another pole inland at Waimate, and I will erect it at its proper place at Kororareka in order to put a stop to our present quarrel. Let your soldiers remain beyond the sea and at Auckland. Do not send them here. The pole that was cut down belonged to me. I made it for the native flag, and it was never paid for by the Europeans.

From your friend,
Hone Heke Pokai."[1]

Honour was now satisfied and the Governor and 'the men who wear red garments' departed from the Bay of Islands.

About this time, however, a new and aggressive Maori comet appeared on the local horizon in the person of Kawiti, chief of the Kawakawa *hapu*, and an old-time pagan warrior whose ancestry in the Ngapuhi was as illustrious as Heke's; his signature had been first in seniority on the Treaty of Waitangi. Kawiti's eagerness to rebel against *pakeha* authority seems to have stemmed solely from an old-fashioned Maori desire to test the fighting worth of the British soldiers, while it is equally clear that many of his followers were only motivated by dreams of loot. Normally Hone Heke and Kawiti would have been rivals for *mana* and dominance in the North, but now Heke was forced to become an ally of Kawiti. Desperately Heke strove to orientate the old pagan

[1] Quoted in *New Zealand's First War* by T. Lindsay Buick.

to a joint struggle that was not directed against helpless settlers for plunder, but against Government oppression. Doubtless in order to emphasise his theme, on the night of 9 January, 1845, he silently entered Kororareka with his tribesmen and cut down the flagstaff yet again.

At Auckland, the exasperated FitzRoy ordered Hulme to return the garrison of thirty soldiers of the 96th to the Bay of Islands and wrote to the Governor of New South Wales appealing for reinforcements; he also recalled HMS *Hazard* from Wellington and directed it to Kororareka where he placed a reward of £100 on the apprehension of Hone Heke. This highly irritated the proud Maori who complained petulantly, but presumably without illusion to Kotiro's insult: 'Am I a pig that I am thus to be bought and sold?'

With Maori humour, he offered an equal reward for the capture of the Governor.

CHAPTER 3
Hone Heke's Flagstaff

IN mid-January, 1845, the *Victoria* landed the returned garrison at Kororareka, also Dr Sinclair, the Government Secretary, who at once insisted, against the vehement advice of local residents who knew Hone Heke's fixation about the flagpole, that another staff should be erected. However, though soldiers or Waaka's friendly Maoris mounted alternate guard on the symbolic spar of timber, Heke's audacity had not been fully calculated. Landing from canoes on the morning of 19 January, he left his armed men at the foot of Maiki Hill while he strode up to brush disdainfully aside Waaka's bewildered men, who, with their Maori values, hesitated to shoot such a distinguished chief for the sake of a piece of timber and coloured cloth. Heke dropped the new staff by severing its stays with his axe and marched calmly off to rejoin his jubilant followers. As they paddled by the *Victoria* to re-cross the Bay, they fired their muskets in the air in happy derision.

The saga of the flagstaff attrition continued. Another and greater was thrown up, its lower portion encased in an iron sleeve for invulnerability against Maori axes, with a ditch dug about it; a blockhouse was also constructed nearby to house twenty soldiers under the youthful Ensign Campbell. Lower down the hill, a second redoubt was built and here three ancient cannon were sited, while yet another defence measure was a stockade to act as a protective rallying point for the town's inhabitants in time of attack.

30

These security precautions were timely, as Hone Heke was now moving to grander designs. His *mana* was high and his war-runners were meeting an enthusiastic response from the young warriors of the Ngapuhi, though most of the chiefs waited aloof to see a positive victory. In March, the alliance between Heke and Kawiti solidified, with the old warrior chief persuading Heke that they were really after bigger issues than chopping down a flagpole; they must eject the *Pakeha* and this meant fighting the soldiers. They set up a joint camp at Te Uruti, near Kororareka, and drifted irrevocably towards conflict, with their marauders beginning to appear on the outskirts of Kororareka after easy loot. At Te Uruti, gentility mingled with savagery in a confused way, as even church parades were held; a Catholic priest celebrated Mass for Kawiti's men, though he was still sturdily a pagan, and the Rev Brown held a service for Heke's followers, taking the text for his sermon from James, IV, 1: 'From whence come wars and fightings among you?' This drew a sharp reaction from his most distinguished worshipper:

'After the service, Heke walked up to the missionary and remarked to him that he had better preach that sermon to the soldiers, who had more need of it.'

Some 600 fighting men had now assembled at the camp, most of the reinforcements coming from the Kapotai *hapu*, and the simple master plan was to attack Kororareka. In accordance with Maori chivalry, no secrecy was attempted and in the town the local experts on native thought and behaviour soon knew what was in the wind. Fortunately, Acting-Commander Robertson of the *Hazard*, the senior officer present, took the rumours seriously and positioned a landed naval gun, with a small protective picquet, at a defile that led to the town from the south-west. Also, on the night of 10 March he sent ashore 45 sailors and marines to strengthen the garrison of 2 officers, 52 NCOs and soldiers of the 96th and the militia of 110 armed citizens.

The night of 10 March was to be crowded with activity and excitement, for hundreds of rebel Maoris were moving towards the township. In the last hour before dawn, Robertson led his naval contingent to the south-western outskirts to dig entrenchments when suddenly they heard the emplaced gun firing ahead of them. Shortly afterwards, as they pressed on, retreating men of the picquet stumbled into the party; they had been overrun and the gunner killed as he tried to spike his gun. Hard on the heels of the fleeing picquet loomed groups of Kawiti's warriors out of the morning mist and a savage fire-fight developed until the sailors and marines collected themselves and with a spirited charge, broke through the enveloping ranks of the rebels. Robertson, who had been wielding a cutlass with great *élan*, was wounded pursuing Pumuka, Kawiti's second-in-command, who discharged a double-barrelled pistol at him. Pumuka was then despatched by two sailors following the Commander, though one of these was killed and the other seriously wounded.

Robertson, now bleeding and isolated from his men, lay down in some scrub; but as a party of rebels was bearing away the body of Pumuka the last Maori noticed him and fired a parting shot which shattered his right thigh. He lay there, abandoned and in agony.

The naval party, with six dead from their brisk and furious encounter, including the Colour-Sergeant of Marines, and their Commander missing, decided to retire to the town. However, their movement was intercepted by another aggressive band of rebels and a fresh action began. The unfortunate Robertson, in the line of fire, endured yet another wound, his other leg being hit. Desperately he managed to wave his handkerchief and was seen by his men; rescued and borne away, he was to linger dangerously ill for many weeks.

Meanwhile, a central attacking column of Kapotai had come into action from the wooded hills at the back of the town with the object of pinning down the soldiers, and this they did with some success. Lieutenant Barclay, of the 96th, moved up most of his uncommitted soldiers to the Maiki Hill blockhouse to answer their fire, while the old guns in the lower blockhouse supported his firing line noisily and gallantly, though against the concealed rebels in the scrub, probably not too effectively. Finally, in the fern about the slopes of Maiki Hill, the many brown bodies of Hone Heke's own men waited for the signal to administer the *coup de grâce*. During darkness they had crept

A photograph of Tamati Waaka *Nene in old age.*

2. *Te Rauparaha, Chief of the Ngatitoa.*

4. *The Flagstaff on Maiki Hill; a photograph taken in 1903.*

Hone Heke Pokai of the Ngaputi.

5. *Kororareka, Bay of Islands, in 1864.*

6. *Colonel Hulme burns Pomare's* pa *at Otuihu; the* North Star *is in the foreground.*

forward, each party keeping in contact with the imitated plaintive cry of the native owl whose sudden and widespread activity failed to excite the blockhouse sentry.

Before dawn, Ensign Campbell emerged from the blockhouse with five armed soldiers carrying spades to dig a trench above a nearby beach. They had hardly begun work when the sound of firing from the initial clash between Kawiti and Robertson caused them to abandon their task and move back towards the blockhouse. Here soldiers were straggling out, buckling on their equipment but mostly unarmed, to watch and listen to the distant action from the brow of their hill. The watching Hone Heke waited until he knew only four soldiers were left inside the blockhouse and then made a rush with his warriors. The sentry opened fire at the surging wave of rebels, but was quickly killed, as were his three comrades inside. The surprised and disorganised soldiers caught in the open retreated to the lower blockhouse, as did Campbell and his working party, after firing one volley at the rebels, for another group of rebels was moving round their flank to cut them off. As the action developed, the sound of Maori axes soon rang out as the hated flagstaff was attacked.

Some of Heke's men now directed their fire at the lower blockhouse where the exposed guns were, but one gun was trained in their direction and silenced them. About twenty Kapotai also stole up to sniping positions, but the gallant Mr Cornthwaite Hector, who commanded and served the guns with two old soldiers, could get no help from the stockade where by now some one hundred and fifty armed men were concentrated in impotent inaction, and so he sallied forth himself with six soldiers. The rebels counter-attacked, the roving gun came into play again, and a bigger, but *ad hoc*, force again issued from the lower blockhouse to hold the ring. But Hector was now grievously short of ammunition, and at least the women in the stockade contributed to the battle by tearing up clothes to make powder-bags.

As the morning wore on, the fighting began to fizzle out, for both antagonists were remarkably inept in any form of co-ordination of their forces; indeed, neither seems to have attempted any overall control. On the rebel side, Kawiti's men,

c

after their dawn battle, remained inactive, making no attempt to press on themselves or to reinforce the Kapotai, while Heke's assault force, having gained Maiki Hill and destroyed the flag-staff, seems to have remained immobile and fixed, contributing only a few stray volleys to the rest of the battle. For the defenders of Kororareka, the loss of Commander Robertson was a grievous blow; command fell on the indifferent combination of the brave but inexperienced Lieutenant Barclay and Lieutenant Phillpotts of the *Hazard*, who, between them, allowed many armed men, including the naval contingent, to remain unemployed in the stockade while Maiki Hill fell through the unawareness of the inexperienced Ensign Campbell, and the courageous Mr Hector had to fight on, unsupported.

Chaotic conditions existed in the overcrowded stockade and when Barclay visited it for more ammunition, he suggested to the badly-wounded Robertson, who was lying there awaiting movement to the *Hazard*, that the women and children should be taken off to the safety of the several ships anchored off Kororareka. Robertson agreed to this sensible proposal but at a later council of war, it seems that a decision was reached, prob-ably not with his comprehension, to evacuate the whole town, including the military force. Hector, for one, was incensed and called for forty men as a counter-attack force to clear Maiki Hill, but Phillpotts, who now seems to have assumed command, refused. The evacuation, begun about noon and watched un-molested by the rebels, went off from the beach in waiting boats to the *Hazard*, the visiting United States man-o'-war *St Louis*, the whaler *Matilda*, the *Victoria*, the schooner *Dolphin* and Bishop Selwyn's lugger, the *Flying Fish*.

At 1 pm, the magazine in the stockade blew up from an unknown cause and the debris from the explosion set alight nearby buildings. The rebels filtered into the township in the wake of the evacuation and happily began looting. As rum casks were broken open and exultantly imbibed, the train of damage spread. When the dashing but erratic Phillpotts fired several salvoes from the *Hazard* into the doomed town, this served only to enrage the rebels and cause more damage to be wreaked. A chief called Te Aho fired much of the remaining town, though the Anglican and Catholic churches and the house of the Catholic bishop, Mgr Pompallier, were deliberately spared.

Bishop Selwyn and the Rev Henry Williams went ashore to the sorry devastation of Kororareka and were treated with great civility by the victorious rebels, being invited to partake of the liberated rum, food and even sweets. In the top blockhouse, Williams found Ensign Campbell's sword and he made the mistake of rowing out to the *Hazard*, saying innocently as he handed it up from his boat: 'Here is something one of you gentlemen has left behind.' He had to sheer off rapidly to save himself and his native boat crew from injury. A more appreciated recovery was a boatload of sacks of flour for the *Matilda* which two of Henry Williams' sons secured from rebels plundering a baker's shop. 'Of course,' said the cheerful Maoris, 'carry away as much as you can. There is plenty for all, and it is only right that the women and children should have something to eat on board.'

Some Kororareka citizens returned ashore during the late afternoon to salvage what possessions they could from their erstwhile homes, but as Phillpotts began another futile bombardment, maddening the rum-soaked rebels, they mostly went rapidly back to the ships; six, who did not, were murdered that night as flames rose in the darkened sky from the dying township. Before these fatalities the fall of Kororareka had already cost the lives of 13 Europeans, with 23 wounded, while the rebels lost 34 killed and 69 wounded.

At dawn, the evacuation fleet, with its crammed cargo of miserable and dispossessed refugees, weighed anchor and crept sadly out from the Bay of Islands for Auckland.

CHAPTER 4

The Red Tribe Attack

THE impressive victory of the Hone Heke-Kawiti rebel alliance at Kororareka cast a chilling fear among the settlements and homesteads of North Island, and certainly at Auckland, where much worrying conjecture on its effect on other major tribes, such as the Waikato and Arawa arose. Robert FitzRoy, however, faced up to the disaster with bluff naval courage and set about strengthening the defences of his capital and arming and drilling a militia. Then, as certain panic-selling of Auckland property was developing, with passages being booked for the placid Australian colonies, a veritable armada began sailing into the harbour; on 23 March, 1845, HMS *North Star*, a frigate of twenty-eight guns commanded by Sir Everard Home, arrived, and on the following day, the transport *Velocity*, carrying 280 men of the 58th Regiment under Captain Grant. Four weeks later, on 22 April, the transport *Slains Castle* beat into the harbour with another 215 soldiers of the 58th under Major Cyprian Bridge. These considerable reinforcements to FitzRoy's parlous military strength were the belated response of Sir George Gipps in New South Wales to his urgent appeal in January. As so often with the British Army, the delay had been caused by finance: in this case, haggling over the price of hire of the transports.

Since the fall of Kororareka, FitzRoy had been under much pressure from the belligerent colonial Press and from Auckland society to mount a punitive expedition against Hone Heke and

Kawiti. He was vulnerable to accusations of this kind because of his handling of the Wairau tragedy which had enraged the citizens of Wellington and Nelson and had even confused the Maoris, who naturally expected him to secure *utu*. However, this unhappy episode needed more than an ordinary Solomon-type judgement; if he had sought out Te Rauparaha and Te Rangihaeata with his very modest military resources, he could easily have been faced with a major Maori uprising, for, whatever the goriness of the massacre, the two chiefs did have a legal case; yet because he did not try to gain *utu*, a Maori view could be that the British must be regarded as timid and hesitant. However, he now had the forces to achieve *utu*, and he briefed William Hulme to set about planning field operations in the Bay of Islands. Another spur to this decision was the arrival of the chief, Paratene, in Auckland, bearing a message from the loyal Waaka Nene, saying that soldiers must return to help him crush Hone Heke.

Tamati Waaka Nene (and it was the saving of the British in this war that the formidable Ngapuhi were so divided), was enraged by Heke's descent on Kororareka; he regarded the rebellion as an unforgivable insult to respected chiefs and elders who had given their word to the Governor to guarantee their disgruntled peer's conduct. Waaka was to become a pillar of the Government's fluctuating military fortunes, forever steadfast, unwavering and brave.

It is interesting to speculate how much the old wars and depredations of Hongi Hika influenced the adoption of clearly-divided positions by the tribes affected by the rebellion. Rumour accused Waaka of siding with the *Pakeha* because Hongi had killed his elder relation, Te Tihi, and had eaten his eyes. Certainly the tribes connected with Hongi's victories tended to flock to Hone Heke, while to Waaka's banner came the surviving forty warriors of the Ngatipou who had almost been exterminated by Hongi, though they had the satisfaction of firing the shot that inflicted the chest wound from which Hongi ultimately died; unfortunately, he had left his English mail shirt off that day. The Ngatipou fought with pitiless ferocity against Hone Heke throughout the war.

While he skirmished with some success against Heke, Waaka's appeal was met on 28 April, when HMS *North Star* and other vessels in company sailed into the Bay of Islands bearing an expeditionary force of some 470 men of the 58th, 96th, Marines and Auckland Volunteers under the overall command of Lieutenant-Colonel William Hulme, of the 96th. Hulme was an alert, intelligent officer who had distinguished himself in the Pindari rising in India in 1817.

The return of British power to the pathetic and blackened ruins of Kororareka was marked with due pomp and ceremony. While the guns of the *North Star* boomed out a Royal Salute, the Band of the 58th played the National Anthem and the Union Jack was hoisted (temporarily, on a very temporary staff). These symbolic formalities over, the troops re-embarked and the modest fleet, towed by rowing parties, moved laboriously up the Bay. Its destination was Pomare's *pa* at Otuihu, as letters of a subversive tone, alleged to have been written by him, had been intercepted on their way to the great chief of the Waikato, Te Wherowhero, and he was to be arrested and taken to Auckland to explain his conduct.

At dawn, as the *North Star* stood off Pomare's *pa*, Hulme was surprised, and doubtlessly relieved, for Pomare was highly connected among the northern chiefs, to see a white flag flying. However, he disembarked his troops according to his assault plan and, after some arrogance about the colonel coming to see him, Pomare and his family were taken on board. An ultimatum was then issued to the *pa* to surrender all its arms, but as it had not been surrounded, this was the signal for all its male occupants to escape into the bush. In exasperation, that evening Hulme ordered the *pa* to be fired. As the holocaust lit up the deepening dusk, much chasing after abandoned pigs and ducks went on by the soldiery who, Major Cyprian Bridge of the 58th sourly noted, were all from the 96th.

Hulme now decided to make his next objective Kawiti's *pa* at Waimio but in poring over the very rudimentary maps he was dissuaded by no less a local expert than the Rev Henry Williams that this approach march would be hazardous and exhausting, so he determined to go for Hone Heke's new *pa* at Puketutu. On

3 May, after briefly meeting the redoubtable Waaka Nene back at Kororareka, he disembarked his force at Onewhero Bay, across the great inlet, and the soldiers, laden with five days' meat and biscuit and thirty rounds of ball ammunition, began trudging inland. This first advance was an arduous and miserable experience: the rude track wandered infuriatingly across the grain of the country which was cut with steep gullies and swampy hollows. Nine miles were covered the first day and at the camp made by a stream for the night, torrential rain soaked the numbed soldiers and ruined much of their food and powder. Cyprian Bridge asserted it was the most miserable night he had spent in his life.

Next day the bedraggled column made a detour of four miles to Kerikeri Mission where it dried out and sheltered during two more days of heavy rain. On the 6th, the march was resumed, struggling through a dense wood along a path cut by pioneers, until at sunset the weary expedition encamped within two miles of Heke's *pa*. Here, at least, some cheer awaited them as Waaka's warriors and their women had constructed fern and palm lean-to shelters for them and the begrimed and grateful soldiers settled down around blazing fires to a nourishing hot meal of pork and potatoes. Waaka was to become a great favourite of the soldiers and was known as 'General Walker'.

At first light next morning, Hulme, without any firepower heavier than the ball ammunition of his muskets except some 3 lb rockets from HMS *Hazard* whose gear had been a sore trial on the overland march, contemplated the formidable construction of a Maori *pa*. He was the first British Army officer of experience to have this sobering insight:

'The *pa* was built on a slight eminence, was square of shape, but zigzagged at the corners in order to bring a crossfire to bear on its assailants. It had three rows of tree-trunk palisades, 15 feet in height, sunk to several feet in the ground, each tree-trunk 5 to 6 inches in diameter, set close together. A mass of stone rubble, collected from volcanic debris strewn about, further strengthened the foundations of the *pekerangi* (or outer fence). The palisading was carefully caulked with green flax to prevent enemy bullets penetrating the apertures. Loopholes were everywhere prepared to facilitate the defence, and to render its storming still more difficult, a deep trench was dug between each of the wooden walls."[1]

At 7 am on 8 May, the bugle sounded the advance and the soldiers, with full packs and shouldered muskets, marched out. Their morale and general preparedness for battle was hardly textbook: it had been another night of pouring rain and there was no food for breakfast. One hour later they stood before Hone Heke's *pa*, typical British soldiers—patient and disciplined in adversity. Their Colonel's plan was to have his main weight before the frontal approach to the *pa*, with a strong storming party on rising ground on the right while Waaka's men covered the left; the rear of the *pa* backed on to Lake Omapere. With his purely infantry force, Hulme's concept of the operation seems somewhat optimistic, but great store was set by the terror, if not destruction, to be wrought by the naval rockets which were being set up, commanded by Lieutenant Egerton of the *North Star*, a mere 150 yards from the *pa*. Considerable Maori interest, both rebel and friendly, was fixed on the rockets, for native gossip said they were 'a species of consuming monster which would go into the *pa* where it would twist and turn about in pursuit of the people until it killed every one'. As a general description of their accuracy and ballistic performance, this was probably a fair estimation. Egerton's first problem was to get his temperamental missiles to hit the *pa*, let alone get them inside it.

The first two rockets soared wildly and ignominiously high and wide of the *pa* while Hone Heke, standing at one of the gates, grinned contemptuously. But the third hit the outer palisade with a resounding crash and penetrated to the middle wall, causing much excitement among the defenders and considerable barking from their dogs. Hulme immediately launched his right-flanking assault party consisting of the Light Company of the 58th, the 96th detachment and the marines and sailors, to seize the high ground. Dashing forth, they survived a fierce fire from the loopholes of the *pa* only to be confronted on their hillock by the dramatic appearance of a force of Kawiti's warriors who had

[1] Buick.

40

fortuitously arrived on the scene. A savage mêlée set in, in which the British gradually drove the rebels off the disputed ground and then fell exhausted, sheltering behind an old Maori breastwork. An hour later, with all twelve available rockets expended, Hulme decided to mount a general attack.

As the soldiers stood ready to cross the start line, a sudden cry from a friendly Maori rent the air: 'Kawiti! Kawiti!' Hulme turned to see behind him the redoubtable Kawiti with about 300 of his warriors. After their repulse, they had worked their way through the bush and were now in force in his rear. Hulme acted calmly and decisively, a typical Victorian commander confronted with a superior native enemy. He addressed a company of the 58th—'About turn! . . . Fix bayonets! . . . Charge!'

If the Maori warrior had shaken the British soldier with the strength of his *pa*, he now exposed himself to an expertise for which the redcoat was renowned: disciplined action in the open field. A veteran of Kawiti's force has set down his vivid impressions of this incident:

'A number of the red tribe who had not joined in the attack on our *pa* came at our people with a rush with their bayonets fixed to their muskets, yelling horribly, grinding their teeth and cursing. Down went Kawiti's choicest warriors, the ground was strewn with them. Alas, it was a fatal mistake. We never tried that move again. Once was quite enough. But it was wrong of the red tribe to curse us. We were doing no harm; we were merely fighting them.'[1]

To succour Kawiti's shattered ranks, a brave rebel chief called Tupori issued from the *pa* with 200 warriors and went for the hill taken by the British. Hulme rapidly re-formed the company of the 58th and sent them to support the defenders of the hill. As Kawiti's men, encouraged by Tupori's bold sortie, also rallied to join in, another savage and confused battle ensued, with both the British and the rebels trying to drive the other down the slopes into the lake. However, the training and cohesion of the British began to tell, and with a cheer they drove the Maoris into retreat. As they pursued those making for the *pa*, they came under heavy fire from the walls and had to desist.

A stalemate followed, broken only by fierce but inconclusive

[1] Buick.

exchanges of fire between the *pa* and the besiegers. It now became clear to Hulme that Heke's *pa* was not going to be breached by his slim resources and he abandoned the operation. The soldiers marched wearily back to their base camp, where they fell out to drop tired and supperless into their beds of fern. Again the rain, now turning to the driving sleet of the New Zealand winter, came down. Next day a stray bullock was shot and slaughtered, and the famished men ate.

Off they marched to Kerikeri Mission Station where organised food awaited the column and the wounded received proper attention. Meanwhile, Hone Heke had given strict orders that the British dead were not to be stripped and summoned the Rev Williams from Waimate to give Christian burial to the fallen. From Kerikeri, the troops trekked down to the river to embark in the *Hazard* and sail down the Bay to rejoin the *North Star* and *Slains Castle* off Kororareka. For this first major trial of strength in the field against the Maori rebels, the British lost 13 dead and sustained 39 wounded, while it is probable that Heke and Kawiti had 20 to 30 killed, with wounded unknown. One of the fatal rebel casualties was a son of Kawiti; he had already lost another in the attack on Kororareka.

Hulme sailed away to Auckland in the *North Star* with his despatches for the Governor, who professed himself well-satisfied. On the performance of the soldiers, faced by the natural valour of the Maori warrior defending his stoutly-built *pa* and unsupported by artillery, and enduring miserable conditions and primitive administration, he could well afford to be generous. However, Heke was left in possession of the field and he and Kawiti had suffered most of their casualties only when they made the tactical error of testing British bayonets in the open. It was not an auspicious opening to the campaign, but 'the red tribe' had acquitted themselves admirably, drawing the admiration of the Maoris, both friendly and rebel. Waaka's men were astonished at the weight of equipment the soldiers carried on the march, and were distinctly repelled by the British custom of carrying stretchers into battle; this they regarded as tempting fate and turning the whole operation into a potential funeral party.

Major Cyprian Bridge was left in command in the Bay of

Islands and on 15 May he decided to mount a private expedition of his own against a *pa* of the Kapotai up the Waikare River where much booty from the sack of Kororareka was rumoured to be hidden. His force of 192 soldiers of the 58th and 100 friendly Maoris under two of Waaka's most competent allies, Repa and Mohi Tawhai, drifted in ship's boats and native canoes on the tide away from the *Hazard*, anchored at the head of the Waikare, but on entering the mangrove creek near the *pa*, the flotilla got into trouble when several boats went aground on the mudflats. This disturbed so many nesting wild duck that their commotion alerted the Kapotai who hurriedly decamped with their loot. As their mud-covered attackers finally staggered towards the *pa* a running fight ensued and the *pa* was burned to the ground. Finally, during the afternoon, Bridge moved back to his boats with no British losses but two friendly Maoris were killed and several wounded in pursuit of the Kapotai through the bush.

Bridge now received a letter from Waaka on 18 May saying that Heke had abandoned his *pa* at Puketutu the day the soldiers had marched away and was now building a new *pa* seven miles farther inland to be nearer his food cultivations, and Waaka urged the major to attack before the construction was too advanced. Bridge could only demur, as he had no authority to venture into such a serious operational task, but literally as he pondered, the *North Star* returned with orders that he was to embark his troops for Auckland.

As the transports *Velocity* and a hired whaling ship were beating out of the Bay, the Rev Williams dramatically intercepted their course to say that Heke was willing to discuss peace. Bridge obligingly left his ship with the missionary but all he secured was a letter from Hone Heke to the Governor, written in the classical mould:

'Friend the Governor:
    I have no opinion to offer in this affair, because a death's door has been opened. Where is the correctness of the protection offered by the Treaty? Where is the correctness of the goodwill of England? Is it in her great guns? Is it in her Congreve rockets? Is the goodwill of England shown in the curses of Englishmen

and in their adulteries? Is it shown in their calling us slaves? Or is it shown in their regard for our sacred places? The Europeans taunt us. They say: "Look at Port Jackson, look at China, and all the islands—they are but a precedent for this country. That flag of England that takes your country is the commencement." After this, the French, and after them the Americans, told us the same. Well, I assented to these speeches, and in the fifth year we interfered with the flagstaff for the first time. We cut it down and it fell. It was re-erected and then we said: "All this we have heard is true, because they persist in having the flagstaff up." And we said: "We will die for our country that God has given us."

If you demand our land, where are we to go? To Port Jackson? To England? Many people took part in the plunder of Kororareka. There were but 200 at the fight, but there were 1,000 at the plundering of the town. Walker's fighting is nothing at all. He is coaxing you, his friend, for property that you may say he is faithful. I shall not act so. He did not consider that some of his people were at the plunder of the town. It was through me alone that the missionaries and other Europeans were not molested. Were anything to happen to me, all would be confusion. The natives would not consider the harmless Europeans but would kill in all directions. It is I alone who restrain them. If you say we are to fight, I am agreeable; if you say you will make peace with your enemy, I am equally agreeable. I am on my own land. I now say to you: leave Walker and I to fight. We are both Maoris. You turn and fight with your own colour. It was Walker who called the soldiers to Okaihau, and therefore they were killed. That is all. Peace must be determined by you, the Governor.

From me

John William Pokai (Heke)."[1]

On 29 May, at Government House, Auckland, Robert FitzRoy read this letter, so typical of Hone Heke with its faint hint of reconciliation but unable to refrain from his old arrogance, and he considered it truculent and offensive. He decided to send back to the Bay of Islands 300 troops with artillery to march on Heke's new *pa*. However, before any move could be made, the *Lady Lee* sailed into harbour from Sydney with the welcome news that the two flank companies of the 99th Regiment under their Commanding Officer, Colonel Henry Despard, were on their way and that the Colonel had been appointed to assume command of all troops and volunteer forces in New Zealand.

[1] Buick.

CHAPTER 5

Ohaeawai Pa

'The principal object of your expedition is the capture or destruction of the rebel chief, Heke, and his supporters, Kawiti, Hira te Pure, Hori Kingi, Te Haratua who, with their followers, should share the fate which their destruction of Kororareka has rendered inevitable . . . My duty to our Sovereign, our country and the well-disposed tribes of New Zealand demand an exemplary chastisement of the rebellious natives . . . A British Officer will, of course, spare and protect the old, the helpless, the women, the children, the unresisting . . .'

So ran the operational directive Robert FitzRoy penned on 6 June, 1845, to Colonel Despard soon after his arrival with his troops in the *British Sovereign*. The new commander lost no time in righting the grievous lack of artillery, probably on Hulme's urgent advice, and he resurrected from the Auckland ordnance depot four obsolete guns whose rotted carriages were hurriedly replaced. He soon had his expeditionary force ready to move, but this commendable desire to close with the enemy was, regrettably, Henry Despard's main military virtue. An officer of much Indian experience, he was of a fiery and impatient disposition which was not alleviated by a generous share of bovine stupidity. His whole choleric outlook and limited military ability were unequal to the command of a joint force with native allies operating in primitive terrain.

The expedition did not start auspiciously when, on 10 June, the *British Sovereign*, with Despard on board, went aground on

Brampton Reef in the Bay of Islands. As she floated free, undamaged, two days later, a battle of some moment erupted inland. In the dim light of the dawn, Hone Heke at the head of 450 warriors descended on Waaka Nene's *pa* at Te Ahuahu, grimly determined to destroy him before the British took the field again.

Heke's approach was detected by an old slave-woman out gathering wood and when the alarm was given, the doughty Waaka sallied out with his men to give battle. When Waaka was taken in the flank by a force under another famous war-leader, Te Kahakaka, his ally, Taonui, also took the field with his followers and during the morning fortunes swayed to and fro. However, Waaka was to carry the day decisively by adopting the traditional British Army tactic of coolly reserving fire until the enemy was almost on them, and then blasting the attacking ranks. Te Kahakaka died of wounds and Heke was badly hit in the thigh, to be borne away defeated and in some peril, as Taonui and his warriors were pursuing and cutting down the routed rebels, to his *pa* at Ohaeawai. Waaka saw to the burial of the many dead, both friend and foe, and acted with that unpredictable Maori chivalry towards the wounded, even sending the rebel chief, Patai, suffering from head wounds, to the Rev Burrows for medical attention.

When Despard heard of Heke's reverse, he determined to move out at all speed to confront the stricken rebel leader at Ohaeawai *pa*. He sent his guns and heavy stores by boats up the inlet to Kerikeri Mission and after commandeering three bullock-drawn drays and two carts, began his march inland on 16 June. Now the old painful struggle with the rude bush tracks, swamps and stony creeks that had harassed Hulme set in, as the crude wheeled transport toiled forward. Despard's constant worry was the progress of his vital guns, two 6-pounders and two 12-pounders. Again, in typical wintry conditions, the weather blew cold and rainy and it was a bedraggled column that trudged into Waimate in the early hours of next morning, with the drays hauling the guns twelve hours behind them. As the rations were inevitably in the transport, the disconsolate soldiers went to sleep hungry, but, at first light, a ton of potatoes that Waaka had sent along as a gift to the Colonel were eagerly drawn on for breakfast.

At Waimate next day, Despard, irritable from the frustrations of the march from Kerikeri, met for the first time Tamati Waaka Nene who came to this rendezvous with 250 warriors. It is typical of Henry Despard's lack of vision that he opened the acquaintanceship of this invaluable ally with some short-tempered and barely polite remarks that the interpreter reported otherwise, and so solidarity with the worthy Waaka was for-tuitously preserved.

The column rested at Waimate for five days, with more and more of the Rev Burrows' chickens disappearing into the soldiers' cooking pots. During this halt, Despard was surprised one day to see about 200 Maoris with a large Union Jack at their head straggling toward the Mission. Their chief proved to be Pomare, now reinstated after the affair of the subversive letters, mainly by the intercession of Waaka with the Governor. He had hardly had his first glass of rum when he observed William Hulme standing in the gathering. He became quite livid and burst out impassionedly, shaking his fist in front of Hulme's face: 'You made me prisoner and carried me to Auckland! You burned my *pa* and drove my people out!' Fortunately for future rela-tions, though Pomare did accompany the expeditionary force to Ohaeawai, the supply of rum was rather parsi-monious in the front line and he drifted away as casually as he appeared.

At dawn, 23 June, Despard led his force out of Waimate on the final leg of the march; his command now consisted of 180 men of the 99th under Major Macpherson, 270 of the 58th led by Major Bridge, followed by 70 soldiers of the 96th under Lieutenant-Colonel William Hulme; then came 30 marines from the *Hazard* under Acting-Commander Johnson and Lieutenant Phillpotts, 80 Auckland Volunteers and finally Waaka's friend-lies; the guns were in charge of Captain Marlow and Lieutenant Wilmot of the Engineers. The going was so difficult that it was sunset before they had covered the seven miles to Ohaeawai. As the column approached, musketry fire indicated that Waaka's scouts had driven in a rebel picquet from a conical hill overlooking the *pa*. The hill, which was to have some significance, was called Waaka's Hill.

Ohaeawai *pa*, which had been greatly strengthened by the constructional genius of Kawiti, now stood before Despard, though without Hone Heke who was lying in the safe obscurity of Tautoro, fourteen miles away, recovering from his wound. Not especially large, the *pa* was built very solidly on rising ground with a small ravine on its west, sudden slopes on the south, a gradual decline on the east and a gentle rise to the north. Each wall was blistered with projections that ensured enfilading fire along any section, and its timbers were young puriri trees sunk six feet in the ground with a height of ten feet exposed and laced together with vines and overhung with thick mattresses of green flax which absorbed musketry balls. Inside the *pa*'s outer wall were the usual two inner walls; between these two walls, which had connecting escape holes, ran a trench, and musketry slits were cut in the middle and outer walls for the defenders manning the trench to observe and fire through. The *pa* also had shellproof shelters and storehouses for its garrison of about 250 and the nearness of the close bush allowed reinforcements and couriers to slip in and out during the mid-winter nights.

Next day Despard set up his four guns on an earth and stone platform and began bombarding, but the shells had little effect. Even when the battery position was moved up to within 200 yards of the *pa*, the elastic and tenacious flax closed up about the shotholes and made it difficult to gauge the extent of any damage. On the night of the 25th, when a 58th grenadier was killed by a musket ball, Despard decided to have a concerted bombardment and attack, but torrential rain cancelled the operation and the storming parties returned lamely to their camp. Over the following days the guns continued their desultory work, ineffective fire fights flared up between the rebels and their besiegers, another abortive attack was stood down and the watching and waiting were enlivened by two rebel sorties which were repulsed, leaving three dead. But by Monday, 29 June, British casualties were slowly mounting: a grenadier of the 99th and a seaman were killed by enemy fire and several wounded.

Despard, ill-tempered and frustrated, now sent for a 32-

7. *Colonel Despard's attack on Hone Heke's* pa *at Ohaeawai.*

8. *Colonel Hulme's attack on Pomare's* pa *at Puketutu.*

9. *A photograph of the site of Ohaeawai* pa *as it looks today.*

10. *The bombardment of 'The Bat's Nest', Kawiti's* pa *at Ruapekapeka.*

pounder from HMS *Hazard* and settled down impatiently in the miserable wet and thundery weather to await it laborious arrival. By Sunday afternoon he could bear the inaction no longer and determined to attack without the heavy gun. All his field officers without exception, including Hulme and Waaka, who told a fellow chief that it made him sick in the stomach to contemplate such a waste of valuable lives, were vehemently against such a suicidal plan. At this *moment critique* in Despard's blood pressure, news came that the vital gun, weighing some $1\frac{1}{2}$ tons, had reached Waimate with twenty-five sailors. In fact it was already well on its way to Ohaeawai and when it arrived later that day, the crowd of curious who flocked about it drew heavy rebel fire and another soldier was killed. That evening the drays returned to Waimate with the wounded.

The whole of that night and the next day were occupied positioning the gun on which so much hope was now pinned. But as the sun shone in a rainless sky, that hope was nearly dashed by a critical sortie from the rebel garrison. Despard was toiling up Waaka's Hill when, to his amazement, he saw a small picquet of the 58th and some friendly Maoris tumbling down towards him pell-mell; the rebels had gained possession of the hill. Turning to his bugler to sound the alarm, he managed to turn out a company of the 58th under Cyprian Bridge and launch it on a circuitous approach to cut off the rebel detachment from the *pa*. But before the 58th could close, the rebels ran into the fern and disappeared.

The upshot of this brisk encounter was that the British flag from Waaka's Hill fell into rebel hands. Later Despard was mortified to see it flying in the *pa* upside-down and at half-mast, below the native flag. This caused an explosion of rage and he was now determined to attack without further delay.

Under the orders of his acting-Brigade Major, Lieutenant Rupert Deering of the 99th, his force assembled at 3 pm for the assault. The advanced storming party of 2 sergeants and 20 soldiers, all volunteers from the three Regimental detachments and, as reality was to prove, dubbed not without reason 'the forlorn hope', was led by Lieutenant Jack Beatty of the 99th; then followed the first assault party under Major Macpherson, 99th,

D

with 40 grenadiers of the 99th and 40 of the 58th, closely supported by seamen and Volunteers carrying axes, ladders and ropes under the colourful Lieutenant Phillpotts; next came the second assault group of the remaining 60 grenadiers of the 58th and 40 men of the Light Company, 99th, under Major Bridge. A support group of 100 men of the 58th and 96th remained in reserve under Lieutenant-Colonel William Hulme, a captain and 40 soldiers of the 58th stood firm on Waaka's Hill, and the balance of the force was under Despard's own command. Waaka's Maoris clustered thickly on the Hill to watch, fascinated, the gory spectacle they knew would unfold.

With a full-blooded British cheer, echoed by a roar from Waaka's Hill, the patient infantry in their tattered red tunics, some barefooted, all carrying a full knapsack even in the assault and still wearing the old-fashioned leather stock, went for the *pa*. Inevitably the north-west corner, the point of attack chosen by Despard, was the strongest part, being of the original *pa* before Kawiti's re-building, and was also defended at that sector by the local chief of Ohaeawai, Pene Taui, and his own *hapu*. As William Free, who enlisted in the 58th Regiment in 1842 and came out to Australia on convict escort duty, to die eventually at the splendid age of 93 at New Plymouth in 1919, says: 'We just went at the strong stockade under orders from a Colonel who did not know his business and who had a contempt for the Maori.'

Within ten minutes, under the horrified gaze of their commander, the slaughter of the attackers was fearful. The rebels allowed the assault to gain within twenty-five yards of the *pa*, then opened fire with devastating effect. Even through that withering fire, brave surviving groups reached the outer wall and some even tore their way through a hole or fell dead at the top of a scaling ladder but these were in turn blasted at close range by shotguns and, most savagely, by an old 9-pounder salvaged from the wreck of the *Brampton*, which, loaded with bullock chain, swathed through the surviving few. Despard ordered the retreat to be blown. The shattered ranks fell away from the carnage, covered by Hulme's reserve, and courageously recovering their wounded as they went. Some forty were killed or died of wounds, including Grant of the 58th, Phillpotts and Beatty. Some eighty were wounded, Major Macpherson seriously. The bodies of the many dead lay before the *pa* all that long, dreadful night which was rent by the shrieking celebrations of the victorious rebels, making the despondent soldiers believe that their missing comrades were being tortured.

Phillpotts, with that strange presentiment men occasionally have, went forward knowing he was going to die. He was an extraordinary character, and one who had shared the excitements and fluctuations of the First Maori War from the onset; he had even been captured riding out from Kororareka when Hone Heke and Kawiti were encamped at Te Uriti. Of bizarre dress, complete with monocle, he was the son of the Bishop of Exeter, yet his antagonism to the missionaries, whom he accused of siding with the rebels, drew a personal rebuke from the Governor. Brave and amusing, popular with his sailors and even with the rebels who called him Toby, he was the *bête noire* of Despard, with whom he made a point of insolently disagreeing on every topic, and the Colonel was not the man to entertain disagreement. An accusation exists against Phillpotts that, irreverent and insubordinate to the last, he told his sailors to discard the axes and ladders they were ordered to carry and retain their cutlasses, but certainly at least one ladder is known to have reached the *peherangi*. He strode to his death with a bared cutlass, hatless, in a sailor's shirt and grey flannels. Certainly eccentric and clearly difficult to superiors, George Phillpotts was an Englishman others would follow without hesitation and of such Empires are made or retained.

For the imperious Despard, the dawning of the next day merely emphasised the gravity of his situation: his major assault had been an appalling failure, his ammunition was now low, and the morale of his men had been badly affected by the bloody repulse. The dead still lay before their eyes for the rebels had received the intermediary, the Rev Burrows, very coolly and curtly told him to come back the following morning. Despard now decided, as impetuously as he rushed to the offensive, to abandon the siege and retire to Waimate. At once, as the rumour circulated in the camp, he was confronted by his protesting allies, Waaka and his chiefs. Grudgingly, for he felt as a British Colonel he could hardly allow himself to be swayed by a pack of savages, he agreed to a council of war that afternoon.

The meeting was heated and acrimonious. Despard upbraided his native allies for not supporting his suicidal attack, while Mohi (Moses) Tawhai retorted what a disastrous effect his abandonment of the dead would have on the minds of all Maoris, both friendly and hostile. Harsh words were hurled about until Waaka calmed the furore by formally requesting two final days for the operation, and probably because he was the one steadying influence among the angry chiefs, Despard reluctantly acquiesced.

Next day, 8 July, the dead were brought in, mainly through the agency of a *pakeha* Maori, John Marmion, a former Botany Bay convict who came to New Zealand in 1817. Haphazard firing broke out again, with the 32-pounder opening up only occasionally due to lack of ammunition, but on the following night a strange silence enveloped the *pa*. In the early hours, Waaka's scouts, whose suspicions had been aroused, crept up to the *pa* and after cautious investigation found it to be deserted. The rebels had slipped away. Blood had been spilt on the *pa* and according to a curious Maori war custom, it was abandoned, as Puketutu had been, despite the British withdrawal. In Maori eyes it was no disgrace to give up a fighting *pa*; victory was measured by the infliction of casualties and the taking of captives.

When the British entered the *pa* they found the mutilated body of the able and energetic Captain Grant of the 58th; parts of his body had been cut away and probably eaten. The burned body of a grenadier of the 99th, wounded and captured before the attack through foraging too carelessly for potatoes, was also discovered, but whether he was tortured or the burns were accidental was never established. Torture, in fact, was not a Maori custom; if anything, they tended to despatch an unwanted prisoner summarily.

By virtue of occupation, despite Despard's abject handling, the operation against Ohaeawai *pa* ended in a hollow victory of sorts for the British. The native flag which had flown triumphantly over the purloined Union Jack from Waaka's Hill was secured by Waaka's men who presented it to Cyprian Bridge as a memento. Ohaeawai was destroyed and after returning to Waimate for a rest, the depleted column went on to the *pa* of Heke's lieutenant, Te Haratua, at Pakaraka on 16 July. On finding that *pa* also empty, Despard again had the doubtful satisfaction of razing to the ground another deserted enemy position. That evening he received despatches in camp summoning himself and Hulme back to Auckland to discuss further operations with the Governor.

Well might the Ngapuhi war-runners fan out through the North proclaiming:

'One wing of England is broken and hangs dangling on the ground.'

CHAPTER 6
The Bat's Nest

THE detachment of the 96th Regiment went with Despard and their Commanding Officer, William Hulme, to Auckland where they relieved a company of the 58th to join their comrades at the Bay of Islands. Meanwhile, much to the embarrassment and annoyance of the Rev Burrows, the main body of the field force settled about Waimate, under the command of Major Bridge who was instructed to remain on the defensive.

At the capital, Despard and Hulme sat on the courts-martial of Lieutenant Barclay and Ensign Campbell, charged with dereliction of duty at Kororareka. Barclay was acquitted, while Campbell was found guilty; however, his youth and inexperience were taken into consideration by the Court and he was merely reprimanded (which may indicate that Despard, the court-martial president, did have some understanding behind his explosive and easily-ruffled exterior).

However, this duty done, the fiery Colonel soon became frustrated and impatient as he waited for the Governor to decide the future course of action. Robert FitzRoy thought that the loss of Ohaeawai *pa* had produced a sobering effect on the rebels, yet he dared not withdraw troops altogether from such a forward position as Waimate in case Heke's and Kawiti's followers really ran amok and destroyed outlying homesteads and missions. His havering was anathema to the unchastened Colonel, who was champing to take the field again, as his military philosophy delivered to Auckland society in that waiting period indicated:

'The New Zealander is not a man who can be treated with any sort of hesitation. He must be talked to with the bayonet.'

FitzRoy, however, was worried about bigger issues than the Colonel grasped, or wished to grasp, namely the loyalty of the other leading Northern chiefs and the consequent threat to Auckland if another important native personality joined the rebel cause. In his dilemma, he would hardly have been human if he did not wish to believe the more cheerful signs, such as another fulsome letter from Hone Heke, dated 19 July, 1845, hinting at a rapprochement.

FitzRoy replied tactfully, but pointed out the destruction of Kororareka and of the lives lost, and asked what Heke intended to do to make amends. As his correspondent thought with some feeling that the Europeans were at fault and ought to do any atonement, this particular peace overture then faded into silence. The breakdown of peace feelers at least suited the bellicose Henry Despard and on 26 August he embarked in the *Slains Castle* with reinforcements for the 99th and some recovered-wounded of the 58th and sailed back to the Bay of Islands.

On 1 September, Despard was back at Waimate with the fresh troops and supplies but his blood pressure immediately rose when he sighted the solid earthworks Cyprian Bridge had constructed, after many rumours of a rebel attack. Despard took this sensible and cautionary measure to be a personal affront to the fighting qualities of the British soldier and ordered the glowering Bridge to demolish such needless defences. However, his extraordinary lack of comprehension about the fighting powers of the Maori at least allowed him to cancel the practice of the whole camp standing-to during the many and unfounded night alarms and he set up inlying picquets instead. This ensured that most soldiers had a sound night's rest.

At the end of September, Despard and his native ally, Waaka, received an important addition to their ranks, Nopera Panakareao, chief of the Rarawas who brought 100 of his prime fighting men, and this auspicious event was celebrated with a grand *haka* and many speeches. Nopera, who had made the celebrated remark at the Treaty of Waitangi about the shadow of the land and the substance, was a reliable and reputable war-leader who even impressed Henry Despard, perhaps not least because on Sundays he observed the Maori chief diligently studying his Bible.

Meanwhile, another flurry of letter-writing set in between Hone Heke, and now Kawiti, too, and the Governor, who laid down the conditions for peace, which included the confiscation of rebel lands. Kawiti was now more amenable to peace than Heke, so beset by bursts of arrogance and intolerance; and doubtless the tragic loss of two sons in the fighting had dampened his campaigning fever, but he replied that he would never countenance the loss of his land. Heke wrote in well-worn style, blaming the war on Waaka Nene's personal blood vendetta. The upshot of this latest correspondence was to reassure FitzRoy that Waimate and other missions would be quite safe from rebel depredations in their own right and he instructed Despard to withdraw the field force to Kororareka where he was to construct a defensive position and await events. FitzRoy was now banking much hope on the peace activities of Archdeacon Henry Williams and the ubiquitous Rev Robert Burrows.

In late October Despard landed his troops on the beach before the blackened ruins of Kororareka: earlier that month he had gained the valuable reinforcement of 214 men of the 58th under their Commanding Officer, Lieutenant-Colonel Robert Wynyard, when their ship, the *Royal Sovereign,* was met off Auckland after the voyage from Sydney by HMS *Daphne* and *Racehorse* and instructed to proceed direct to the Bay of Islands. As Despard set about making the few standing buildings habitable as billets, he seems to have ignored the Governor's instruction to restore the fateful flagstaff and flag to Maiki Hill. However, he soon stopped work on constructing defensive redoubts—such anathema to his offensive creed—when he heard the startling news that a new Governor had been appointed.

The new man was Captain George Grey, a former officer of the 83rd Regiment who had made an early reputation in epic explorations of the Australian deserts and latterly as a successful Governor of South Australia. Young (not quite 34 years old), able, intelligent and forceful, and a man of some erudition who was to take a deep interest in the Maori language and culture, he was destined to become one of the great Victorian proconsuls of Empire, with a train of achievements in Australia, New Zealand and South Africa. When he landed at Auckland on 14 November to the booming of guns and military ceremonial, it was perhaps fitting that among 'the quality' who bowed before him at the levée at Government House after his swearing-in was none other than that strong arm of the Queen, Tamati Waaka Nene, resplendent in naval officer's uniform with sword and a colonel's cocked hat with plumes. Robert FitzRoy took his supercession with well-bred equanimity and briefed his successor fully; the missionaries were aghast to see him go but the New Zealand Company and the settlers, smarting from his indictment of the Wairau incident and deeming him a Maori-lover, were jubilant. Possibly it was the influence and pressure of the Company's investors in England, waiting in their counting houses, country seats and rectories for profits from the land speculations, that caused FitzRoy's removal.

The bellicose dreams of Henry Despard were soon to be given substance as the new Governor energetically slipped through the administrative work awaiting him and sailed a few days later in the East India sloop-of-war, the *Elphinstone*, to the Bay of Islands; he was quick to see that the main problems currently lay there. When he disembarked on 24 November at Kororareka, he was again met with due military formality but, on this occasion, also with Maori ceremonial. A tremendous *haka* was performed until which time Waaka, formally attired in his mixture of naval and military finery, was impressively dignified and sedate. When the *haka* began he discarded his veneer of *Pakeha* propriety, drew his sword and threw himself into the frenzy and passion of the war dance. British officers who saw this transformation with astonishment and affectionate amusement, relate that, in his gyrations, Waaka had great difficulty with his sword scabbard.

Four days later, Grey addressed a large concourse of Maoris among the ruins of Kororareka and while he repeated with some emphasis the Queen's protection for their lands, he delivered an ultimatum to the absent Hone Heke and Kawiti that they must come to terms within days or the war would be renewed. It is interesting that the friendly or neutral chiefs spoke unanimously against Heke; they advised the Governor that he should not hesitate to resume hostilities as Hone Heke was 'a man of many thoughts'. To this final offer, Heke sent a wordy but unequivocal rejection but Kawiti was inclined to haver:

From the Ruapekapeka,
29 November, 1845.

'Sir, The Governor,
  Salutations to you. Formerly I was a good man to the Europeans, but the Ngapuhi were so eager to fight with me. They are the people who formerly killed Europeans. If this war was solely yours and the natives had not part in it with you, our peace would have been made; but as for the natives fighting, perhaps it cannot be made straight, because Waaka is constantly naming his dead. You do not understand this. Waaka's fighting is not for your dead. No, it is for those who were killed long ago—on account of Hao, of Tuahui, Tihi and Poaka. These were killed long ago. Sir Governor, the thought is with you regarding Waaka that he returns to his own people at Hokianga. Do not be hasty about the land. Land is enduring but man is perishable. Friend, I have no desire to write to you, but you may write if you are pleased with my letter. Sir, if you say that we do fight, it is well. If you say "cease", it is well; but do not say that you will not yield some portion of your thoughts.

From me,
From Kawiti."[1]

More correspondence ensued, and the *North Star* was anchored discreetly in the Kawakawa river to receive the submission of the two rebel chiefs in case of a change of heart, but then Grey learned that ammunition-gathering and fortifying was going on apace in the rebel territory and he realised that the letters were merely a time-gaining device. He ordered Despard to take offensive action and sailed back to Auckland to attend to urgent matters that affected the modest colonial war effort: the raising of more Volunteers, supplies for the field force, and most important of all, forbidding the sale of arms and ammunition to natives, a highly lucrative commercial venture that some Auckland merchants pursued indiscriminately with few questions asked.
  Despard undertook his operational mission with typical war-

[1] Buick.

like enthusiasm and energy. The new objective crystallising for the campaign was Kawiti's own *pa* at Ruapekapeka, 'the Bat's Nest', alleged to be a veritable Gibraltar of Maori military construction and the topic of much discussion throughout Maori encampments in the North how the British would fare against it. Kawiti, true to his original simple decision to enter the rebellion to test British fighting prowess, had complained to Hone Heke with some feeling that so far all the fighting had been done on Heke's land. Now he, Kawiti, wanted some glory too.

By 12 December, by ship and route march, Despard had concentrated his whole force, with guns and heavy stores, at the pleasant *pa*, amid orchards and gardens, of an enemy of Kawiti's, Tamati Pukututu, at the very head of the Kawakawa river. The next week was spent, after a reconnaissance by Despard and Captain Marlow of the Engineers, broadening a track through dense high fern that would take the drays hauling the guns to the next staging post, Waimio. On 14 December the *Elphinstone* sailed back into the Bay of Islands with the Governor on board, and he went forward to be with the troops. Grey was a man of action who preferred the field to the office and, as befitted his old profession and as the son of the Commanding Officer of the 30th Regiment who fell in action at Salamanca in 1812, he doubtless thrived on the smell of powder; however, apart from this personal inclination, his presence could be explained by two other reasons: he wished to be on hand for sudden peace negotiations or, possibly briefed by FitzRoy, he may have been apprehensive about the shortcomings of his field commander.

On 22 December Lieutenant-Colonel Wynyard led the advance guard out from Puketutu to Waimio, a mere five miles distant but over the usual arduous country. Next day the main body followed under Despard, with the drays and guns struggling laboriously along the primitive track now awash from heavy rain and in deep mud, pulled by bullocks and also hauling on drag-ropes to the 32-pounders, some sixty hardworked seamen and soldiers. The expeditionary force against the Bat's Nest was now quite formidable—the Naval Brigade under Commander Hay numbered some 33 officers and 280 seamen; the Infantry Brigade consisted of 80 Royal Marines under Cap-

tain Langford, 20 officers and 543 men of the 58th under Wynyard, 7 officers and 150 men of the 99th commanded by Captain
Reed, 42 Auckland Volunteers under Captain Atkyns, all supported by a sizable ordnance of two 32-pounders, two 12-pounders,
one 18-pounder, one 6-pounder brass gun and four light mortars
which were to prove invaluable for dropping bombs into the
objective. Mainly seamen manned the guns but from the *Elphinstone*, diverted on Grey's own responsibility from transit to India,
were an officer and fifteen gunners of the Bengal Artillery. With
'the men in red garments' and the sailors were 450 friendly
Maoris under Waaka and his doughty confederates: his brother,
Patuone, Mohi Tawhai, Nopera Panakareao and Repa.

After three days of enforced rest at Waimio, where torrential
rain saved the soldiers and seamen from marching out on
Christmas Day, on the 27th Grey and Despard stood at last
before Kawiti's stronghold, the Bat's Nest. It was a daunting
sight, lying on a narrow ridge protected by a deep and abrupt
ravine from the open approach along which the British force
had advanced. Despard set about turning the ravine by cutting
a track through the bush and concentrated on getting his guns
up from Waimio. As his men became more wearied from track-
building and the bullocks exhausted from gun-hauling, yet
another reinforcement arrived at his forward camp, a final company of the 58th from the notorious Australian penal settlement
of Norfolk Island.

With his considerable artillery in position, Despard began a
steady harassing fire, seeking to wear down the rebels in the *pa*
through the terror of shells and rockets bursting about them.
Two mornings later, when fog silenced the guns, some rebels
crept out and caught a Volunteer pioneer, wounding him
critically. Repa led a charge of friendly Maoris to intercept the
rebels on their way back to the *pa*, but had three fingers of one
hand shot away. Later, when the sun broke through, Kawiti's
personal red and white standard, with the sun, moon and stars
depicted in the white half, was seen fluttering bravely over the *pa*.
In New Zealand's first war, flags and flagstaffs were certainly
passion-rousing to a disproportionate degree, and Despard, again,
was far from immune. As he regarded this latest entry into the

vexed flag controversy, he was rescued from his emotional volcano by Lt Bland toppling the flagpole to the ground with a single superbly-aimed shot. In the morning sky, a young moon with a distinct bright star was then seen and this coupled with the summary demise of the rebel flag, had a profound effect on credulous native minds, not the least that of the otherwise redoubtable Kawiti.

During the next few days, Despard began advancing his guns steadily nearer the *pa* and by 2 January, 1846, he had established his breaching battery of the two 32-pounders in a clearing masked by fern and protected by a stockade wall a mere 400 yards from the *pa*. That afternoon a strong force of rebels sallied out to attack the feared big guns but Waaka's men were launched by Despard with unusual prescience at the sortie, possibly to test the sincerity of his native allies, and a running battle developed until dusk when the superior tactics of Waaka in the centre and Nopera and Mohi Tawhai on the wings began to envelop the rebels and they retreated into the *pa*, leaving 7 dead and 13 wounded, while the friendlies sustained only five wounded. Waaka and his men celebrated this sharp little victory with a great *haka* that shook the ground well within earshot of the *pa*; Repa's missing fingers could be said to have been royally revenged. Over the next seven days, two more gun positions were established, including another 32-pounder dragged up from the *Castor*.

On 9 January a recovered Hone Heke slipped into the Bat's Nest with sixty followers from his new *pa* at Hikurangi, twenty miles away, where Taonui and 100 friendly Maoris had been watching him until he eluded their vigil; he had heard that the British preparations for a final assault were now almost ready, and again, confidently expected that the 'red tribe' would advance on to the muzzles of the rebels' muskets and be destroyed. On the following day, at 11 am, a concerted bombardment roared out from every British gun, shrouding the *pa* wall in smoke and dust as the defenders took shelter in their dug-outs; even Hone Heke was shaken by its intensity. As the day and the violent bombardment wore on, Heke's keener tactical sense caused him to urge Kawiti to abandon the *pa* and draw the enemy into the bush away from their big guns and cut them down there. But Kawiti refused to give up his *pa* without returning the fight. The outer wall was beginning to break up, but behind, as stout as ever, were the other two wall systems.

With breaches now opening in the outer wall, Despard decided, despite the Ohaeawai debacle, to attack, and a storming force of 200 was quickly mustered. But Waaka and some of his chiefs, especially Mohi Tawhai who again was vehemently forthright to Henry Despard ('How many more soldiers do you want to kill?'), ran over to him and protested bitterly against the folly of assaulting at this stage and, quite out of character and probably because of Grey who trusted the Maori allies and listened to them, he reluctantly agreed. The gunners continued with a harassing dropping fire but that night another unusual silence, with no baiting calls from the rebel sentinels, settled over the *pa*.

The next day was Sunday and in one of the typical but quite extraordinary situations that happened in the First Maori War, it transpired that Hone Heke and most of the rebels, who were Christians, were outside the *pa* in the bush holding a service. A band of Waaka's men under another brother, Wiremu Waaka Tutau, shrewdly guessing what had happened, crept up to the battered outer wall and deduced that the *pa* was almost deserted. In response to their frantic silent signals, a number of soldiers sprinted up to the *pa* led by Wynyard and hard on his heels came Henry Despard with Denny and 100 men of the 58th. Quickly they began infiltrating through the breaches and the mouseholes of the inner walls and inside they found Kawiti and a mere handful of fellow pagans dozing blissfully in their trenches. Surprised, Kawiti and his few stalwarts stood to arms but could only fight their way desperately out through a back entrance.

Meanwhile, the dutiful Heke and the Christian rebels, dramatically disturbed at their devotions by the sound of musket fire coming from the direction of the *pa*, rushed back and found that they had to fight fiercely to try to regain their own fortress. For some four hours a firefight raged but the soldiers were too wily to be drawn into the bush after the rebels; some seamen did charge from the *pa* but were quickly killed in the bush. Finally, the dispirited rebels made one last attack, mainly to recover their dead and wounded, and then melted away into the bush in full retreat.

Again, somewhat fortuitously, Colonel Henry Despard was left the victor in the field and next day he began demolishing Ruapekapeka, 'The Bat's Nest'. On inspection the British found that it warranted its native reputation, as it was honeycombed with subterranean tunnels, well-constructed dugouts and shelters, and probably only a crisis over food and water could have affected a long siege. In the actions that raged about its possession, the British lost 12 killed and 30 wounded, while on the rebel casualty lists at least twelve chiefs were known to have been killed and their overall losses were probably heavy.

With the capture of the Bat's Nest the rebellion in the north ended. Hone Heke and Kawiti fled to Pomare's *pa* but received cold comfort from this worldly cousin who now saw clearly how the wind was blowing, and he offered only temporary refuge and food. As the two rebel chiefs moved to the more inaccessible points of their lands and awaited further advances by the 'men who wear red garments', the real statesmen to emerge out of the débris of war was Tamati Waaka Nene, the Ngapuhi chief suspected of fighting to avenge old scores. He went in the brig *Victoria* to plead with the Governor at Auckland for clemency for the rebels and he was successful. Grey was not disposed to seek heads and harsh retribution and moreover, with native troubles brewing in the south, it was politic to gain peace in the north. He granted free pardons to Heke and Kawiti and renounced the seizure of their lands threatened by both FitzRoy and Despard. Waaka summed up the whole affair with his usual native perspicacity when he heard the Governor make this decision, for he grasped Grey's hand and said: 'You have saved us all.'

Grey's magnanimous peace undoubtedly did placate savage passions and time worked the final healing process. Waaka, Hone Heke and Kawiti were even reconciled, and finally, Kawiti, with Te Haratua and Pomare, was converted to Christianity; perhaps the moral of sleeping-in on Sunday mornings had not been lost on him. Hone Heke died from consumption in 1850, slightly

63

mellowed but still difficult, and Kawiti from measles in 1853. It was indeed fitting, if not ironical, that his son, Maihi Paraone Kawiti, was to re-hoist the British flag on Maiki Hill in January, 1858, when the old bitterness had died and a new spirit of co-operation and brotherhood with the *Pakeha* had developed.

It is also interesting to speculate whether Sir George Grey saved the Maoris with his peace, or Waaka Nene the *Pakeha* with his influence on the Governor. For British rule in New Zealand was later to enter a second, more widespread and difficult period of native unrest and wars, and if the numerous and warlike Ngapuhi had not stayed loyal and aloof from the later conflict, the Queen's Government and European settlement could have been in great jeopardy. When the powerful Waikato tribe set up the Maori King movement in the Fifties, their emissaries promised Maihi Paraone Kawiti the Governorship of the North if the Ngapuhi backed the régime. But the Ngapuhi remembered that they had eaten Waikato and replied: 'Kuini Wikitoria' was their 'Kingi'.

Young Kawiti then went along to hoist the Queen's flag on Maiki Hill.

CHAPTER 7
Smouldering Embers

LIKE every Victorian colonial governor, Sir George Grey was acutely conscious of his slim military resources and the end of the war in the North could not have happened more opportunely. Ominous signs of unrest were now occurring in the south part of North Island. From an unhappy culmination of reckless land deals by Company agents and growing greed by local Maoris, outlying homesteads in the Hutt Valley leading into Wellington were being intimidated. Inevitably the instigator of this native aggression was that savage character, Te Rangihaeata.

As a garrison to enforce the peace in the Bay of Islands, 300 men of the 58th Regiment encamped about James Busby's damaged old residency at Waitangi, while the rest of the expeditionary force sailed back to Auckland. At the capital the two flank companies of the 99th were joined by another company from Australia under Major Edward Last and a few days later, on 26 January, 1846, their Commanding Officer embarked for Sydney to resume command of his Regiment; 'much,' as one caustic officer remarked, 'to the satisfaction of the troops in New Zealand'. However, the stay of the veterans of Ohaeawai and Ruapekapeka in the comparative civilisation of the drawing-rooms and taverns of Auckland was to be brief, for Maori depredations in the Hutt Valley began to grow more serious. As defences were being thrown up about Wellington and the Militia called out, 400 soldiers of the 58th, 96th and 99th, with two gun detachments of the Royal Artillery, embarked at Auckland under the command of Lieutenant-Colonel William Hulme to reinforce its garrison of 180 men of the 58th and 96th. Only the influence of the devoted missionary, Octavius Hadfield, and the friendly chief of the Ngatiawa, Te Rangitake, prevented the ferocious Te Rangihaeata from moving on the settlement.

The arrival of this strong military force was not too soon, as the situation rapidly deteriorated from the pillaging of crops and intercepting supplies to the murder of a settler and his son. Martial law was proclaimed and Hulme deployed up the Valley to protect the exposed farms. Desultory brushes with Maori raiders developed, until in April an imaginative offensive operation launched two companies, one each from the 58th and 99th, under Major Edward Last by sea to Porirua, on the west coast above Wellington, to establish a force in rear of Te Rangihaeata's forays. However, as Last cautiously spent several weeks setting up a stockaded base camp as soon as he landed, the rebel chief also used the time constructively to build a strong *pa* four miles away to checkmate the British landing. Meanwhile, another force of the 58th under Captain Russell set about making a road from Wellington to the Porirua outpost, divided into subalterns' parties of fifty men each two or three miles apart and working always with their arms piled beside them.

When their crops were gathered by May, the dissident Ngatitoa, joined by Upper Wanganui adventurous spirits, began moving in force over the countryside again. One hour before dawn on 16 May a war party 200 strong under the Upper Wanganui chief, Te Mamaku, crept up on Boulcott's Farm garrisoned by about forty-five soldiers of the 58th under Lieutenant G. H. Page, mainly in a stockaded barn but also in the farmer's cottage, outhouses and a tent alongside. In the chilly pre-dawn light the prowler sentry realised that the bushes on the farm clearing by the riverbank seemed to be getting strangely nearer and he just had time to get one shot away before he was rushed and tomahawked as he tried to re-load. The cottage where Page and two soldiers were sleeping and the exposed tent were also in this initial charge:

'At a given signal, the ropes of the tent were cut, and as the soldiers struggled out from beneath the folds, they were set upon by the Maoris. Drummer Allen seized his bugle and managed to sound the alarm when his right arm was almost severed by the blow of a tomahawk. He seized the bugle with his left hand and bravely completed the call and continued sounding until hacked to pieces."[1]

Four dead soldiers lay with the courageous boy soldier, but three wounded escaped to the stockade, as did Page, armed with pistol and sword, who fought his way with his two men from the cottage to the main barn. Once together the 58th detachment fought with the steady discipline of Regular soldiers, each section firing through a part of the light fence and then retiring, on relief by another section, to reload in the barn. Eventually, Page, with some brashness, led most of his men out with fixed bayonets to close with the enemy and as this action was developing, a party of Hutt Militia fortuitously arrived and Te Mamaku's warriors retreated across the river to dance a furious war dance of some frustration before retiring into the forest.

After the action of Boulcott's Farm, Te Rangihaeata moved up the Horokiwi valley to his *pa* at Porirua where only artillery, with the usual great delay in getting forward over the rude bush tracks, would shift him. However, the offensively-minded and resourceful Sir George Grey now set about mounting an excellent *coup de main* against Te Rauparaha who, professing innocence of any complicity with his terrible nephew's activities, was living with the Ngatitoa of Taupo on the northern arm of Porirua harbour. During the night of 23 July the darkened HMS *Calliope* slid noiselessly into the harbour and 150 armed soldiers, marines and sailors rowed to the shore. The old warlord was seized in his sleep and frogmarched, protesting violently, to a waiting boat and the man-o'-war and borne off to Auckland. There he was eventually released to a form of town arrest, through the inter-cession of Potatau Te Wherowhero and, inevitably, Tamati Waaka Nene, and paraded happily about the capital dressed in naval captain's uniform. In 1848 he was allowed to go to Otaki and died the following year.

This dramatic seizure of Te Rauparaha shook Te Rangihaeata

[1] *The History of the Northamptonshire Regiment, 1742–1934* by Lt-Col Russell Gurney.

for the simple Maori reason that one week before, when staying in his uncle's house, he had a bad dream and filled with foreboding, pleaded with the old man to leave that place of danger. But Te Akua, the old warrior's chief wife who had accompanied him through many vicissitudes since the tribe had been driven south from Kawhia twenty-five years ago by the Waikato, was ill and he refused to leave her. So, strangely, Te Rangihaeata abandoned his Porirua *pa* and withdrew up the recesses of the Horokiwi valley. Major Last, now reinforced by a company of the 65th Regiment from Van Diemen's Land to some 250 rifles, including Hutt Militia, some bluejackets from HMS *Calliope* and a party of Wellington armed police as well as the 58th and 99th companies, and led by 150 Ngatiawa under Te Rangitake dressed in blue serge blouses with big letters 'VR' in white on back and front to mark their friendly status, followed him up and on 6 August came in sight of a strong *pa* well-sited on a daunting hill. In the advance, at one of the abandoned rebel camps, a soldier of the 65th Company found in a *whare* the bugle of young Drummer Allen and returned this honoured relic to the 58th.

An impetuous approach to the *pa* cost the lives of Ensign Blackburn, 99th, and two soldiers, and a thorough reconnaissance by Last, mindful of the bloody lessons of the past, decided him that the *pa* was too forbidding for any frontal assault and he contented himself with lobbing bombs from his three light mortars into its perimeter. This waiting tactic was an intelligent decision as, four days later, Te Rangihaeata again took to the forest and Te Rangitake and his Ngatiawa set off to harry him. Te Rangihaeata withdrew far into the deep flax swamps, streams and lagoons of the Horokiwi, rich with eels and wild fowl, to a last retreat called Paeroa where he was allowed to subsist unmolested with a hundred diehard followers. In 1856 he, too, died of measles:

'So passed a type of the old pagan order, a true irreconcilable, averse to anything of the white man's but his weapons of war. He was seldom seen in any dress but the picturesque native garments of flax; and a commanding figure he was, tomahawk in hand, standing 2 inches over six feet, draped in a finely woven and beautifully patterned *parawai* or *kaitaka* cloak.'[1]

[1] *The New Zealand Wars and the Pioneering Period* by James Cowan.

With the complete negation of both Te Rauparaha and Te Rangihaeata, Sir George Grey might reasonably have hoped for a lasting peace for the troubled North Island, but now, in late 1846, another crisis of classical New Zealand colonial mould arose at the small New Zealand Company settlement of Wanganui, on the west coast between Wellington and New Plymouth: 200 settlers had been promised land by the Company that the local Maoris still claimed, and 4,000 tribesmen in ugly mood gathered on the Wanganui river. The Governor despatched Captain Laye and 180 men of the 58th to Wanganui and Laye set about erecting a stockade to protect the town.

Some months of uneasy calm followed, to be savagely broken in May by the brutal murders of a settler's wife and three children at an isolated farm; the settler and his 16-year-old daughter, both wounded, escaped. When the five murderers were captured, a war party of 700 warriors gathered to rescue them and so Captain Laye, who seems to have been a man of some decision, promptly convened a court-martial composed of his subalterns and hanged four of the accused without delay. An attack came in almost at once, but the garrison repulsed it. The next day, 20 May, Grey sailed from Wellington in the *Inflexible* with two companies of the 65th and took the field himself at Wanganui. Some sporadic skirmishing set in until July, when the recalcitrant Upper Wanganui sued for peace, again through the influence of Potatau Te Wherowhero and Tamati Waaka Nene.

As Wanganui was to be the last unhappy spasm of the First Maori War, it was fitting that the splendid Waaka participated in the final act of mediation.

Sir George Grey now faced the formidable task of lifting the bankrupt, stagnant and war-ridden Colony into peace and prosperity. His obvious and immediate problem was the reform of land purchase. The land question particularly bedevilled the North Island where the density of the Maori tribes was considerable and where most Europeans settled. In the first eight years of Grey's first governorship, some 30,000,000 acres of Maori land were bought in the South Island for £13,000 while a mere

3,000,000 acres in North Island cost £36,500. An encouraging feature, however, of the late 1840s was extensive settling of the empty South Island where Nelson had been the only settlement since 1841; Scottish Presbyterians founded Otago and Anglicans Canterbury, somewhat to the irritation of Grey who disliked the concept of sectarian enclaves.

Meanwhile, with the approach of more tranquil days, the military establishment in the Colony thinned out to return to Australia. In January, 1847, William Hulme took the two 96th companies back to rejoin their Regiment at Hobart, and in August Edward Last embarked the three 99th companies for Sydney. The 58th, mainly about Auckland, were to soldier on in New Zealand until 1857 and the 65th, fully arrived by January, 1847, were destined to see many years of service and campaigning in the Colony.

With the years the economy picked up dramatically; Auckland was booming with land speculators from Australia and the introduction of sheep farming, especially in South Island, was going well; the exports of timber and foodstuffs to the Australian colonies increased. Soon the colonists began feeling for political power and the Constitution Act of 1852 by the Imperial Government brought a real measure of independence from Whitehall. The 26,000 Europeans in the Colony, however, were much governed; each of the six provinces of Auckland, Wellington, New Plymouth, Nelson, Otago and Canterbury had their own Provincial Council, while a central government for the Colony consisted of an elected General Assembly and a nominated Legislative Council. The Governor retained the power of veto over all legislation and Grey was particularly careful to ensure that Native Affairs were reserved to him. He was pleased and relieved that the recent war did not appear to have bred any longstanding rancour as such, but he was astute and sensible enough to appreciate that resentment over land was as volatile as one of the indigenous hot springs that bubbled and simmered and sometimes violently erupted. In his awareness and sympathy of the Maori problem, he devoted much energy to the promotion of schools and hospitals for the native peoples and to assisting their agriculture with gifts of grain, flour mills and carts.

In December, 1852, Grey returned to England on leave and while there was appointed Governor of Cape Colony. The new Governor of New Zealand was Colonel Thomas Gore Browne, a former Commanding Officer of the 41st Regiment in the First Afghan War and lately Governor of St Helena. As, in those leisurely days, he did not reach New Zealand until September, 1855, the popular Colonel Wynyard of the 58th Regiment acted as the interregnum, and it was under his aegis that the General Assembly met for the first time. Soon the reservation of native questions to the Governor became a fertile source of clashes between him and the very new and brash colonial Ministers. On the political scene it must also be mentioned in passing that Edward Gibbon Wakefield came to New Zealand, his colonial brainchild, in 1853 and, after being elected to the Wellington Provincial Council, went on later to the General Assembly; he died in the Colony in 1862.

The new Governor's assumption of office coincided with an interesting and far-reaching Maori political experiment, the King movement. Its author was Wiremu Tamihana, the intelligent, articulate chief of the Ngatihaua, one of the main Waikato tribes, and an austere Bible expert. He had visited England in 1851 and had absorbed the concept of a monarch or supreme leader as a source of unity and power to be applied to his sadly-divided race. Many proud Maori notables saw with dismay the erosion of the tribal system, the degrading use of Maori women by white men and the working of a colour bar except in the churches; moreover, though a Native Secretary was meant to administer Maori affairs, the bias was more humantarian and charitable than practical and effective and, in fact, a rebuff to Tamihana in Auckland in 1857 by Native Secretary Donald McLean over a request for a loan to build a flour mill gave much impetus to the King government. Big inter-tribal meetings that year in the Waikato and the following year near Auckland brought about the proclamation in April, 1858, at Rangiaowhia, in the Waikato, of Potatau Te Wherewhero as the first Maori king. The famous old warrior of the native wars was supported by most of the powerful and numerous Waikato and Taupo tribes and some east coast tribes; while the Ngatiawa and the Taranaki of the west coast were receptive to the King idea, they regarded Potatau with some coolness as, in true Maori tradition, they remembered he had ravaged their lands. The settlers and the Government viewed the Maori king concept, not unnaturally, with considerable reservation as they saw that it had the built-in power of preparing a united front for war.

Grey's successor, a highly-principled, conscientious and religious man, was unfortunately not of his calibre; it was said, as some illustration, that George Grey mixed with the Maori chiefs and enjoyed their company, while Thomas Gore Browne subjected them to clerks; Wiremu Tamihana's brush with Donald McLean, an ambivalent character who also held the all-powerful and lucrative post of Land Purchase Commissioner, over the flour mill loan is indicative. Gore Browne soon marked his tenure of office with a drastic error of judgement: in 1857 he repealed Grey's longstanding law forbidding the sale of arms and gunpowder to Maoris and it is estimated that, over the next three years, Maoris spent the considerable sum of £50,000 in the purchase of arms. This concerted effort clearly pointed to a definite objective in view. Even in 1855, the writing on the wall should have been clear to Gore Browne when only the prompt arrival of three companies of the 58th at New Plymouth averted a serious civil war among the Taranaki tribes over land disputes.

It was in the fertile Taranaki littoral where the explosive mixture lurked to ignite a chain of wars in the Colony for the next ten years. Some 3,000 European settlers stared resentfully and covetously at 1,750 Maoris occupying 2,000,000 acres, 1/100th part of which was actively used. In the vexed land question, right and wrong, and natural confusion and irritation, persisted among both races, and A. H. Reed in *The Story of New Zealand* puts the situation very well:

'The Company really wished to be fair to the natives, and proved it in a practical way by setting aside, and reserving for their benefit, one tenth of all the land that was bought. That tenth, after the land was settled by the white man, became of greater value than the whole had been before his arrival . . . What Wakefield and his fellows did not understand was the Maori's attachment to his land, even those parts that seemed quite unused;

that he hunted pigs, snared birds, and harvested berries in the forest; that he fished in the streams and the lakes, and he knew every hill and valley by name. Nor was it known how hard to understand were the Maori land laws; how every chief, every tribe, and in some degree every individual member of the tribe, had his own rights; how both the conqueror and conquered, and the very slave who might be permitted to return to his distant home after many years, had their rights. Certainly it was explained to the Maoris, as far as possible, that when land was sold they gave up all their rights to it, except the tenth part specially reserved. How much of what was told them they might not have properly understood, how much they understood but found it convenient to forget, can only be guessed. However that might have been, there was trouble in plenty laid up for the Pakehas, who made the big mistake in thinking they had come in possession, so simply, of all this land.'

In Taranaki, where the drift to war was to begin, the land situation was even more complicated than elsewhere, as the local Ngatiawa had only returned in force to their ancestral lands in 1848 after being driven off by the invasions of the Waikato, and it was to be one of the tragedies of the controversy that the principal antagonist against the settlers and the Government was to be Te Rangitake, now with the anglicised name of Wiremu Kingi (William King), the gallant ally against Te Rangihaeata in 1846–47, and a cool, intelligent old chief who was in reality a genuine friend of the *Pakeha*. The flashpoint of the quarrel was 600 acres at the mouth of the Waitara River, twelve miles north of New Plymouth, that was urgently needed to settle new immigrants. At a meeting in 1859, which the Governor attended, a minor chief, Te Teira, offered to sell the block to the *Pakehas*, but Wiremu Kingi, his tribal senior and leader of the local Maori Land League, immediately forbade the sale. Gore Browne, merely trying to get at the nub of the matter, then asked Kingi if he owned the land, whereupon the Ngatiawa chief and his entourage walked out. Gore Browne, not unreasonably, took this as an insult, though Kingi was merely demonstrating in the Maori fashion, rather dramatically, that he had spoken his last word. However, the Governor was a fair man and he retired to consult his native affairs experts in Auckland.

Meanwhile, the situation in Taranaki deteriorated as settler determination to have the Waitara block carried the day; the land was purchased from Te Teira, who appeared to all, including the Governor, to be the legitimate owner, though later rumour had it that the sale was done with malice aforethought as he bore a grudge against Kingi. But when surveyors went out on 20 February, 1860, to parcel up the block into small holdings, they were molested and their pegs uprooted by Kingi's men, and they retreated hastily to New Plymouth. There, Brevet-Lieutenant Colonel G. F. Murray, the commander of the local garrison from the 65th Regiment, consulted the civil authorities and declared martial law on 22 February.

When Governor Gore Browne heard of the proclamation of martial law in New Plymouth he ordered Colonel C. E. Gold of the 65th to prepare to embark his Regiment for field service in Taranaki. On 1 March the 65th landed at New Plymouth from the steamer *Airedale*, and Gore Browne, who had accompanied them, immediately tried to re-open negotiations with Wiremu Kingi in an honest attempt to avert conflict. But Kingi feared the protective custody fate of the late Te Rauparaha and declined.

HMS *Niger*, a screw corvette, also arrived off New Plymouth on 1 March which was clearly a great day for the settlement for the warship too landed a detachment, as the *Taranaki Herald* happily reported:

> 'They marched up from the beach with their Band playing and the sailors dragging the gun, and were greeted with a hearty cheer from the townspeople on passing over the Huatoki bridge.'

But sterner affairs were soon at hand. On 5 March Colonel Gold marched out to the disputed territory with four companies of his Regiment, modest detachments of the Royal Artillery and Royal Engineers, fifty seamen and Marines from *Niger* with their 12-pounder gun, and a body of Volunteer horsemen. The war was on.

CHAPTER 8

Rebellion in Taranaki

'In essence these settlements were frontier outposts. Each of the capitals was a ragged and sprawling small town of rutted and unreliable streets, scattered weatherboard houses, stores and hotels, mostly ill-planned and often ill-sited. They served as centres of commerce, law and culture for a penumbra of small farms and limitless sheep runs cut out of bare plain and standing forest. In their primitive way they concentrated and distilled the fashions of England. Officials, soldiers, traders and well-to-do farmers set the social tone, blundered with their wives down unlit streets of mud to formal dinners and balls. On a fine day they might promenade along the foreshore and greet each other to the music of a military band. Visiting ships brought, besides more settlers, letters and newspapers from home; gentlemen and their ladies pored over the news and the fashions that had been fresh in London some six months before. But old as the news might be, it stirred nostalgia for distant refinements.'[1]

NEW PLYMOUTH was such a typical 'capital' in 1860 with a population of about 2,500, but now crammed with refugee settlers who had fled with their families from the Maori terror in the outlying districts. It was for these frightened and worried families that the patient, disciplined British soldiers marched out to the Waitara.

On the first night out Gold encamped his column ten miles north of the capital and next morning came on a small rebel *pa* a mile distant. When he advanced it was found to be abandoned and he had barely destroyed it when another *pa* of considerable strength was discovered on the Waitara block, with 100 hostile

[1] *The Story of New Zealand* by W. H. Oliver.

Ngatiawa under the war chief Hapurona, who came down to dance a defiant *haka* before the British camp.

At midday on 17 March, Gold moved out to attack the *pa*, known as Te Kohia or the L *pa* from its shape, with three companies of the 65th supported by two 24-pounder and one 12-pounder howitzers and a rocket tube, and his advance screened across the fern-covered plain by the Taranaki Mounted Rifles. As the force halted 800 yards from the *pa* and the guns were positioned, the rebels blew a horn in defiance and warned off Mr Parris, the Native Commissioner, when he rode forward with a letter of mediation. The guns, served by twenty Royal Artillerymen, and the naval-manned rocket tube opened up, and as the shells and rockets burst about the *pa*, a red war flag was run up by the defenders. The guns bounded forward to close the range to 400 yards, with the infantry moving in support. The rebels replied with a brisk small-arms fire, which the 65th in extended order returned, but the weight of the artillery fire began to tell, and some rebels were seen slipping away. These fugitives were charged by the excited young Volunteer horsemen firing their pistols, but their eagerness drew them too close to the rifle and musket fire from the *pa* and one Volunteer fell mortally wounded, to be carried gallantly to the rear under fire by a 65th soldier and a seaman. The artillery bombardment brought the rebel flagpole crashing down, with the rebels' flag draping itself over the palisade where it was seized by a soldier of the 65th and a seaman from *Niger*. Dusk fell on the action and the British formed a leaguer of the guns and their weapons to lay down on their arms in the field, though the rebels kept up a sporadic fire during the night. At dawn the guns moved up to a point-blank 150 yards range and again bombarded to open a breach, but the assaulting 65th found the *pa* deserted; the rebels had slipped away down a deep gully to the river.

The minor success of the L *pa*, due to the power of the British artillery, and where British casualties were only 1 killed, 1 died of wounds and several wounded, hardened settler feeling in New Plymouth to demand a final confrontation with the rebellious Ngatiawa and resolution of the bitter Waitara land question. Gold's command had increased considerably and this inspired belligerence; he now had 500 men of the 65th, with his company at Wellington also en route, small RA and RE detachments, a contingent of seamen, Marines and Marine Artillery from HMS *Niger*, 300 Militia, 180 Taranaki Volunteer Rifles and Mounted Rifles. Moreover, it was known that the Governor had written to Australia for reinforcements from the 12th and 40th Regiments.

This victorious mood was shattered by the news that the Taranaki tribe south of New Plymouth had also now caught the infection of rebellion and Gold hurried back to the township with most of his force, leaving only two companies under Captain J. Barton to hold the disputed Waitara block. This was a disturbing development as the farmers in the southern settled districts had been pinning their hopes on the traditional enmity between the Ngatiawa and the Taranaki. On 27 March the situation deteriorated rapidly when three European men and two boys were shot and tomahawked to death at Omata, a mere $3\frac{1}{2}$ miles from New Plymouth. The intense excitement and alarm raised by the Omata murders caused Gold to despatch a column next day to rescue outlying families remaining in the area.

The rescue expedition, consisting of the Light Company, 65th Regiment, 28 seamen and marines from *Niger*, 103 Taranaki Rifle Volunteers and 56 Taranaki Militia under the command of Brevet-Lieutenant-Colonel Murray of the 65th, did not set out until 1 pm and Murray's orders from Gold were to be back in the township by dusk. The soldiers and sailors led by Murray marched down the main road as enemy were expected to be blocking it, while the Volunteers under Captain Brown were to move along the beach to Waireka, gather in the isolated families and move across country to join the Imperial troops on the road. This tenuous plan had an inevitable fate: the trained and well-armed Regulars met no opposition at all while the large, amateur band of Volunteers, barely trained and armed with old smooth-bore Brown Bess muskets and muzzle-loading Enfields ran into serious trouble. When the mouth of the Waireka was reached, many Taranaki and newly-arrived Ngatiruanui came running down from their *pa* a mile inland at Kaipopo to attack. As the action developed, Brown, who had no military experience whatever, handed over command to his Adjutant, Captain Stapp, an ex-58th Regiment corporal from Hone Heke's war, who with his old regimental comrade from the 58th, now Colour-Sergeant W. H. Free, the critic of Colonel Despard after Ohaeawai, became the cool organiser of their defence against the growing numbers of hostile Maoris ringing them in, ably seconded by Captain Harry Atkinson of the Rifle Volunteers.

Meanwhile, Murray, moving inland, heard the firing and sent Lieutenant Urquhart with twenty-five soldiers of the 65th and Lieutenant Blake's bluejackets who joined in the battle with zest, though Blake was soon seriously wounded. The Volunteers had now gathered in a perimeter about Mr John Jury's farmhouse above the beach and with well-aimed fire, desperately kept off the enemy filtering in strength down the river bed and covered gullies to the sea. Their ammunition ration, a bare thirty rounds per man, with no reserve, was now running low and Stapp urgently passed orders out to conserve it for the concerted rush he expected when the evening light began to fade.

Murray was also thinking of sunset which was now near, but for the pedantic reason of Gold's orders. After he had sounded the 'Retire' three times to summon Urquhart, that reluctant subaltern finally had to obey though he left some men with the Volunteers, and in the most reprehensible manner Murray began to march back to New Plymouth, leaving the Volunteers to fight their battle. However, succour was on its way in the welcome shape of Captain Peter Cracroft of the *Niger* and another sixty seamen and marines who had landed when they heard the alarm guns of Marsland Hill stockade, New Plymouth, sounding after young Frank Mace had ridden in from the Waireka, and now, guided by Mace, Cracroft and his men, itching for a fight, were moving as quickly as they could to the field of action. The light was fading when Cracroft came on the rebel *pa* at Kaipopo, now weakened by many who had dashed off to attack the Volunteers on the coast-line, and he immediately attacked it with great elan. He spied rebel flags floating over the *pa* and so his simple but effective battle orders for the assault were: 'Ten pounds for the man who pulls down those flags!'

The seamen, brandishing their cutlasses, swarmed over the

palisade and Coxswain Bill Odgers was the first in to hack his way through the tomahawk-flailing ranks of the enemy, to capture three flags and also to gain the first Victoria Cross of the Maori Wars. Cracroft only had four wounded, due to the bad light spoiling the defenders' aim, but his close quarter onslaught once inside the *pa* left sixteen Taranaki dead in their trenches. The excellent side-issue of his attack was its timing, for then the beleagured Volunteers, down to their last few rounds, were bracing themselves for a final assault by the enemy about Jury's farmhouse when the sound of the assault on Kaipopo drew all the rebels dramatically away. Captain Stapp, Harry Atkinson, Free and the Volunteers were puzzled, though greatly relieved, as they knew Murray had gone, and while the moon was setting, retreated on Omata stockade with their casualties, with the eight soldiers of the 65th left with them and some of Atkinson's men forming the rearguard. British losses were 2 killed and 12 wounded during this afternoon and evening of crisis, though the Taranaki and their Ngatiruanui allies probably suffered between 30 and 50 dead, mainly from the accurate fire by the defenders of Jury's farmhouse.

Great relief was felt in New Plymouth when the missing Volunteers tramped wearily in very late that night, having been met by another relief column of soldiers and settlers, and next day *Niger* proudly flew her three captured rebel flags. But public scorn and anger ran highly against Murray's conduct and also Gold's orders and eventually, over twelve months later, a military Court of Inquiry, presided over by Colonel Trevor Chute, Commanding Officer of the 70th Regiment, was convened to inquire into Murray's execution of his duty at Waireka. However, the proceedings and findings were conveniently lost from public sight when they were sent away from New Zealand for consideration by higher military authority.

April was mainly devoted to organising and drilling the Militia, though Gold did lead a column down to the Tataraimaka block, another troubled settled area fifteen miles south, where a truculent *pa* was burned. That same month he received substantial reinforcements from Australia in response to Gore Browne's entreaties: the *City of Sydney*, *City of Hobart* and *Wonga-*

wonga brought four companies of the 40th Regiment and two companies of the 12th. The steam corvettes HMS *Pelorus* and *Cordelia* came too, while the Colony of Victoria sent her total fleet, her pride and the first Australian warship, another steam corvette HMVS *Victoria*.

The upshot of Cracroft's brisk little victory at Kaipopo was to break the encirclement of New Plymouth. But the intelligence reaching the Governor and his advisers in Auckland was grave; all the signs indicated that the Ngatiawa's defiance about the Waitara block was arousing Maori passions so vehemently that tribal differences were being discarded. Waireka was such an example, while from the King country news came that Potatau Te Wherowhero alone restrained the Waikato, though he had to assent to the urgent demand of the fierce Rewi Maniapoto to lead a war party of his tribe to the Waitara. So down the traditional route of the Mokau river by canoe came the Ngatimaniapoto, who then marched along the coast by White Cliffs to the Waitara.

Meanwhile, the companies of the newly-arrived 40th Regiment also marched out to Waitara to relieve the 65th and Major Nelson of the 40th assumed command. His operational task, apart from ensuring the inviolability of the bitterly-contested 600 acres, was to watch and, if possible, disperse the inevitable concentration of rebels who, with the constructional genius and military energy of their race, had erected another seemingly impregnable *pa* nearby. This particular masterpiece by Wiremu Kingi was in fact a double-*pa*, known as the Puketakauere *Pas*, standing in echelon on a ridge flanked by deep gullies full of brambles and thick, entangled bracken and dropping away into a swamp near the Waitara river. Not only had Wiremu Kingi chosen his field of battle admirably in the Maori tradition, he had shown the military world before the American Civil War the value of fire trenches against the increasing power of artillery and small arms fire. He had sited weapon pits for his riflemen before the *pas*.

Major Nelson was certainly offensively-minded (the regimental history of the 40th relates that the rebels later called him '*taipo*' or 'devil' because he was always harrying them), but at this stage it could also be said that he was very newly-arrived in New

Zealand. The more he studied the Puketakauere *Pas*, the more they lured him to attack. In late June, he determined to assault Puketakauere, and in this decision he was probably aided and abetted by a splendid nineteenth-century character, Captain Beauchamp-Seymour RN, of HMS *Pelorus*, who was ashore with sixty of his sailors and marines in the Waitara camp. A strikingly sartorial figure, complete with monocle, Beauchamp-Seymour was nick-named 'The Swell of the Ocean'; happily, he was to survive (just) the coming battle to become Lord Alcester.

Nelson's plan of attack for the fateful 27 June, was to advance, after a preliminary bombardment by his two 24-pounders, with three columns from 350 men of the 40th and the naval contingent: he would lead one column frontally while the other two worked around either flank. Such a naïve and optimistic plan against such strong objectives, with his assault dissipated into three columns, was playing into the trigger fingers of Wiremu Kingi and his waiting marksmen and also those rebels armed with shotguns and old fowling pieces for the close quarter work.

The British attack was slaughtered. At 7 am, the advance went forward; by 1 pm it had recoiled, broken, to the haven of Waitara camp with 30 dead and 34 wounded. The enemy trenches before the forward *pa* cut down the lines of the 40th and the naval contingent, though Beauchamp-Seymour and his spirited sailors and marines carried the first trenchworks before point-blank fire and tomahawk counter-attacks forced them to give ground and retreat, with the gallant Swell of the Ocean badly wounded in the leg. The two 24-pounder howitzers under Lieutenant Mac-Naghten, which had not made much impression on the *pas* in their preliminary bombardment, now covered the retirement with case shot. But it was the two flanking columns who suffered the most. Struggling through the sucking mud of the gullies, soaked by winter rains, and clawing their way through thick brambles, they were attacked at close quarter by ferocious parties of Ngati-maniapoto and Ngatiawa wielding long-handled tomahawks. When Nelson sounded the Retire, many of the wounded had to be left in the gullies to be despatched by the blood-maddened rebels.

'We killed them in the swamp,' says a Maori who fought there. 'We used chiefly the tomahawk. Such was the slaughter of the

F

soldiers in that swamp that it came to be called by us Te Wai-Kotero (meaning a pool in which maize and potatoes are steeped until they are putrid); this was because of the many corpses that lay there after the battle."[1]

Some mystery concerns the full circumstances of the abortive Puketakauere attack. Two days earlier, Nelson had sent in one of his officers to get approval for his plan and next day Gold sent him as reinforcements another company of the 40th and Beauchamp-Seymour's contingent from *Pelorus*. It is clear that Nelson, as his assault went awry, due to the enemy attacking out of the bush, looked anxiously for the arrival of a co-operating column from New Plymouth under Gold. The fact remains that Gold did march as far as the flooded Waiongana with four companies of the 65th and two guns that morning, but, as incomprehensively as his subordinate Murray at Waireka, he then turned about to march back to New Plymouth, an order that caused the men of the 65th, according to one correspondent, to hiss him.

When the sea mails reached England in September, the nation was shocked to hear of another military disaster in New Zealand. On 13 September, 1860, *The Times* carried a long report of Puketakauere from the *Sydney Morning Herald*, which in turn had drawn heavily on the *Taranaki Herald*'s account, and this hinted heavily that the unfortunate Nelson had been let down by his superior commander from New Plymouth. In a letter to *The Times* published on 19 February, 1861, Gold, now a local Major-General commanding the Auckland district, angrily refuted this charge; he had given up command of the 65th on 1 October, 1860, but this was not necessarily connected with any censure as, such were the patriarchic tours of duty Commanding Officers had in those days, he had been commanding the 65th since 1845, and his promotion would seem to preclude any label of disgrace. The crucial part of his letter read:

'. . . I had neither the knowledge that such would take place, nor had I arranged any combined movement whatever with him. I had the day before sent him all the reinforcements I could spare from New Plymouth. It is true I made a reconnaissance as far as Mahoetahi, where I was anxious to form an outpost, but

[1] *The New Zealand Wars and the Pioneering Period* by James Cowan.

(independent of the river being impassable) I could not have advanced further without endangering the town and its 2,000 women and children . . .'

This quickly drew a sharp rejoinder on 20 February from Nelson's brother in England, an Adjutant of Rifle Volunteers, who stated he had documentary evidence from his brother that Gold knew of the attack; the despatch of reinforcements on 26 June, the day before, would certainly seem to imply this. And his last point: 'By some coincidence, the Major-General did move out with troops in the direction of Waitara on the morning of the attack.'

One senior person rather nearer to New Zealand, who was also profoundly disturbed by the Puketakauere defeat, was Major-General Thomas Pratt, General Officer Commanding in Australasia. The news reached him in Sydney on 12 July, 1860; six days later, he embarked the rest of the 40th Regiment under Lieutenant-Colonel Leslie for New Plymouth and several days after, he also sailed with his small headquarters. Thomas Pratt was a Lowland Scot, then sixty-three years old; he had been gazetted to an ensigncy in the 26th Foot in 1814 and saw active service in the Low Countries at the end of the Napoleonic Wars. He commanded his Regiment in the Opium War in China, 1840–41, particularly at the attacks on Canton and the advance on Nanking; he subsequently served in India. He had been commanding in Australia since 1856.

At New Plymouth, Pratt found an unhappy military and civil situation as he doubtless expected. The 40th and 65th Regiments were now deployed in a line of blockhouses about the town, with some advanced outposts and occasional roving columns. New Plymouth itself was very overcrowded and insanitary, and Gold had ordered that the refugee women and children should be evacuated to Nelson but many of the wives refused to leave their men. Moreover, the atmosphere between the Army and the citizens was becoming unpleasant; the Army began to harbour suspicions that they were meant to do all the fighting to win more land for the colonists who meanwhile waxed prosperous on military contracts for foodstuffs, haulage and billeting, while with the *Pakeha* New Zealanders, the abandonment of the

Volunteers at Waireka by Murray was hard to forget and now the Puketakauere disaster, to which apparently even the overall military commander himself had contributed, bred more loss of confidence.

The fortunes of the Taranaki campaign had now fallen back to the outer works of the town's crude defences, though a third company of the 12th Regiment under Major Hutchins, which disembarked on 23 July, did march out four days later to the Waireka to construct a redoubt to halt the encirclement of the capital. This challenge to enemy-held territory duly led to their investment during 11–23 August, when any movement drew hostile fire and each wood and water detail provoked a skirmish, but then the rebels gave up and moved away.

The cold and rainy weather, however, rather inhibited the offensive plans of both hostile Maori and 'the red garments', and Pratt judiciously set about reorganising his command, now some 3,500 strong, though 900 were local militia of limited value only for the defence of the town. The logistic support of his force was difficult, as the west coast was notorious for its lack of safe harbours and certainly New Plymouth was no exception: no ship could linger on account of the wild seasonal gales and the surf. The many ravines and watercourses wending their way to the coast, especially from the great snow-capped watershed of Mount Egmont, 8,000 feet high, made movement laborious for artillery and heavily-loaded carts in the mud and rain torrents of the winter. The terrain lent itself naturally to the elusive, lightly laden and mobile Maori; even the so-called 'open country' of the settled area was mainly broken plains covered with a thick growth of fern. Then came 'the bush', a closely-matted growth of timber and brambles, especially in the gullies where a path had to be hacked through the thick growth. To cope with this rugged environment, the British soldier had discarded the unsuitable tight red tunic, old-fashioned stock and shako for a loose fitting blue serge jacket and forage cap.

Governor Gore Browne, not unnaturally, pressed his new com- mander to avenge the defeat of Puketakauere with some urgency and with the early signs of Spring and favourable campaigning weather, Pratt marched back to the Waitara in force on 10

September with a column of 1,400 men of the 12th and 65th Regiments. He found the bloody field of Puketakauere deserted but with heavy marching over rough tracks and the broken, exhausting country, he sought out three rebel *pas* and after light skirmishing, destroyed them. He wisely desisted following up the rebels as they melted away in the forest. On 18 September, he despatched another punitive expedition of the 12th, three companies of the 65th, with gunners, sappers and Volunteers, under Major Hutchins, south from New Plymouth to check rebels raiding the Tataraimaka settlement area and some eight minor *pas* were razed before the soldiers returned to the provincial capital.

Pratt now began to move out against tougher rebel positions. On 9 October, he personally led a force of 1,000 of the 12th and 65th again to the south some eighteen miles away to the banks of the Kaihihi river where three strong *pas* stood, and he showed his own unique tactic of sapping up to the *pas*, rather than launching the usual bloody frontal assaults of the past. Laboriously, but steadily, the saps dug their way to the palisades and though the work drew heavy and frustrated fire from the defenders, each *pa*, strongly and skilfully built, with the final *pa* even holding an underground hospital as well as the usual plethora of rifle pits connected by covered passages, was found abandoned when the sap finally reached it. For the minor cost of five casualties, Thomas Pratt had captured three major *pas* with sweat, not blood.

Back in New Plymouth on 5 November, after this almost bloodless victory, the General received some startling and alarming intelligence. It was reported that the Waikato were crossing the Waitara in force and next morning would be at Mahoetahi, eight miles from the town and three from the Waitara redoubt. King Te Wherowhero was now dead and the young men of the Waikato, jealous of the Ngatimaniapoto success at Puketakauere, could no longer be held. Pratt acted with resolution: at dawn next day, two columns began to converge on Mahoetahi, one from Waitara under Colonel Mould, Royal Engineers, the other under his personal command, 900 strong from the three Regiments and two companies of Taranaki Rifle Volunteers, supported by two 24-pounders of the Royal Artillery.

Both columns were timed to arrive at Mahoetahi at 8.30 am but the main force from New Plymouth, though it had to cover the longer distance, met better going and splashed across the Mangaoraka stream first, with the *pa* one and a half miles distant. The guns were hauled forward and sited, and as their bombardment developed, the usually circumspect Pratt ordered a general assault when the Volunteers had worked their way about the other flank; he had discerned that Mahoetahi was a disused *pa* in a state of disrepair which the Waikato, despite the inherent beaver-like Maori military quality for *pa*-building, could not have hoped to restore in face of his prompt appearance. Two companies of the 65th went for the *pa* and gained entry, with savage hand-to-hand fighting ensuing. Then Mould's Waitara force came up on the *pa* and attacked from a third side, and the enemy resistance broke into a rout, though the Waikato warriors individually fought hard to retreat into the haven of the swamp. Pratt on this occasion followed up through the swamp and forest, and the Waikato lost some 49 dead; British casualties were 4 killed and 15 wounded.

Pratt left a garrison of 300 at Mahoetahi and marched the rest of his force back to Waitara and New Plymouth. He was then beseeched by an anxious Government to send troops to cover Auckland, as it was feared that the powerful Waikato, frustrated in Taranaki, would turn on the Colony's capital which their lands bordered only forty miles distant. Four companies from the 40th and 65th hurriedly sailed after a hazardous embarkation over powerful surf in a steam sloop for Manukau, the western port of Auckland, with a rough passage en route. But the alarm was groundless, and as the 2nd Battalion of the 14th Regiment began arriving at Auckland from Cork on 29 November, the New Plymouth troops were soon re-embarked and tossed and crashed against great, billowing waves on an equally wild return passage.

But Wiremu Kingi and his Ngatiawa, with their Waikato allies, were far from done on the Waitara. Five miles up the river, three more *pas*, Matarikoriko, Hiurangi and Te Arei, of the first order in construction and siting, appeared. On 28 December, Thomas Pratt again moved out from Waitara camp, where he left a garrison of 300 men, to destroy this new and formidable challenge.

The General at once commenced his classical sapping technique before Matarikoriko and by last light of the next day had raised his first redoubt 800 yards from the *pa*. He left mainly the 40th and 65th in the field and marched back the other half of his force for administrative convenience to nearby Waitara camp. That night the rebel Maoris moved about in some strength and kept up a harassing fire on the redoubt, which they clearly saw as an ominous portent of Pratt's now well-known tactics to get within point-blank assaulting distance with minimal casualties, but at dawn, when the General came up to visit his forward post, a white flag was flying over the *pa*. The chaplain went forward to speak to the senior rebel chief who reminded him it was Sunday and his men 'did not wish to desecrate the Sabbath by spilling blood'. An armistice was duly agreed for the day and large numbers of Waikato emerged from the *pa* and moved about openly before it, while the not-so-pious British laboured on to finish their redoubt and some foraged, quite unmolested, for potatoes in a field by the *pa*. Next morning, Matarikoriko was found abandoned with 12 enemy dead buried inside; British casualties had been 3 killed and 22 wounded.

The patient saps dug on to the next *pa*, Huirangi, and at the redoubts before it, a brisk fight developed from a concerted rebel counter-attack on 23 January. The *Taranaki Herald*, in its issue three days later, graphically describes the scene:

'The Waikatos, labouring under the delusion that they could easily conquer and capture the advanced redoubt occupied by the headquarters of the 40th, at 3 am on the 23rd madly attempted to rush. it. The 40th were just getting under arms at that hour, and they gave them a warm reception. A body of some sixty or eighty men ensconced themselves in the ditch and kept up a rapid fire on the defenders, whose heads they could see in bold relief against the clear morning sky. Colonel Leslie directed the regimental call of the 65th and the "advance" to be sounded, and Colonel Wyatt, having on the first shot being fired, got his men under arms, forthwith despatched two companies under the command of Captain Macgregor to their assistance, and directed the detachment 12th Regiment, under the command of Captain Miller, to proceed in support. As this force passed No 2 redoubt they were cheered by the 40th, and, advancing at the double, Captain MacGregor directed Lieut. Urquhart to take the Light

Company 65th around the base front of No 3 Redoubt and clear the ditch, while he took the rear base. The bayonets were soon fixed, and did their work well.

In the meantime, Colonel Wyatt directed Captain Miller to advance and close upon the enemy, which he did, though wounded . . . Captain MacGregor's and Lieut. Urquhart's men now opened a crossfire on the Waikatos from the ditch, and the 40th, firing over them from the parapet, soon put them to flight. The enemy tried to cover their retreat by a brisk fire from their rifle pits, but the shelling being too much for their feelings, they desisted by 7 am.'

Pte Cooper, No 10 Company, 65th Regiment, had a particularly busy time:

'Having passed round to the advanced works, mounted over the gabions, he came in immediate contact with the enemy occupying the extreme left ditch. He first shot one man and, after loading again, bayoneted another, when, in rushing on, the cap fell off his gun and consequently he had only his bayonet to rely on, with which he succeeded in doing great execution, knocking down with the butt of his rifle those who opposed him; but, his rifle breaking, he was struck to the ground wounded.'

This spirited fray, where the rebels were venturesome to tackle the British regular in the open field, rather than letting him come to the stout defences of their *pa* and aimed fire, cost the Waikato 34 known dead and 6 wounded. But their plan had been a sound and dangerous one, using the cover of darkness to position a large assault force in the ditch outside No 3 Redoubt with their marksmen posted to keep down the defenders' fire. When their stormers went in, the situation was confused and dangerous and only the prompt appearance of the counter-attack force of the two companies of the 65th and the company of the 12th taking them in the flank redressed and restored an ugly situation. The British lost sixteen killed and wounded, but now their strength had soared to 1,500 as two companies of the 14th Regiment had arrived from Auckland.

The indefatigable Pratt sapped remorselessly on against Huirangi, with the work resuming next day, quite unswerving in his objective, despite the disruptive rebel sortie, the heavy fire directed at the work and, even more distracting, word reaching him that other tribes were now threatening New Plymouth. By

3 February, his No 6 Redoubt had reached within fifty yards of the rifle pits before Huirangi, but his mole-like military tactics were too much for the Waikato: they abandoned Huirangi without a final fight and retired to the final *pa*, Te Arei.

As amateur military engineers of considerable ability themselves, the Maoris doubtless appreciated Pratt's sapping technique, but clearly this deviation from what they expected the British soldier, whom they regarded as brave but stupid, to do was unnerving. However, though the sapping caused much misgiving, it was turned, with the typically broad outlook of the Maori making war, to some advantage for both antagonists. Bundles of green *manuka* were needed in some quantity by the toiling British for overhead protection as they sapped close to the marksmen in the makeshift towers in the *pa* or up nearby trees, and years later, an aged former rebel chief related that as they were always short of necessaries such as food or blankets in the beleaguered *pas*, the rebels would steal out at night to cut *manuka*, hand it over to the friendly Maoris serving with General Pratt, and these broadminded intermediaries sold the *manuka* to the British, kept part of the payment themselves, bought what the rebels needed from the British commissariat and delivered these goods to the rebels when they rendezvoused the following night to collect another *manuka* consignment. 'All this,' said the old chief, 'did no one any harm, and when the General's sap got too near the *pa* to be comfortable, well, the Maoris flitted away some dark night and built another one somewhere else.'

The rebel Waikato had other diversions to lighten their state of siege. Among their nefarious military equipment were some bugles, captured or purloined, and at night their keen amateur buglers would imitate the British Army calls. As, at that time, each Regiment had its own bugle calls (not standard calls throughout the Army, as shortly was to happen), this lighthearted enemy practice initially caused considerable commotion and confusion; for instance, the 12th Regiment's 'advance' was the 65th's 'extend', the 65th's 'close' was the 12th's 'commence firing'. Keen ears gradually became attuned, as this psychological warfare wore on, to detect the crucial difference whether the bugler came from Suffolk or Yorkshire or the Waikato.

The final objective, Te Arei, was inevitably a daunting task. A subaltern of the 12th describes it:

'It could be seen from the redoubts, and native report had it that it was the strongest and best defended *pa* in the country. It certainly was a well-selected situation; in the first place, between our position and the very thick bush, there was a mile of perfectly level ground from which the fern had been removed, and just on the border of the dense bush, there were numbers of well-constructed rifle pits, covered over and quite invisible, which extended for about a mile. Behind the pits there was a dense bush, so thick with undergrowth that but for some paths, eighteen inches wide, made by the natives, there was no means of penetrating it, except by cutting down the underwood. Round the *pa*, which stood on a considerable rise, there was a cleared space, and more rifle pits. The river Waitara, with steep banks, almost cliffs, protected the position on the right and left, and at the rear there was more thick bush."[1]

Meanwhile, as Thomas Pratt deliberated on Te Arei, a company from the 57th Regiment, which had arrived from India at Auckland, landed at Waitara from HMS *Cordelia* on 28 January and marched inland to join the field force.

On 10 February, Pratt moved against Te Arei. At dawn, the 40th and two companies of the 65th advanced in extended order against the strongly-manned intermediary rifle pits and Captain Strange, a company commander of the 65th, fell mortally-wounded among five other 65th casualties. The British seized a small, fern-covered hill that commanded the whole line of rebel trenches, stretching some 2,000 yards, and dug in to construct Redoubt No 7 and occupy it that night. Outflanked, the Waikato abandoned their rifle pits that had covered the expanse of open ground so admirably and now Pratt set his force, consisting of 12th, 14th, 40th, 57th and 65th detachments, the herculean task of hacking a route through the tangled bush for his guns to close with Te Arei. This gruelling approach, which took two days, was not merely sheer toil since hand-to-hand fighting broke out in the dense bush when the Waikato fell on the toiling soldiers. British casualties were twelve killed and wounded.

[1] *The History of the 12th (Suffolk) Regiment, 1865–1913* by Lt-Col E. A. H. Webb.

On the 14th, Pratt was ready to begin his relentless sapping forward. As the familiar work proceeded, the Waikato in the *pa* shouted to the soldiers to come on and fight. On 5 March, the rebels issued out from the *pa* to attack the head of the sap, firing heavily, but though the soldiers crouched with fixed bayonets ready to receive a concerted rush, none came. It was a nerve-racking time, as the surrounding bush was ideal to harbour out-flanking sorties, and the tensed-up soldiers would have been relieved to have been loosed at the rifle pits and the *pa*.

However, it was fitting that the stronghold of Te Arei, under the methodical command of Thomas Pratt, was to be no bloody Ohaeawai or Puketakauere. Its aura of impregnability was to fizzle out against this commander who demanded much sweat and hard work from his soldiers but who conserved their lives, if in a somewhat ponderous way. On 11 March, when No 8 Redoubt was complete and the sap within 200 yards of Te Arei, the rebel chiefs proposed a truce. Pratt agreed for a period of three days as he knew that Capt Mercer's battery of modern 12-pounder Armstrong field guns and 10-inch and 8-inch mortars had arrived at Auckland on 4 March, and was straining every muscle to reach the war in Taranaki. On 13 March, Mercer with a half-battery and the mortars—he left the other half at Auckland to await 180 horses from Australia—landed from surf boats at the mouth of the Waitara from the *Victoria*, and two mornings later, the guns and mortars were in action against Te Arei, as Pratt had hoped.

When hostilities were resumed, on the night of 16 March, the Waikato again tried to destroy the sap but three were blown to pieces on booby-traps. This was the last desperate offensive bid by the defenders of Te Arei *pa*, now feeling trapped and isolated by this ever-patient General, but skirmishes and clashes dragged on for two more nights. The following night Colour-Sergeant John Lucas of the 40th won the first Victoria Cross of his Regiment. When deployed as skirmishers to the right of the Redoubt, his detachment was ambushed by a marauding rebel party and he held the position until dawn, despite five casualties, including his officer.

However, on the night of 18 March, after a hard day in which

Lieutenant MacNaghten RA was shot dead and a captain of the 65th wounded, the 12th were on outpost duty when their Officer Commanding, Major Hutchins, was informed that two chiefs from Te Arei wished to see him. The two emissaries were duly sent to the rear where they told Pratt that it was the desire of the rebels 'to talk of peace'. Next day, a white flag was run up over Te Arei. The last shots of the Taranaki rising of 1860–61 had been fired.

With the return of peace to the strife-torn province, where some 176 homesteads had been destroyed, the Governor came hurrying back to Taranaki with terms that were meant to appeal to both settler and Maori: he was determined to restore or compensate the plunder taken from the devastated farms, and he promised the defeated Ngatiawa a fresh investigation into the Waitara purchase, about which he clearly had latent pangs of conscience.

With the peace also came a new commander of the troops in New Zealand, Major-General Duncan Cameron CB. Sir Thomas Pratt, with a well-earned KCB for his solid and workmanlike achievement, returned to his command in Australia. 'Come and fight!' had taunted the Waikato chief, Wetini Taiporotu, from Mahoetahi, as he had doubtless heard of the sapping technique which was also the subject of ribald comment in New Plymouth, and Pratt did. Among the notable Waikato chiefs who lay dead at Mahoetahi after the British bayonets had swept through was Wetini Taiporotu.

The defeated Ngatiawa submitted to the Queen, but an unrepentant Wiremu Kingi slipped away with the departing Waikato. Though an uneasy peace settled over Taranaki and a chilling abundance of war clouds over the hard-tried North Island seemed to have been stayed, the tragedy of the triumph of British military power against the Ngatiawa and their erstwhile allies was that the antipathy of the Waikato was merely stiffened and the King movement considerably strengthened as a rallying point against visibly-increasing *Pakeha* pressure.

The central plains of the Waikato and the King country now became the new centre of gravity.

CHAPTER 9
Uneasy Days

Oɴ 30 March, 1861, that indefatigable reporter of the early New Plymouth scene, the *Taranaki Herald*, announced the presence of another popular Regimental Band:

'The Band of the 57th Regiment will perform on Tuesday next, at 4 o'clock pm.

Programme

March	*Jubilee*	Lindpainter
Overture	*Czar and Zimmerman*	Lortzing
Quadrille	*Bombastes Furioso*	Moore
Selection, opera	*Satanella, the Power of Love*	Balfe
Waltz	*Beloved Star*	Laurent
Finale	*Louisa Miller*	Verdi
Schottische	*Pretty Little Girl*	Divoure

—Mr. Philip Galea, Music Master.'

While the 57th's Band played a series of concerts for the culture-starved citizenry of crowded New Plymouth, other Regiments were soon withdrawn from Taranaki. The 57th, who had arrived only for the closing actions of the rebellion, remained to protect the province as it struggled back to normality.

The destination of the 12th, 14th, 40th and 65th Regiments was Otahuhu, nine miles outside Auckland, to cover the capital from the menacing Waikato frontier only forty miles away. In June, the 70th Regiment also landed at Auckland to swell Major-General Duncan Cameron's command and five months later, had a mild experience of the turbulence of New Zealand colonial life when a company under Major Ryan was despatched to Otago, in the South Island, where disturbances had broken out in the Dunedin area among the European gold miners. In Australasian history, miners were traditionally a wild and unruly lot; in July of that year, a company of the 12th Regiment remaining in New South Wales had to march to the Lambing Flats gold diggings where the miners, enraged that more diligent Chinese coolies were washing gold out of alluvial claims they themselves had abandoned, were maltreating the Chinese, which included cutting off their pigtails.

Meanwhile, politically, the Maori King movement, entrenched firmly in the Waikato country, was gradually gathering momentum and beginning to show its power. A colonial Minister of Native Affairs of those days, William Fox, wrote a strong view:

'An elected king, a very young man of no force of character, surrounded by a few ambitious chiefs who formed a little mock court, and by a bodyguard who kept him from all vulgar contact and from even the inspection of Europeans, except on humiliating terms; entirely powerless to enforce among his subjects the decisions of his magistrates; an army, if it might be called so, of 5,000 to 10,000 followers scattered over the country but organised so that large numbers could be concentrated at any one point on short notice; large accumulated supplies of food, of arms and ammunition; a position in the centre of the island from which a descent could be made in a few hours on any of the European settlements; roads prohibited to be made through two-thirds of the island; the large rivers barred against steamers so that nine-tenths of the country was closed against the ordinary means of travel and transport; the Queen's law set at utter defiance; her magistrates treated with supercilious contempt; her writs torn to pieces and trampled underfoot; Europeans who had married native women driven out of the King's districts, while their wives and children were taken from them, unless they would recognise and pay an annual tribute to the King; all this accompanied by an exhibition of the utmost arrogance and undisguised contempt for the power of the Queen, the Governor and the Europeans.'[1]

The young King was Tawhiao, the son of Potatau Te Whero-whero, who died from influenza in June, 1860. The King movement was anathema to the Governor, as it was to the entire

[1] *The War in New Zealand* by William Fox.

colonial population, naturally apprehensive of this native genie in their midst. Such fears were initially lost on the Imperial Government, and certainly in the days of the old King, the Colonial Secretary, the Duke of Newcastle, took a very cavalier view. He said blandly: 'If they merely honour their king, whether his name is Potato or Brian Boru, and commit no breach of the Queen's peace, I agree with Sir William Martin that such folly should be left to the influence of time.'

The Governor soon began to be drawn into a lengthy discussion with the movement's architect and king-maker, Wiremu Tamihana, who dazzled him with speeches studded with scriptural texts when he attended a meeting of chiefs at the King capital, Ngaruawahia, at the juncture of the Waikato and Waipa rivers, on 3 June, 1861. Later, in a letter on the subject of restitution for the devastated Taranaki farms, Tamihana accused British troops of eating the settlers' cattle and selling their horses. Gore Browne considered this allegation unforgivably impertinent and said of Maori law that 'its aptest symbol is the tomahawk'. The stolid and upright Gore Browne was clearly moving towards war to scarify the King canker, but at this stage the Duke of Newcastle decided that the drift to another eruption of violence in New Zealand had to be arrested. On 6 September, 1861, the Colonial Secretary informed Gore Browne that he was being transferred to the Governship of Tasmania, as notorious Van Diemen's Land was now innocently called.

His successor, dramatically, was Sir George Grey, recalled from Cape Colony, where, apart from his local achievements, he had rendered great service in 1857–58, pushing every soldier he could lay his hands on to India during the crisis of the Mutiny. He disembarked from HMS *Cossack* in Auckland on 26 September and Thomas Gore Browne, called Governor Angry Belly by the Maoris, sailed for Australia on 3 October. His intransigence over native affairs or, more accurately, his inability to break through the weighted advice of his colonial ministers, and especially his heavy-handedness over the Waitara purchase which had led to another expensive native rising, probably told against him in the deliberations of the great men sitting in the cloistered calm of Whitehall. Strangely enough, Grey was viewed with more apprehension by the King-ite Maoris than Gore Browne; he was reckoned to be stronger and more subtle.

Grey moved with his customary energy to dampen down the confrontation that was inexorably developing between the Government and the King-ites. But despite his innate sympathy for the Maori dilemma, he was deep-rootedly against the King-concept and both the Waikato and the Ngatimaniapoto sensed this. Grey was quite aware of the well-grounded fears of the settlers, and moreover the King-ites were becoming increasingly arrogant. However, he strove for a peaceful solution and as he stressed the wastefulness of colonial wars to Crown and colony, the Duke of Newcastle and the Colonial Office fully backed his endeavours. His plan for New Zealand was the classic British Imperial device of indirect rule. Again, in the best British tradition, the area that had given the earliest major trouble, the Bay of Islands, became the first (and successful) selection for this experiment. The fierce and powerful Ngapuhi, in this Second Maori War, were to become what the Sikhs were to the hard-pressed British in India during the Mutiny; after defeat in an earlier war, they remained loyal to their recent conquerors in a crisis of momentous proportions when their hostile intervention would have been a calamity.

Indirect rule was meant to infiltrate that Maori diehard fastness, the Waikato, and onward to the hinterland of the unyielding Ngatimaniapoto. In theory, it had much to offer to salve the honour and conscience of both Maori and *Pakeha*. However, in the unmapped wilds of the King country in the centre of North Island, ingrained and passionate suspicions of *Pakeha* intentions were not to be swayed. The King-ite Maoris saw British military power building up ominously, for some 6,000 Regular troops— six Regiments of the Line supported by Royal Artillery and Royal Engineers—were now stationed in the Colony. This concentration of troops, mainly on the northern Waikato frontier, became the final disenchantment; for Grey decided to cut a military road from Drury, where the road south from Auckland stopped after winding its way for 25 miles through pleasant farms and homesteads, over the final fifteen miles through the Hunua forest to the great Waikato river. This road, to be built by

11. *The 57th Regiment under Colonel Warre in action on the Katikara River in the Tataraimaka Block, June, 1863.*

12. *The destruction of Orakau* pa *which marked the end of the Waikato war, April, 1864.*

13. *The defiance of the defenders of Orakau.*

soldiers, could only have one purpose to the simple and unso-phisticated Maori mind: it was a red dagger working relentlessly to accomplish the demise of the tribes of the Waikato.

Work began on the road in December, 1861, as the hot, dry summer came along, and each Regiment was allotted a certain number of miles of road to make. For the stolid and disciplined British soldier, recruited from the stews of London or the grow-ing industrial cities or the rustic poverty of the countryside, and who was paid a pittance for a performance on which a great Empire depended, the task had its compensations. Lieutenant Mair, of the 12th Regiment, writes:

'The work for the road parties was hard, but the pay was good and the duties not heavy, as, besides our regimental guards, we only had to take the precaution of having a captain, two subalterns and a hundred men on picquet duty. At the end of six months, the road being completed, we all returned to our old quarters, where huts had been erected.'[1]

As the Regiments went into winter quarters at Otahuhu and Auckland, leaving three companies of the 70th to complete work on the Queen's Redoubt at Pokeno at the end of the military road, the Governor continued to strive for a political solution. In January, 1863, he journeyed, with considerable courage, unescorted to Ngaruawahia to meet King Tawhiao, Wiremu Tamihana and other notables. When asked if he was working against the Maori kingship, he perhaps revealed his real attitude too starkly for his hostile audience, many of whom wished him to commit himself in this vein: 'I shall not fight against him with the sword, but I shall dig around him until he falls of his own accord.'

To ease one smouldering Maori grievance, Grey re-opened the Waitara question with a fresh investigation and, typically, it was in Taranaki province that the cause of more strife flared up just when a gesture of considerable proportion was about to be made to placate Maori feeling. On 3 May, 1863, Grey's hard-headed Ministers grudgingly accepted the inquiry's finding that injustice had been done at Waitara and with equal reluctance agreed to return the land to the Ngatiawa. On 4 May, in

[1] Webb.

G

Taranaki, 2 officers and 6 NCOs and soldiers of the 57th Regiment were murdered in an ambush.

The ill-fated party was from the Tataraimaka Block, eighteen miles south of New Plymouth. If the Waitara was open to inquiry, the Tataraimaka, lost during the recent conflict, was not and six weeks earlier, on 24 March, the 57th under Col Warre had marched out to Poutoko, on its southern boundary, to reclaim it and began building St Patrick's Redoubt. On the 29th the Governor, accompanied by Lt-General Duncan Cameron and his Minister for Native Affairs, had arrived at New Plymouth and, on studying the tense situation in the Tataraimaka, sent for more troops—Capt Mercer's Royal Artillery battery, whose 100 horses, guns and wagons were landed over the open surf beach without loss by local boatmen, three companies of the 70th under Col Mulock and a company of the veteran 65th who came down from Auckland in HMS *Harriet* and *Eclipse*. With these reinforcements the General marched out with his own column on 4 April, also to the southern boundary of the Tataraimaka, and began building St George's Redoubt.

It is clear from this considerable show of force that opposition was expected. But though no organised Maori resistance materialized, the deep undercurrent of antagonism soon erupted into violence. The history of the 57th Regiment describes a regimental tragedy:

'On 4 May, 1863, Colour-Sergeant Samuel Ellers, Sergeant Samuel Hill, Ptes Edward Kelly, John Flynn, Bartholomew McCarthy and Patrick Ryan were sent from Tataraimaka on escort duty, having in charge Private William Banks, a prisoner to be brought to trial by Court-Martial at New Plymouth.

Lieutenant Tragett (57th) and Staff Assistant-Surgeon Hope (late 57th, recently transferred to the Staff) accompanied this escort, but without any idea of danger, the Rebel Maoris, up to this time, having been in the habit of bringing vegetables and supplying the Troops at the Redoubt. On reaching the Wairau, a small stream half-way between Tataraimaka and Poutoko, the escort was suddenly fired upon by an ambuscade of 30 or 40 Rebel Natives and the whole party were killed or wounded.'[1]

[1] *Historical Records of the 57th, 1755–1878* by Lieutenant-General H. J. Warre, CB.

Pte Kelly, though wounded, managed to escape into the fern and stagger to St Patrick's Redoubt at Poutoko, where a flying column immediately set out for the Wairau. There the mutilated bodies of all the ambushed party were found, including the prisoner, Banks, but not Pte Ryan's. His body was subsequently found concealed in a hole nearby after information from a prisoner. The ambush, which was tantamount to a Maori declaration of war, was probably meant to catch more distinguished victims, possibly even the Governor; certainly the General and Col Warre were also journeying in the area at that time. Bands of hostile Maoris now began entrenching and constructing a *pa* on the far bank of the Katikara River, a boundary of the disputed Tataraimaka, and a mere half a mile from St George's Redoubt. In April the implacable Rewi Maniapoto had sent a chilling exhortation to the restive tribes of the Taranaki: 'Kill the *Pakeha*!'

While Sir George Grey, recognising the inevitability of war, wrote to England for reinforcements, his military commander set about ridding the Tataraimaka of the defiant *pa* on the Katikara, held by 600 rebels. At 6 am on 4 June, a rainy, wintry morning 400 men of the 57th under Colonel Warre, with the four companies of the 65th and 70th in support, crossed the Katikara while Mercer's battery of powerful 12-pounder Armstrong guns and the guns of HMS *Eclipse*, anchored in the mouth of the river, crashed down on the rebel defences. The weight of the artillery and naval gun support was overwhelming and though the rebels fought doughtily, the 57th, burning with rage to avenge their murdered and mutilated comrades, went through with the bayonet with ferocious dash. For the loss of twelve casualties, including three dead, the British won a salutary success in the first engagement of what was obviously going to be an ever-widening war. Some twenty-eight Maori bodies were found, including a senior chief, Hori Patini.

The irony of the victory, however, was that, due to the strategic pressures of the mounting crisis in North Island, the Tataraimaka Block had to be abandoned yet again. On 20 June Duncan Cameron sailed back to Auckland in the *Eclipse*, taking all the reinforcing troops except one company of the 70th which was left under command of Colonel Warre and the 57th, again the sole guardians, with the local Militia, of the province. To compensate the 70th, their detached company at the Dunedin goldfields returned on 16 June and after a sojourn at Camp Otahuhu marched out to the Queen's Redoubt on the Waikato River.

Though the Waikato was soon to claim the attention due to a major military offensive, Taranaki continued to endure the alarms and minor depredations of guerrilla warfare, of ambushes, settler murders and rebel raiding parties. Colonel Warre, forced to husband his main strength around the approaches to New Plymouth, was in touch by telegraph with his outlying posts and redoubts about the town, of which the main and most exposed was St. Patrick's at Poutoko. With his limited resources, he had to evacuate St George's and another at Oakura in the Tataraimaka area. A crisis such as frequently beset Warre occurred in October when he learned that a major rebel attack was planned on the Redoubt at Poutoko. Though parties of rebels were demonstrating north of New Plymouth to divert him, he decided to reinforce Poutoko. Two weak companies of the 57th, about 100 men, under Brevet-Major Shortt, set out along one bush track while Warre, with another 100 Militia under Captain Harry Atkinson, of Kaipopo and Mahoetahi fame, moved along another route.

As both columns converged on the Redoubt, commanded by Major Butler, the operation ran into serious trouble and again the history of the 57th recounts a sterling tale of determination and courage by these Regular and Volunteer soldiers of Victorian days:

'Major Butler, with a small party of the 70th Regiment, having gone out to reconnoitre, had been seriously engaged with a very superior number of Maoris who advanced with considerable determination, driving back Major Butler's party (with some casualties) towards the Redoubt; the companies under Major Shortt arrived at the moment when, embarrassed with his wounded men, Major Butler was endeavouring to force his way back to Poutoko. Although very inferior in numbers, Major Shortt did not hesitate to cut his way through the rebels, whom he took by surprise in the rear and inflicted considerable loss. Major Butler quickly recovered his ground, and being joined by the Volunteer

Militia under Colonel Warre, was able to drive the natives off the plateau and into the deep ravines, from which, being densely covered with bush, it was not possible to dislodge them. During this attack so gallantly repulsed upon the north, another party of 200 or 300 natives crept up the gullies on the south side, with a view to surprise the Redoubt; these were met by Lieutenant Mills, in charge of the small garrison, whose effective fire, with that of the Howitzer permanently defending the Redoubt, soon obliged the rebels to retire. This severe engagement, in which the Maoris far outnumbered the Troops, was not brought to a successful termination without loss. Ensign Powys was severely wounded, Sergeants S. Harvey and P. Bourke being dangerously, and Corporal Rae, Privates W. Reeves, F. Flinn (died of wounds), H. Cain, M. Foley very severely, and Drummer Dudley Stagpool slightly wounded. Major Shortt was highly commended for the gallant manner in which he led his party right through the rebel Maoris upon whom he inflicted heavy loss.

The conduct of the Volunteer Cavalry, acting as guides and escort, under Capt Mace, was also deserving of special notice. When ammunition failed, these men rode up to the Redoubt, and returned, through a very heavy fire, carrying the ammunition (tied up in clothes) in their hands, and several instances occurred of the removal of wounded men on the horses of the mounted orderlies.

Ensign Down and Drummer D. Stagpool were recommended for, and eventually received, the Victoria Cross for their gallant conduct in rescuing a wounded comrade from the clutches of the rebel natives, and many other soldiers behaved with marked courage and coolness, when nearly surrounded by a howling multitude of naked savages, whose loss on such occasions it is always difficult to determine; the killed and wounded being dragged off the field, and carried off (by the women) to a place of safety. That the Rebels suffered severely was evident, not only by the size of the pit in which they—during the night—buried their dead, but by the procession of carts, evidently bearing off their wounded, which were seen later in the evening winding their way to Kaitake, a very strong position in the neighbouring mountains.[1]

[1] Warre.

CHAPTER 10

The River War: The Waikato

WAR fever was in the air in Auckland during the winter of 1863. The fresh outbreak of Maori violence in the Taranaki encouraged a voluble political lobby of land speculators and businessmen who demanded the crushing of the King movement and the opening up of the great Waikato plains. As the Crown had ceased to be the sole purchaser of Maori land in 1862, land could be confiscated from the rebels and thrown open to settlers, with the speculators in the van. In the triumphant wake of the Army, commerce would also follow.

In tenor with this belligerent mood, a selective ballot of single men was conducted in Auckland, after a call-up in June, by Colonel Mould, RE, late of the Taranaki campaign and recently the builder of the Great South Road. Though 400 were taken to back up the Regular troops, many of these were retained in local defence duties as the policy now was to recruit a more professional and mercenary volunteer who would live hard in the bush, undistracted by cares of family or job. Recruiting went out to enlist 2,000 diggers from the Australian goldfields with the enticement of confiscated land as bounty, and was quite successful; this idea of military settlers to occupy land exposed to native attack obviously came to Sir George Grey from his experience of the Boers in the South African veldt. Also, some swashbuckling characters were drawn to the excitement that New Zealand offered, such as the Prussian, Gustavus von Tempsky. After a colourful career in Mexico and the Californian diggings, he was to lead a company of an excellent auxiliary force, the Forest Rangers, who specialized in deep patrolling and scouting, living frugally in the rebel-held forests for many days without even the glimmer of a campfire to betray their presence, but well-armed with carbine, revolver and bowie knife. The two companies of the Forest Rangers were first class complements to the British regulars.

As Manukau harbour, Camp Otahuhu and the posts along the Great South Road bustled with military activity, a certain air of political desperation, however, pervaded Auckland. Power and importance were gradually, but steadily, slipping from its grasp. The new and expanding centre of wealth and population and, consequently, electoral influence, was South Island, enjoying a boom gold rush after the discovery of gold near Dunedin in 1861 when the population of Otago soared from 12,000 to 27,000 within the year; also wool was fetching high prices and the flocks in the peaceful South Island, where very few Maoris lived, were increasing rapidly. Auckland province, though stimulated by a war economy, was more dependent on crops and cattle and con- sequently considerable frustration and resentment built up against the denied Maori-held heartland.

As Otago and Canterbury grew in size and affluence, followed more slowly by Nelson and Marlborough, resentment about pay- ing taxes to finance wars in North Island also mounted in vehemence; one angry Otago faction even demanded secession. Auckland was not able to sustain this challenge as the 1860s went on; the overall population of South Island rose from 50,000 to 159,000 while the North Island, embattled with its native wars, went on more cautiously from 42,000 to 97,000. Inevitably, to placate the southern shift of power, the capital moved to Wellington in 1865. Finance was becoming an acrimonious sub- ject in several quarters, not only inflaming inter-provincial jealousies and prejudices but also the Imperial Government was becoming somewhat irritated by having to pay the costs of New Zealand's perennial wars from the purse of the British taxpayer when the London Stock Exchange boomed with tales of gold and wool fortunes being won in the Colony.

However, while the financial arguments dragged out their protracted course, the Imperial Government responded without demur to Sir George Grey's request for 3,000 reinforcements. In April, 1863, the 2nd Battalion of the 18th Regiment, raised five years earlier at Enniskillen, at the time of the Indian Mutiny, sailed from Portsmouth as a routine relief for the 65th, but as the 2/18th landed at Auckland in July the long service 65th was ordered to remain in New Zealand to meet Grey's demand for extra military help. Meanwhile, War Office clerks scratched out in copperplate-hand orders for the Commander-in-Chief, HRH The Duke of Cambridge, to sign and then to be borne by fast sailing ship to far-distant stations of the Empire: the 43rd Regiment at Calcutta, the 50th in Ceylon and the 68th in Burma were placed at orders to move to New Zealand.

The 18th did not dally in the modest fleshpots of Auckland after their long sea voyage but marched out to Otahuhu the day after their disembarkation. The urgency was dictated by the imminence of the campaign the General Officer Commanding was about to launch against the Waikato. As a Regiment newly arrived after three months at sea and unfamiliar to New Zealand conditions, the 18th were deployed initially on protective duties.

'The battalion received their campaigning kit: Officers and men were provided with blue serge "jumpers", haversacks, water-bottles and pannikins; all ranks carried a blanket and waterproof sheet, rolled and slung over the left shoulder; the men were armed with Enfield rifles and bayonets. Five days later the column marched through Drury to the Queen's Redoubt, a work that commanded the crossing of the Waikato at Te Ta. A detachment of two hundred of the 18th under Captain Inman was dropped at Drury to hold that post on the line of communication and a few days later the whole of the battalion appears to have been echeloned along the bush track between Drury and the Queen's Redoubt.'[1]

With his communications secured and dispositions made to protect isolated communities from marauding bands striking toward Auckland, Duncan Cameron assembled a punitive expedition in early July, 1863, to invade Waikato territory; the pretext for this offensive action was to forestall the build-up of enemy

[1] *The Campaigns and History of the Royal Irish Regiment, 1684–1902* by Lieutenant-Colonel G. Le M. Gretton.

reported over the other side of the frontier, with alleged aggressive intent on Auckland. Consequently, on the night of 12 July, 400 soldiers set off, led by an advance guard of the 12th Regiment, across the Mangatawhiri stream, a Rubicon that the Kingite Maoris declared meant war if crossed, and entered the King country. Simultaneously, 300 men of the 65th, under Colonel Wyatt, crossed the Waikato on 13 July at Tuakau and established Alexander Redoubt on the high cliffs dominating the river.

The main column was soon in action. On 17 July some 300 Waikato were entrenched on the Koheroa range in the path of the advance and Cameron hurried forward to take charge of the attack himself. The General, who nine years earlier had led his own Regiment, the 42nd Highlanders, up the Alma, advanced twenty paces in front of the leading assault ranks, armed only with his walking stick. The attack was made by 300 men of the 14th, under Lieutenant-Colonel Austen, supported by 150 of the 12th and 104 of the 70th, and though the Waikato Maoris fought gallantly, they were driven from their positions at the point of the bayonet, losing 30 to 40 dead. British casualties were 3 dead and 10 wounded, all from the 14th; their Commanding Officer was slightly wounded.

After this spirited encounter, the force pushed over the Koheroa hills along the Waikato to Whangamarino and erected a stockade in sight of the dominating rebel position at Mere Mere, overlooking the river. Cameron still kept his headquarters at the Queen's Redoubt, for the considerable problem of supporting large forces in the roadless, undeveloped terrain of the King country was exercising his staff. The obvious axis of advance was the great river itself, but there was a delay in obtaining suitable shallow-draught vessels.

Meanwhile, as his advanced post at Whangamarino drew the fire of snipers and a sentry from the 12th had his thumb tomahawked off by a rebel who stalked him and tried to seize his rifle, his various detachments on the British side of the Waikato were having an active time with raiding war parties. On 22 July a party of the 18th Regiment was surrounded at Kiri Kiri and was in desperate straits when a rescue column of the 65th from Tuakau came up opportunely to their entrenched knoll and poured rapid fire at the many besieging rebels: 'The regimental call of the 65th, and the "Fire" was now sounded by Lieutenant Pennfather, which was answered by the 18th with a loud cheer.' The rebels were driven off, taking their casualties, and the 65th lost one soldier killed.

The 65th were engaged in another exciting rescue operation on 7 September, when Captain Swift took Lieutenant Butler and fifty men from Tuakau to go to the relief of friendly Maoris being attacked at a post called Cameron seven miles lower down the river. At 4 pm, savage fighting ensued against a numerous enemy war party, and Swift was cut down, mortally wounded, leading a bayonet charge, and Butler was also wounded in the next charge. Colour-Sergeant MacKenna, well supported by Lance-Corporal Ryan, took over with great coolness and having got the wounded officers to a place of safety, returned to the fight: 'with one loud huzza we charged, burning to avenge our officers.' Fortunately for the outnumbered soldiers, the early New Zealand dusk intervened and they lay on their arms, with four soldiers wounded, as well as their two officers, and two comrades dead. During the night the gallant Swift died and MacKenna hid his body in the bush; next morning the Colour-Sergeant led his party away, carrying their wounded. Fortunately, they soon met two companies of their Regiment under Brevet-Lieutenant-Colonel Murray hurrying forward to their assistance. Swift had reported his intention to the Queen's Redoubt, and Duncan Cameron, on hearing of it, at once ordered out the two companies in support.

Another particularly severe action occurred at Pukekohe on 14 September, only a week after the fight at Cameron, when 3 officers and 43 men of the 70th under Major Ryan relieved a detachment of the Forest Rangers cut off by a numerous and well-armed enemy. The 70th lost 2 dead and 6 wounded.

By October, Cameron had two vessels, the paddle steamer *Avon* and the gunboat *Pioneer*, with four armoured barges, and he was now ready to move against Mere Mere. On 3 October the remaining companies of the 12th Regiment under Lieutenant-Colonel Hamilton arrived from Sydney and marched out to Whangamarino. Lieutenant Boulton, of the 12th Regiment, relates in his diary how his battalion at Whangamarino was suddenly placed at short notice to move without tents and in light marching order:

'On the afternoon of the 27th, the gunboat *Pioneer* arrived at the Bluff, having steamed up the River Waikato with perfect impunity under some heavy firing, and she brought some large bulletproof boats for the conveyance of troops, and also two 40 pounder Armstrong guns. She looked very grand, being 140 feet, with accommodation for 500 men, and is quite bulletproof.'[1]

On 1 November an assault force of 550, detachments from six Regiments, embarked and under the personal command of Duncan Cameron, sailed up the river to Mere Mere. The advance of the small armada was apparently too much for the rebel garrison; they abandoned their positions and melted southward through inaccessible, rain-soaked country. Boulton gives the following description of the scene:

'We landed immediately, most of us up to our necks in water, and ran up the hill, as far as the *pa* and the flagstaff. Not a single man was to be found, and so this famous stronghold, with its innumerable rifle pits and other defences, fell into our hands without a blow; we found two of the enemy's guns and another is supposed to be in the river. Dusk now approaching, we proceeded to make large fires, and be as comfortable as possible with nothing to eat and no blankets on a very cold night with occasional showers. The next morning whilst anxiously awaiting the arrival of rations and bedding, the *Avon* came up about daybreak with a few blankets and some rum, and was followed at 8 o'clock by the *Pioneer*, bringing a portion of the 12th baggage, lots of provisions, and 400 men of the 18th and 70th Regiments. We now set about pitching our tents on the slope of a hill leading down to the river, a very pretty spot, and there being only two tents for nine officers, three of us commenced to build a hut, which was sufficiently complete to sleep in by the evening. On the 3rd, we commenced to build at Mere Mere (under the superintendence of an officer of the Royal Engineers) a redoubt on flagstaff hill for 200 men which was occupied on the 11th by a detachment of 3 officers and 50 men of the regiment.'[2]

Cameron used November judiciously to achieve two aims: firstly, to clear the raiders who came out of the Hunua forest to

[1] Webb.
[2] ibid.

attack his supply convoys on the great South Road and terrorise farms in the area and, secondly, to build up Mere Mere as the base for the next stage of his advance up the great river. In mid-November he despatched Brevet Lieutenant-Colonel Carey, of the 18th Regiment, in command of six companies, two each from the 12th, 18th and 70th Regiments, with 50 Volunteer horsemen and 300 militia, by sea from Auckland to the Firth of Thames to build a line of blockhouses between the Thames and the Waikato, as he was convinced that the rebel marauders came from the country about the estuary of the Thames. This force saw no fighting but much hard work, and within two months had established a chain of posts, Miranda, Esk and Surrey Redoubts, to link up with the strategic Queen's Redoubt.

Duncan Cameron, meanwhile, reconnoitred upriver in the gunboat *Pioneer*, with *Avon* in attendance, probably for navigational experience and, after twelve miles, came on what was clearly a very strong rebel position at Rangiriri, sited with tactical excellence across the isthmus that ran from the river to Lake Waikare. The *Pioneer* shelled the rebels who replied gallantly but futilely with rifle and musketry fire, then the two steamers turned about and returned to British-held territory. Meanwhile, preparations went ahead at Mere Mere. On 19 November two companies of the 40th and two companies of the 65th landed with provisions and stores for 1,200 men.

On 15 November the 50th Regiment from Ceylon disembarked at Auckland under the command of Lieutenant-Colonel Waddy. Their regimental history nicely gives the proper perspective on going to war in a Victorian campaign:

'and marched the next day to Camp Otahuhu, new Colours having been presented previous to landing by the Colonel's wife.'

The 50th, as new arrivals, took over the static but vital task of responsibility for the Great South Road: Headquarters and three companies were at Drury, two companies at Queen's Redoubt, and one company at each of the posts along the intervening stretch of road: Shepherd's Bush, Martin's Farm, Williamson's Clearing and Razorback.

The stocking and reinforcement of Mere Mere on 19 November

was not without portent: next day, Cameron advanced against Rangiriri. His plan was simple and well-founded: a main frontal assault would be supported simultaneously by a force landed in the enemy's rear from the *Pioneer* and *Avon*, attended by four gun boats under the command of Commodore Sir William Wiseman. At 7 am on 20 November marching columns set off from Mere Mere along the right bank of the Waikato, while 300 men of the 40th remained on board the *Pioneer* ready to move up river for their amphibious landing in rear of Rangiriri. It was a considerable force Cameron had in motion against the Maori fortress: 407 all ranks of the 65th, 85 (on land) of the 40th, 112 of the 12th, 184 of the 14th, 52 gunners of Captain Mercer's C Battery, 14 sappers and 90 sailors and marines from HMS *Eclipse*, *Miranda* and *Curacoa*.

At 3 pm the British formed up for the attack behind a hill 600 yards from Rangiriri (which ominously translated as 'Angry Heavens') and the history of the 14th Regiment sets the battle scene:

> 'The works consisted of a long line of high parapet with double ditch, extending from the Waikato to Lake Waikare, the centre of this line being strengthened by a square redoubt of very formidable construction, the ditch being twelve feet wide and—reckoning from the sole of the ditch to the crest of the parapet—eighteen feet deep. The strength of the work was not known until it was attacked, as the profile could not be seen from the river or the ground in front. Behind the left centre of this main line, and at right angles thereto, was a strong line of rifle pits facing the river, and obstructing the advance of the troops in that direction. About five hundred yards behind the front position was a high ridge, the summit of which was fortified by rifle pits.'[1]

After a preliminary bombardment from the two 12-pounder Armstrong guns, the British assault lines went forward. On the right were 200 men of the 65th, with their stormers thrown out, followed by a ladder party of 72; on the left, the 12th and 14th detachments, while in rear and in general support came a company each from the 40th and 65th. Battle was soon joined, the stormers scaled the parapet of the rebels' first line and, charging on up the hill, also carried the second line of rifle pits. Mean-

[1] *Historical Records of the 14th Regiment* by Captain H. O'Donnell.

while, the 40th on board the *Pioneer* and *Avon* were landing, delayed by a strong wind and adverse currents, and with his first fifty men ashore, Lieutenant-Colonel Leslie scrambled up to the dominating ridge in rear of the main enemy redoubt.

But now, as the rebel outer lines were overrun in strength and the British regiments lapped about the central redoubt, a serious check, with a heavy rate of casualties developed. A deadly fire poured out from the redoubt, which scythed into four main and desperate assaults to get a lodgement into it. Brave men jumped into the ditch but found that their scaling ladders were too short; even so, some clawed their way up to the parapet, only to fall back, shot down. A particularly gallant assault was Captain Henry Mercer, Royal Artillery, leading thirty-six gunners armed with swords and revolvers who were also repulsed with loss, including Mercer, badly shot through the jaw. This bloody affair was distinguished by the chivalrous courage of a Waikato chief, Te Oriori, who jumped down into the great ditch from the safety of the parapet and though himself hit three times, bore a wounded officer away to safety. The ninety-strong naval contingent, under Commander Mayne of the *Eclipse*, launched the last forlorn hope, as Cameron continued to press the attack, but made no headway and fell back, after sustaining many casualties, Mayne being severely wounded in the hip.

Dusk mercifully set in and the soldiers bivouacked on the wet ground, 'disgusted and disheartened' as the diarist of the 12th Regiment relates, 'and kept awake by a chorus of bullets throughout the night'. The Regiments had reason to be dispirited: the 12th had lost 1 officer and 5 soldiers killed and 19 wounded from 5 officers and 107 men who went into action; of the 14th, Lt-Col Austen and Capt Phelps were to die of their wounds, while 5 soldiers were killed and 9 wounded; the 40th had 8 killed and 13 wounded, while the hard-tried 65th sustained 3 officers and 13 soldiers killed and 33 wounded. The gallant Mercer was also shortly to die of his wound after being evacuated to Queen's Redoubt where his wife was present to read his last pathetic message, written in pencil, as he was unable to talk: 'Do not grieve for me. I die contented, and resigned to God's will.' Two officers of his Battery won the Victoria Cross at

Rangiriri: Assistant Surgeon William Temple who rushed forward to tend him and other wounded, and Lieutenant Arthur Pickard RA who repeatedly risked his life after the repulse of the attack to give water and comfort to the wounded.

It was a sorry night for Duncan Cameron and his field force. After early success the attack came to savage grief through the adaptable genius of the Maori for military construction. Not only was the Rangiriri position superbly sited both tactically and strategically, but the surprise effect of the formidable central redoubt, caused by its lack of silhouette, coupled with the deep ditch engirdling it, showed that the power of modern artillery and the rush of many brave men under covering fire could be negated by this astute native enemy.

Like Despard before him, Cameron fortuitously found respite from his military dilemma. At dawn a white flag was run up over the redoubt; after the stiff fight they had endured, the rebels' ammunition had run out. In the extraordinary way British soldiers have, they went forward to shake the hands of the warriors whose fire had raked their ranks the evening before, and Duncan Cameron made a speech exhorting the Government to give decent treatment to the prisoners, who included the brave Te Oriori.

With 39 British dead and 93 wounded, Rangiriri was a bloody victory. A cool mind, with hindsight, could say that having realised the strength of the central redoubt and suffering the first repulse, Cameron should have desisted from pressing further assaults and merely laid siege to it, waiting for it to fall from that Achilles Heel of any Maori *pa*, lack of water. Doubtless he was to some degree at fault, but command and control in that embattled scrubland was not easy. Line of sight was difficult, runners conveying orders got lost or took a long time, and the assault, having broken through two defence lines, could only have come up to the redoubt disorganised, with each Regiment determined to break in for its own glory.

The defenders lost fifty dead and probably many of their wounded were removed during the night in the usual skilful Maori way, but 183 prisoners were taken, including many influential Waikato chiefs, and 220 stands of arms. However, the main significance of the fall of Rangiriri was that the fortress door of the King country had been forced open and after leaving a garrison to consolidate his rear, Cameron set his infantry marching up the banks of the Waikato, past deserted native villages and abandoned cornfields. By 9 December he had occupied the modest King-ite capital, Ngaruawahia, and the British flag flew over King Tawhiao's rude palace as the enemy withdrew forty miles up the Waipa to build new *pas*. Duncan Cameron waited at Ngaruawahia to regroup for the next stage of his advance and the 12th Regiment's history describes the scene when Lieutenant-Colonel Hamilton arrived by steamer with his headquarters:

'At this station were the General and his staff, a battery of Armstrong guns, some RE, about 750 of the 40th and 65th Regiments and a large staff of Commissariat. The King's palace, here, consisting of one large room with a portico, is now the guardroom, where eleven native prisoners are confined. There are large cultivations of potatoes here, and the camp is pitched in a potato field. The surface of the soil is covered with a light sand, and the dust is perfectly blinding.'

Meanwhile, at Auckland, the 43rd Light Infantry disembarked from India in mid-December and marched out to Camp Otahuhu, and the 68th Light Infantry came in January. These reinforcements relieved the 50th in the posts along the Great South Road, and Cameron now brought that Regiment into more active field work. On 20 December the 50th concentrated at Otahuhu and in early January marched to Onehunga to embark for Raglan, a small bay on the flank of the Waikato country. There the 50th landed and began cutting a track from the head of the Waitatura valley to link up with the advance of the main force from Ngaruawahia, now moving along the right bank of the Waipa.

'The Waikato at this time was alive with small craft. Little river steamers panted upstream, sometimes towing barges filled with soldiers. Slim gunboats attracted the admiring gaze of friendly natives, whose canoes crowded the river, carrying stores to the British camps. The river bank was astir with marching soldiers, Forest Rangers, bullocks dragging heavy artillery and ammunition wagons along the rough roads.'

On 28 January, Cameron, now Sir Duncan after his victory at Rangiriri, came up against the strong rebel *pa* of Paterangi and

14. Two soldiers of the 65th Regiment guarding the body of one of their officers – from a sketch by Gustavus von Tempsky.

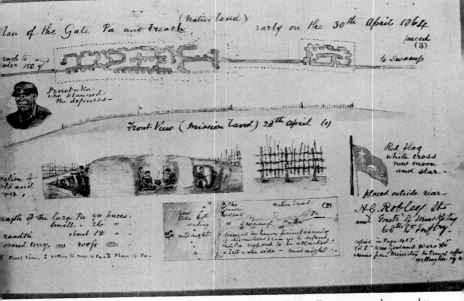

15. *Plan of the Gate pa, Rawiri's stronghold at Tauranga, drawn by A.G. Robley of the 68th Regiment.*

16. *Maori prisoners taken at Weraroa pa on board a prison hulk in Wellington harbour.*

deployed his column on the high ground at Te Rore, on the *pa*'s left flank. Though he had some 2,000 men from the 12th, 40th, 50th, 65th and 70th Regiments, he appreciated Paterangi's solidity and wisely refrained from assaulting, especially as he now had to wait for his artillery and laden stores wagons to join him laboriously over the barely existent tracks. The newly-arrived 50th were blooded, losing two soldiers killed, when a bathing party from both the 40th and 50th were ambushed in Mangapiko creek on 11 February, and a large scale hand-to-hand encounter developed when 200 reinforcements were rushed up under staff officer Brevet-Lieutenant-Colonel Sir Henry Havelock VC of Indian Mutiny fame, mainly from the 40th and Forest Rangers. Captain Charles Heaphy, Auckland Volunteers, though wounded three times, protected a wounded 40th soldier under fire and was to gain the Victoria Cross for his bravery. After several hours of fighting the Waikato withdrew, leaving 28 bodies. The British suffered six killed and seven wounded.

When his heavy stores came up, Cameron decided to mask Paterangi and the nearby *pa* of Piko-Piko with the 12th and 50th detachments and at noon, 20 February, he set off for the defended village of Rangiaowhia which he surprised at dawn next day, capturing it with light casualties, though Colonel Nixon, a former 39th Regiment officer now commanding the Defence Force Cavalry, was shot dead. That same day he brought up the 50th from Te Rore as Colonel Waddy had discovered from his colonial scouts that Paterangi was being evacuated, and similarly, Havelock found Piko-Piko abandoned; the sudden British descent on Rangiaowhia, which was a sharp and unpleasant affair with women and children dying in the burning village, had clearly disturbed the rebel tribesmen. Soon a report came in that large numbers of the rebels from Paterangi were digging in on a ridge by the road to Rangiaowhia.

Cameron decided to attack at once. Two companies of the 70th, supported by two guns, drove in the rebel skirmishers thrown out a mile forward of the position and then the 50th, supported by the 65th and remainder of the 70th, dashed forward and carried the position with some brilliance. For most of the approach the 50th moved on a four-man front down a narrow

H

113

track hemmed in by high fern and impenetrable *manuka* scrub to debouch into open ground 100 yards from the enemy rifle pits. The 50th charged and swept over the rebel entrenchments with the bayonet, killing 40 and capturing 4 wounded before the tribesmen broke and fled towards the Maungatautari ranges. The 50th lost 1 dead and 11 wounded, while the 70th had only three wounded and drew well-earned praise in Cameron's despatch to Sir George Grey.

This spirited success had a dampening effect on rebel morale and Cameron guessed that the Waikato tribes and their Ngatimaniapoto allies were at their last ebb of resistance. Accordingly, on 22 March, he shifted his headquarters and the main weight of his field force from Te Awamutu and the Waipa eastwards to the Upper Waikato. With him, to the site of modern Cambridge, went the 50th, 70th, the Forest Rangers, 50 men of the Naval Brigade and some Royal Artillery, while Brigadier-General Carey, with the 40th and 65th, remained at Te Awamutu.

But it was to be near Te Awamutu that the last and gallant resurgence of Maori defiance in the Waikato occurred. In the delightful pastoral setting of Orakau, only six miles away, amid fields of wheat, orchards of cherry, quince, apple and almond and gardens of potato, melons, pumpkins and marrow, all depicting how much the Maori owed to the *pakeha* for the great variety in his diet, 300 rebels, with women and children, began constructing a *pa* and digging in under the redoubtable Rewi Maniapoto himself. He commanded a curious, though singly-motivated force of both pagans and Christians: about 50 Ngatimaniapoto, 20 Waikato, 100 ferocious Urewera, 100 Ngatiraukawa and even 20 Ngatikahungunu from distant Hawke's Bay.

'Among the warriors was an old tattooed chief of cannibal days, clad only in a flax mat, his hair done up in a top knot with feather decorations. One of the chiefs had been on the Victorian goldfields, and they placed him in charge of the inner defences.'

When on 30 March Carey heard from his scouts of the rebel activity at Orakau, he moved with the 40th and 65th, a company of the Forest Rangers, a company of 1st Waikato Militia and two 6-pounder Armstrong guns to be in position about the *pa* at dawn the next day. The Armstrong guns roared out but Orakau was strong; the incredible ant-like military energy of the Maori ensured that the effect of the shot was offset by massed bundles of fern and flax. Carey mounted two assaults but each time the ring of fire from the *pa* and rifle pits drove the attackers to ground. On 1 April 200 men from the main force, including a company of the 70th, reinforced Carey and more drama was added to the tense situation by the approach of a rebel relief force of Waikato and Ngatiraukawa. But despite a *haka* being danced in the *pa*, the British vice about Orakau was too firm. Next morning, while a fog enveloped the battlefield, a sortie from the *pa* to make contact with the nearby rebel force was beaten back by the vigilant soldiers. Still, the full demands of duty were tempered with mercy:

'That night a British sentry saw a woman stealing down towards a spring in the swamp below, and guessing rightly that she was risking death to take water to the wounded, to his credit be it said, he pretended not to see her.'[1]

With the failure of his assaults and bombardment, Carey fell back on the tried technique of sapping. By the third morning, the head of the sap had reached near the outer trenches, and British grenades, lobbing over from the sap, began to take effect. The Armstrong guns also now began to tell with the weight and accuracy of their fire and two breaches were opened in the *pa* walls. Duncan Cameron, who was now on the scene, ordered the Cease Fire to be blown and in this eerie silence, sent one of his two staff interpreters, Mr William Mair, forward to the head of the sap to speak to the enemy. William Mair, who with his younger brother, Gilbert, became a hero of these wars, wrote an account of these tense historic minutes which James Cowan quotes:

'I got up on the edge of the sap and looked through a gap in the gabions made for the field piece. The outwork in front of me was a sort of double rifle-pit, with the *pa* or redoubt behind it. The Maoris were in rows, the nearest row only a few yards away from me. I cannot forget the dust-stained faces, the bloodshot eyes, and shaggy heads. The muzzles of their guns rested on the edge of the ditch in front of them. One man aimed steadily at me all the time—his name was Wereta.
Then I said, "Friends, listen! This is the word of the General:

[1] *The New Zealand Wars and the Pioneering Period* by James Cowan.

115

Great is his admiration for your bravery. Stop! Let the fighting cease; come out to us that your bodies may be saved."

'I could see the Maoris inclining their heads towards each other in consultation, and in a few minutes came the answer in a clear, firm tone: "Friend, I shall fight against you for ever, for ever!"

Then I said, "That is well for you men, but it is not right that women and children should die. Let them come out."

Someone asked, "How did you know there were women here?" I answered, "I heard the lamentations for the dead in the night."

There was a short deliberation, and another voice made answer: "If the men die, the women and children must die also."

I knew it was over, for there was no disposition on the part of the Maoris to parley; so I said "It is well; the word is ended," and dropped quickly into the sap.

Wereta, the man who had been aiming at me, was determined to have the last say in the matter, and he fired at me. His bullet just tipped my right shoulder, cutting my revolver-strap and tearing a hole in my tunic. Wereta did not survive his treachery long, for he was killed by a hand grenade soon after.'

But for all their proud spirit, Rewi and his warriors were in a critical condition. Many parched throats testified to the lack of water, their ammunition was almost gone and food, due to the haste in which the *pa* had been thrown up, was scarce. In a *korero* with his chiefs, Rewi took a dramatic decision in keeping with their cry of no surrender: they would fight their way out.

As a diversion one chief was sent out to call for more discussion in front of the *pa*. Then the thin cordon of the 40th about the rear of the *pa* saw an amazing spectacle: calmly advancing from the confines of the *pa*, with the women and children held protectively in the centre, was the whole garrison in one compact body under Rewi. The sheer audacity of the movement allowed the concourse to approach the astonished cordon and begin bursting through it before the soldiers started shooting into its flanks. The rebels now broke up and ran, still shielding their women and children, for the refuge of the swamp and the bush, but the Defence Force Cavalry came galloping up to pursue and cut them down, as also did the Forest Rangers, running through the bushland to intercept the fugitives. Only about sixty rebels escaped, including Rewi surrounded by a devoted bodyguard, and at least one Maori woman was shot by a British soldier, despite William Mair trying to save her.

Cameron watched the final act of Orakau *pa* admiringly, as he had done at Rangiriri. Once again, the price of success was not light, for the British lost 17 killed in action or died of wounds and 52 wounded. But for the rebels it was a disaster, as the flight from the *pa* developed into a running massacre. Some 120 were killed, mostly in the pursuit, and 26 prisoners taken. Orakau broke the Waikato and Ngatimaniapoto resistance with some finality. When Cameron returned to his troops before the Maungatautari ranges, where he had fully expected the last stand to be made, reconnaissance now showed that the *pas* in the defiles were abandoned and empty. The Waikato war was over.

Fittingly, Orakau was the last fight of the veteran 65th, though they were to lose Ensign Chaytor mortally wounded, and three soldiers killed, and two officers and six soldiers wounded. Their long and arduous service in New Zealand built up a unique and chivalrous relationship with the rebel Maoris, who called them the 'Hickety-Pip', the nearest a Maori tongue could get to pronouncing Sixty-Fifth. On occasions, when they were the leading regiment in an attack, a warning would be shouted from the rebel parapet: 'Lie down, Hickety-Pip, we are going to fire.' Also, their picquets seemed to come in from night outpost duty fresher than others, as they would call out to the rebel sentries to ask if there would be any fighting that night. Often the reply would come, and they knew the Maoris would keep their word: 'Not tonight—too wet and cold. We'd better all go to sleep. Goodnight, Hickety-Pip!'

At a garrison parade at Camp Te Awamutu on 18 June, Lieutenant-General Sir Duncan Cameron presented the Victoria Cross to Colour-Sergeant, now Ensign, MacKenna, 65th Regiment, for his bravery at Cameron; unfortunately, the Victoria Cross for Corporal Ryan could not be presented as he had been tragically drowned, trying to rescue a comrade.

A tablet in St John's Church, Te Awamutu, aptly writes FINIS to the whole Waikato campaign:

'This tablet was erected by soldiers of the 65th Regiment as a memorial to the New Zealanders who fell in the actions at Rangiaowahia on 21st and 22nd February, 1864, and at Orakau on 31st March and 1st April, 1864. "I say unto you, love your enemies." '

CHAPTER 11

Action at Tauranga

In April, 1864, at Tauranga, Bay of Plenty, Lieutenant-Colonel Greer, the Commanding Officer of the 68th Light Infantry, was shaken to receive a message from Rawiri Puhirake, a senior chief of the Ngaiterangi, that simply said: come out and fight. Rawiri also forwarded a code of conduct he had drawn up for the proposed conflict: civilians would not be molested, prisoners treated with kindness, and the dead respected. He added that for the convenience of the soldiers, his tribesmen had thoughtfully constructed a track eight miles long that led directly to his *pa*.

Greer was a hot-tempered Irishman who ruled the 68th with the strong-handed despotism common to Victorian commanding officers, and doubtlessly his 'large fuzzy whiskers with moustaches that went straight into them', quivered with rage at the impertinence. But he had his orders, which were to remain on the defensive.

The Army had come to Tauranga on 22 January, 1864 when HMS *Miranda* and the steamer *Corio* landed 700 men of the 43rd and 68th Regiments under Lieutenant-Colonel Carey, 18th Regiment. Their primary task was to protect the Mission Station at Te Papa which had been abandoned in July, 1863, at the outbreak of the Waikato war but re-occupied that December. When Cameron had paused with his Headquarters at Ngaruawahia that Christmas, he had clearly given much thought to the situation about the periphery of the Waikato. Though his rear was secure, with Auckland well-protected by his dispositions along the Waikato River and the Great South Road, and by his redoubts stretching from the Thames estuary, he had intelligence that the east coast tribes were affected by the King mystique and were providing fighting men for the Waikato. Though the Arawas, between the Waikato and the Bay of Plenty, remained staunchly pro-British, like the Ngapuhi in the far north, Tauranga was a sea outlet for the Waikato and local bonds were deep and strong.

The 43rd and 68th encamped in the clover fields about the Mission and then proceeded to raise two redoubts, Monmouth and Durham. For the next three months, life was uneventful and on 11 March, Carey, described by a 68th officer as 'the most fussy, uncivil commanding officer I ever came across, most vacillating and undecided', left for Auckland. Greer became the senior officer in the area.

But in April the Ngaiterangi warriors who had been fighting with the Waikato began returning to their own lands and immediately occupied some of their old *pas* to confront the soldiers at Tauranga. It was then that Rawiri sent his challenge. When no attack transpired, he sent another message in a disappointed but still courteous vein to say that as he had apparently taken up a position too far away for the soldiers, he would build a *pa* much nearer. The site he had selected was to become famous as the Gate *Pa*. S. G. P. Ward, in *The Story of the Durham Light Infantry*, describes the ground:

'Te Papa Mission (which was founded in 1838 by the same Archdeacon Brown who, in 1864, still conducted it, entertained the troops and took the Sunday morning services), stood at the tip of a narrow tongue of land about three miles long formed by the muddy saltwater estuaries of the Kopurererua stream on the west and the Waimapu on the east. The boundary between the Mission and the Maori lands ran across the base of the peninsula at its narrowest part, and was marked for all its length (say 500 yards) by a ditch. Where it was crossed by the ridgeway track leading south from Te Papa to the ranges a strong timber gate had been placed. The spot was well known to Europeans as the Gate *Pa* and the Maoris as Pukehinahina.'

From the middle of April, Rawiri's tribesmen set to work with the usual Maori military zeal, constructing a stout, oblong *pa*, well-palisaded and holding a redoubt, which they dug out with fire trenches and shelters, behind the boundary ditch which they also deepened. While they toiled, Greer's men came down the peninsula to watch, which would appear to be stretching interpretation of the defensive orders to overtolerance. However, Cameron, a mere forty miles to the west on the Upper Waikato, reacted strongly at the news of Rawiri Puhirake's boldness and the appearance of the Gate *Pa*. He issued orders for a massive reinforcement of 900 infantry to join Greer's force and himself set off for Tauranga. Among this redeployment was the rest of the 68th who were hurriedly withdrawn to Auckland, embarked in HMS *Falcon* and landed at Tauranga harbour late in the evening of 21 April.

That same day hostilities had flared up at Maketu, fifteen miles down the coast, where a company of the 43rd with some militiamen of the 3rd Waikato Regiment, under Major Colville, 43rd, garrisoned a redoubt aptly named Fort Colville. A small party, including Colville, was ambushed at a ford two miles away but escaped back to the Fort where Colville turned out a column to engage the marauders. A running fight developed back to the ford, with both firing lines building up as the day wore on, the British to about a hundred men of the 43rd, 3rd Waikato and the Forest Rangers, with some friendly Arawas, the Maoris to a strength of about 300. At dusk Colville retired to the Fort, with the loss of three soldiers of the 43rd and one Royal Engineer killed. As usual, the enemy casualties were not fully known but were not considered to be light.

On 25 April, another company of the 43rd arrived from Tauranga and two days later, Fort Colville was seriously invested by numerous rebels, mainly Whakatohea and Ngatiporou attracted from the south by the mischief the Ngaiterangi had in hand at Tauranga. However, HMS *Falcon* now hove in sight from Tauranga, accompanied by the steamer, *Sandfly*, bearing the ubiquitous Sir Duncan Cameron with some of his staff. The *Falcon* shelled the rebels, and drove them back into the forest. Four hundred Arawas, under Major Hay, set out in pursuit killing about 50 and capturing nine prisoners and 40 stands of arms.

Cameron now turned his attention to the Gate *Pa*. On the

evening of 17 April, the 68th Light Infantry with the Moveable
Column, a special force composed of selected veterans of New
Zealand warfare from the 12th, 14th and 65th Regiments under
Major Ryan of the 70th Regiment, encamped 1,200 yards from
the *pa*. Next day, the guns and mortars were brought up, aided
by a large contingent of seamen and marines from Sir William
Wiseman's squadron. Then Headquarters and five companies of
the 43rd, commanded by Lieutenant-Colonel Booth, joined. By
the evening of the 28th, a formidable array of the British Army
had assembled before the Gate *Pa*, as the muster rolls show:

General Staff	5 officers.
Medical Staff	3 officers.
Naval Brigade	4 field officers, 6 captains, 7 subalterns, 36 sergeants, 5 drummers, 371 rank and file.
Royal Artillery	1 field officer, 1 captain, 3 subalterns, 1 staff sergeant, 1 sergeant, 43 rank and file.
Royal Engineers	2 rank and file.
Moveable Column	7 officers, 6 sergeants 4 drummers, 164 rank **and file.**
43rd Light Infantry	**1 field officer, 6 captains,** 15 subalterns, 3 **colour sergeants,** 17 sergeants, 12 buglers, 250 rank and file.
68th Light Infantry	3 field officers, 6 captains, 15 subalterns, 3 colour sergeants, 34 sergeants, 21 buglers, 650 rank and file.

A total of 1,694 all ranks, supported by 5 Armstrong guns, 2
howitzers and 8 mortars, confronted the absurdly brave Rawiri
Puhirake and 300 Ngaiterangi warriors.

As dusk set in, a feint was made frontally on the *pa* to cover
the first phase of Cameron's plan: the 68th, led by Mr Purvis,
a local settler, and a Maori sergeant of police called Tu, moved
silently in single file down the eastern flank of the peninsula and
headed through the night to the ground in rear of the *pa*. It soon
started to rain but, after three-quarters of a mile staggering
through sucking mudflats, by 10 pm and two hours before moon-
rise the 68th were on the large spur running away behind the
Gate *Pa*. By 3 am, Greer had his company fully deployed in a
wide semi-circle about 700 yards from the *pa* and as the soldiers
lay on their arms on the wet ground, they could hear the Ngaite-

rangi singing and making speeches, unaware that they were surrounded. At daybreak, thirty seamen from HMS *Curacoa* reinforced the 68th's cordon.

At 7 am, Cameron opened up a heavy concentration from his artillery which continued battering the *pa* throughout the day. One of the 6-pounders was dragged across the swamp to high ground on the enemy's left where it successfully enfiladed the *pa*, though occasional 'overs' from all the guns caused three casualties among the 68th and some shifting of company positions. By 3.30 pm the *pa* was considered to be sufficiently broken down by the guns to be ripe for assault and half an hour later, as the afternoon light was fading, the attack went in, directed on a large breach torn in the centre of the *pa*. The storming column consisted of 150 men of the 43rd with another 150 seamen and marines from HMS *Harrier* led by Commander Hay, the whole assault commanded by Lieutenant-Colonel Booth of the 43rd. Another 300 of the 43rd and Naval Brigade were to follow in support.

Through the rain the waiting 68th saw the rocket signal for the assault go up and heard the cheer of the stormers as they charged. Surprisingly, the breach was gained with little loss, as the inner trench behind the palisade was unmanned by the enemy, and a human torrent of soldiers and seamen poured into the *pa*. But then a withering fire at almost point blank range seared into the press of jostling, shouting attackers who were probably so jammed together that very few could aim their weapons. The defenders were firing from a labyrinth of trenches and dug-outs in the depth of the *pa* and their devastating opening volleys cut down almost every officer, naturally in the van of the attack. Lieutenant-Colonel Booth and Commander Hay fell mortally wounded, with Captain Glover and Ensign Langsland of the 43rd who led into the breach, and many others dropped about them.

Severe hand-to-hand fighting soon developed as the British, in the haze of gunsmoke and over the unknown ground, attempted to close with the enemy. However, the extreme confusion and the breakdown of effective leadership became overwhelming. What happened next is not clearly known, but apparently the cry went up: 'They're coming in their thousands, retire!' Probably a large number of the Maoris, seeking to abandon the *pa* after having inflicted enough casualties on the attackers to satisfy honour, were driven back by the heavy fire and surprise appearance of the 68th encircling the rear, and it is thought that their return panicked many of the leaderless into thinking that a massive counter-attack was being mounted. A jumbled rush of soldiers and sailors surged into a rout as men now struggled to get out of the *pa*. Lieutenant Garland of the 43rd vainly fought to regain control of the seething mass, aided by seven others of his Regiment who were later to receive the formal appreciation of HRH The Field-Marshal Commanding-in-Chief from distant Horse Guards: two of these were were Ensign J. B. Garland and Colour-Sergeant W. B. Garland. It would be interesting to know if all three Garlands were related.

Among several other heroes who relieve the disgrace of Gate *Pa* was Surgeon W. G. N. Manley who had served with the Royal Artillery at Sevastopol. He volunteered to accompany the assault column and when Commander Hay fell, he carried him out of the *pa* to attend to him, then returned to treat the many wounded inside. He was the last man to leave the *pa* and for his bravery and devotion to duty, he was awarded the Victoria Cross. Manley, in those days when medical officers bore arms, was a Victorian soldier who attracted action. That October he joined the 12th Regiment and in the following year was awarded the Royal Humane Society's Medal for saving a man's life.

Another who was among the last to leave was Captain Jenkins RN, who had fallen into a deep trench so packed with Maoris that they were unable to use their tomahawks or load their firearms. The Captain laid about him with his heavy ship's telescope and somehow managed to struggle out and escape. The battered spyglass was picked up in the trench by the Maoris and in due course was returned by Rawiri.

Meanwhile Captain Grace, with the 68th, tells in his diary of a confused and uncomfortable night from the time they heard the cheer go up at 4 pm for the attack:

'which cheer was re-echoed by the various companies of the 68th, and I got into the midst of a heavy fire, bullets falling all round me. I found Greer had left the *whare* and had moved my company

123

and a part of Spratt's so I could not find them. But getting into some fern I got fired at so often that I rejoined Casement's company whom I advised to make his men lie down, as the fire was very hot—which he did.

Presently about 20 Maoris were seen coming up and they were driven in by the fire of the company. Soon afterwards I heard Shuttleworth saying "All the 68th this way", and I joined him, and he assembled all the detached parties for the assault. We then heard that the storming party of the 43rd and sailors had been repulsed and Ensign William Clarke, 43rd, shot through the shoulder, joined us. Colonel McNeil a.d.c., gave an order not to assault but to hold the spur we were on for the night. A sailor joined us who had gone through the *pa*. We had to remain where we were. Greer soon afterwards joined us. The great mistake throughout the day was that the Maoris were not allowed to escape, but we should have let the storming party get well in before we attempted to show ourselves. All night it rained in heavy showers. No grog, no food, and many alarms.

At daylight we were moving off to our different posts when we heard that the Maoris had evacuated the *pa* during the night. I went up there, passing many dead on the way. Some wounded were in the *pa*—those who were too bad to be moved. Amongst them was a scripture reader of Archdeacon Brown's of Te Papa."

During that wet and miserable night, after the disordered remnants of the attack had streamed back, Cameron dug in a hundred yards away from the *pa* and sent a runner back to Tauranga for another company of the 43rd. But, as Grace has remarked, during the blackness of the night the Ngaiterangi slipped away through the extended lines of the 68th. At daybreak, when the British entered the deserted *pa*, they found that Booth and the other British wounded, true to Rawiri's manifesto, had been cared for. Craving for water, they were tended by a Maori Samaritan who stole out, at considerable risk of a British bullet, to fetch them water from a spring. The identity of this charitable hero is not quite certain: it was possibly Heni te Kiri-karamu who was the only female in the Gate *Pa*, or perhaps Henare Wiremu (Henry Williams) Taratoa who was born in the Bay of Islands, baptised by the Rev. Henry Williams and after attending Bishop Selwyn's College in Auckland, became a teacher at Otaki and later at Tauranga.

[1] *The Story of The Durham Light Infantry* by S. G. P. Ward.

As the dying Booth was being carried away, he pathetically tried to salute Cameron and apologise for having failed to execute his orders. The repulse at the Gate *Pa* was an ignominious disaster for British arms and Cameron must carry a large burden of the blame. Why he decided that the assaulting column should be drawn from two different elements, the 43rd and the Naval Brigade, is hard to understand. In the chaotic conditions of a breached *pa*, still being staunchly defended with hand-to-hand fighting and point blank fire, it would have made more tactical sense to employ one disciplined and cohesive force, such as the 68th who could have provided both the assault and supports under their own officers. It was perhaps attractive to have this large battalion carry out the task of rear cordon, but on balance, a second-best of different detachments could have been accepted as no British cordon had ever yet contained parties of Maori rebels filtering away on a dark wet night. Perhaps the 68th did show themselves too prematurely in the fading light of that tragic evening, causing the withdrawing defenders to turn and re-enter the *pa*, but this would seem to have been the plan. Grace mentions that they were formed up to assault, which presumably means that the 68th were required to ensure that the enemy was wholly bottled up, rather than waiting for them to run on to their fire. Again, Cameron, with his considerable experience of Maori behaviour in war, should have thought this aspect out more thoroughly.

The British losses were heavy and reflect the gory mêlée inside the *pa*. The 43rd lost 5 officers killed and 4 wounded, and 9 NCOs and soldiers killed and 23 wounded; later 2 officers and 4 men died of their wounds. Of 9 officers who dined with Archdeacon and Mrs Brown at Te Papa Mission the night before, only Assistant Surgeon Manley was to come out of the action unscathed. The Naval Brigade lost 4 officers and 40 seamen and marines killed and wounded. Total British casualties, including the other regimental detachments who held the ring, were 120. Inside the *pa*, 20 rebel dead were found and 6 wounded, though these prisoners stated that a large number of the dead and wounded had been carried off in the night in the Maori tradition.

Left in this dubious possession of the field, Cameron proceeded in his ponderous way to erect a redoubt on the site of the Gate *Pa* and another across the western estuary at Te Huria (or Judea). However, grave news from Wanganui and Taranaki now claimed the General, and he sailed away with most of the troops at Tauranga. Greer was left once more in local command, and he maintained company garrisons at the Gate *Pa*, Judea and Maketu.

But the considerable moral victory of the Gate *Pa* for Rawiri Puhirake and his Ngaiterangi was to be their undoing. The winter rains closed down active operations by rebels and soldiers but on 21 June, patrols brought Greer news that a large concentration of hostile Maoris were digging-in a single line of rifle pits across a ridgeline at Te Ranga, only four miles from the Gate *Pa* where the track from Tauranga headed into the forests in the south. Greer, whose orders were to prevent the establishment of any *pas* in his vicinity, moved into the field with a force of 594 all ranks to engage the enemy before their labours developed another Pukehinahina. As the rebel force was estimated to number about 600 Ngaiterangi and Ngatiraukawa, he sent back to Te Papa for the one 6-pounder Armstrong gun and every man in camp, another 230, who marched in his wake.

Contact was soon made as Greer's column approached Te Ranga and his skirmishers drove in a body of rebels who advanced to meet the soldiers. Greer then extended the 43rd, at a strength of 239 all ranks, and two companies of the 68th and kept up a brisk fire fight with the rebel trenches until, two hours later, the gun and the reinforcements came in sight. As soon as this reserve was near enough and the gun positioned, Greer sounded 'the Advance' and the 43rd under Major Synge, two companies of the 68th under Captains Trent and Casement, and a detachment of the 1st Waikato Militia under Captain Moore moved into the attack in light infantry order. Major Shuttleworth, 68th, commanded the supports, including two companies of the 43rd who had worked their way to some high ground across the gully on the right flank to enfilade the enemy trench line.

The attack was executed with relentless determination.

'The 43rd had a reputation to retrieve, the 68th a name to sustain, and the struggle was savage. Captain Trent fell severely wounded in the right arm as he led the two companies forward. Lieutenant Villiers-Stuart, one of the first into the pits. in a personal encounter with a Maori armed with an Enfield rifle and bayonet, was bayoneted by him but managed to cut him down with his sword. Corporal Byrne, the Inkerman V.C., the first of his company into the pits, had spitted his man but was about to be tomahawked by him when Sergeant John Murray, who had already accounted singlehanded for a pitful of eight or ten Maoris, ran to his assistance and cut the man down.

The fight was very even until Shuttleworth, 400 yards away, releasing the supporting companies and the two 43rd companies on the right flank at exactly the critical moment, rushed at the pits driving everything before him.'[1]

The British burial parties were later to inter 107 Maori dead. Among the bloodied and forlorn bodies lying in the trenches was the courageous Rawiri Puhirake whose leadership had been so brilliant at the Gate *Pa*. With him lay Henare Taratoa and on Taratoa's body the soldiers found the rules of conduct he and Rawiri had drawn up and had so honourably maintained. The legend (or Heni te Kiri-karamu's) taking water to the British wounded at the Gate *Pa*, caused Bishop Selwyn, in later years in England to commemorate this act of compassion and chivalry by placing in the chapel of Lichfield Cathedral a stained glass window depicting water being brought to King David from the well of Bethlehem.

With the 43rd, Major Colville, of Maketu, was the first into the line of the rifle pits but on his right, Captain F. A. Smith was severely wounded fighting in the trenches at the head of his company and another 43rd company commander, Captain H. J. Berners, was also seriously wounded near the rifle pits. However, despite the ferocity of the close quarter fighting, British losses were not too heavy: 10 killed and 39 wounded.

'All much pleased', wrote Shuttleworth in his diary on return to Te Papa, which was reached at 6 pm that evening. 'All say the best thing done this campaign.'

[1] Ward.

There was much in what the admirable Shuttleworth noted down. Not only was it discovered that Greer's energetic offensive action had forestalled a major rebel attack on Tauranga but some weeks later, on 25 July, 133 Maoris, including many chiefs and notables, came to Tauranga to make their submission to Greer. The decisive defeat of Te Ranga had broken the last will and hope of the rebellion in the north that had been sustained by the King movement; indeed on 17 May, Wiremu Tamihana had surrendered on behalf of many Waikato and only King Tawhiao, Rewi and other intransigent supporters withdrew, unyielding, into the inner recesses of the wild Ngatimaniapoto country.

Captain F. A. Smith, 43rd, and Sergeant John Murray, 68th, each received the Victoria Cross for their gallantry at Te Ranga. In modern Tauranga, Monmouth Redoubt is still clearly delineated, while Durham Redoubt survives as Durham Street. On the historic ground once occupied by the Gate *Pa* is now the suburb of Greerton.

Meanwhile, in the aftermath of Te Ranga:

'Tranquillity settled once more on Tauranga. The 68th took out their cricket stumps again while the war went on in the west.'

CHAPTER 12
The Menace of the Hauhaus

In Taranaki, the lull of several months that followed the retreat to Kaitake of the rebels investing Poutoko Redoubt was abruptly shattered on 28 February, 1864, by the murder of a settler, Mr Patterson, only three miles from New Plymouth. With his limited resources, Colonel Warre had maintained a commendable control over the territory through his system of outposts sustained by flying columns, of which his own Regiment, the 57th, was the mainstay. He had now, however, been reinforced by 600 new-style Volunteers, the military settler looking for his bounty of land. The local militia was being disbanded except for three companies called Bush Rangers. Warre despatched the military settlers to re-occupy the abandoned redoubts of Mahoetahi in the north and Oakura in the south.

With Cameron's main forces engaged in the Waikato, the spirit of the offensive was infectiously in the air and, in March, Warre received permission from the General to move in force against the hostile Taranaki at Kaitake.

The action did not open auspiciously. Major Henry Butler, commanding the southern outposts of the 57th watching Kaitake, took his reconnaissance too close and accurate fire from the rifle pits flanking the *pa* killed one soldier and wounded a Gunner subaltern and four other soldiers. As Warre's reconnoitring was so thorough, however, he encircled Kaitake with some skill and his attack on 24 March, delivered simultaneously from several quarters by his force of mixed Regulars and Volunteers, totalling

I

420 men, was a brilliant success. By 10 am, Captain Corbett's Volunteers from Oakura Redoubt were in position on the right flank of the *pa*, after a most exhausting approach march through dense bush and gullies for many hours and Captain Harry Atkinson's company of Bush Rangers from New Plymouth had penetrated deeply to the right rear of the *pa*, having been guided by Lieutenant C. M. Clarke, 57th Regiment, who had explored a circuitous track. When the bombardment of the half-battery of Armstrong guns, sited across the Oakura river 1,500 yards away under Captain Martin RA, started a fire enveloping the *whares* and the battered stockade in smoke and confusion, a general attack was mounted. From the left of the *pa*, where they had climbed high ground to enfilade rifle pits on that flank, came two companies of the 57th under Butler; another company of the 57th under Captain Russell charged frontally, supported by the indefatigable Captain Frank Mace and his Taranaki Mounted Volunteers, while hard by Corbett on his flank came a further company of the 57th, another of the 70th and a company of the Bush Rangers. Before the concerted assault, which cost only four wounded, the enemy retired rapidly, as they tended to do when they knew they were enveloped, and the wild, mountainous bush closed about their escape.

'The capture of Kaitake was a severe blow to the rebel natives; it was one of the strongest of their fastnesses, admirably placed on the borders of impenetrable jungle, and commanded about 2 miles of open level ground land between the mountain range upon which it was situated and the sea. Nothing could pass safely between the Tataraimaka block of land and New Plymouth so long as the rebels held Kaitake.'[1]

However, in the unpredictable fortunes of New Zealand bush warfare, though a party of celebrating settlers, including a woman, were to drink champagne in the fallen stronghold a day after its occupation, four days later an ambush, a mere 150 yards away, killed one soldier and wounded another.

Just when it seemed that Taranaki was being firmly held while the Waikato campaign drew to a successful close, it was in this turbulent province that the war was to degenerate to a more

[1] Warre.

130

savage and bestial phase that was to permeate through most of North Island. In 1864, a half-crazed, self-styled prophet named Te Ua Haumene, of the Taranaki tribe near Cape Egmont, began preaching with demented vehemence a new religion, 'Pai-Marire', 'the good and the peaceful'. Te Ua was a former slave whose boyhood had been spent in the care of the missionary, John Whiteley, and Pai-Marire was a confused mixture of the old pagan beliefs and incantations and Christianity, with dashes of Judaism thrown in as a makeweight, for Te Ua was an avid reader of the Bible, particularly the Book of Revelation. The central emblem was the *niu*, or flagstaff, about which the devotees marched, chanting absurd and meaningless jargon, ending with the chorus: 'Hau! Hau!', sounding rather like the bark of a dog. The Maori, who had a flair for apt nickname, called Te Ua and his adherents Hauhaus.

Pai-Marire had a deeper meaning and impetus, however, than superficial exhibitionism and a return to the old darkness of superstitious beliefs. The Hauhaus gained widespread support because they offered a panacea for the nationalism of tribes apprehensive about the land pressures of the *Pakeha*; moreover, to the *hapus* whose villages were grief-ridden from the losses of their young men in the Taranaki, Waikato and Tauranga, *utu* was temptingly offered. The King movement was losing its potency under the shocks of military defeat and this new religion carried a built-in hostility to the *Pakeha*.

A hard-working medium in Te Ua's outpourings was the Angel Gabriel and in April, 1864, Te Ua, translating Gabriel's latest instruction to him, launched his religion on its inglorious political and military path. On 6 April, Captain T. W. J. Lloyd, 57th Regiment, took 53 soldiers of his own Regiment and 41 military settlers from the Kaitake redoubt to the Te Ahuahu district to destroy any native crops there to assert the principle of local *Pakeha* land ownership. Lloyd was reckoned to be an excellent officer, having been Adjutant of the 57th for many years, but he was a newcomer to active service in New Zealand and at the foot of the Te Ahuahu hill, while Lieutenant Clarke and twenty men of the 57th were absent destroying a nearby maize crop, he made a fatal mistake: he piled arms and failed to post sentries.

131

Te Ahuahu was the site of an old *pa* and in a trench system along the hillside heavily masked by dense fern lurked Hauhaus, crouching with their firearms and long-handled tomahawks. As the soldiers rested, out of the fern burst the Maoris, crying: 'Pai-Marire, hau, hau hau!' Lloyd shot down three with his revolver before he himself fell and in the mêlée seven soldiers and Volunteers were killed and twelve wounded before the British were able to hack their way out. The eight bodies were horribly mutilated by the Hauhaus and decapitated for the heads to be smoke-dried and shrunk. Thereafter, Lloyd's head was paraded from village to village to adorn the *niu* pole and celebrate the victory.

'The white soldier's head (it is known now that it was Captain Lloyd's) was passed round from hand to hand in the Pai-Marire ceremonies at the foot of the *niu*. It is described as that of a fair-whiskered man with a shaven chin on the fashion of those days. The head had been thoroughly dried in the *mokomokai* or *pakipaki-upoko* process. Its bearer, the prophet Matene, was a tall man with long hair and a flowing black beard. He led the people in their newly learned chantings, and round and round the sacred mast the half-crazed devotees marched. In their procession they came closer and closer to the *niu*, until many of them embraced it, one after another, and revolved about it, whirling round and round until they sank at its foot in a fit of giddiness and religious mania. The white man's head was passed from hand to hand among the frenzied worshippers, and there were some extraordinary scenes of fanatic fury. Some of the people, particularly those who had lost relatives in the Taranaki War, gnawed the dried flesh in their demonstrations of hatred and revenge. One, a handsome young woman, who had been brought up in Mr Booth's family and who was regarded as a quiet, gentle girl, was so overcome by the new madness that she snatched the *pakeha*'s head from her neighbour at the *niu* and bit the flesh of the neck with horrible savagery. The people, indeed, were transformed by Matene's teachings; the appeal to the feelings of revenge swept them along irresistibly, and made them easy instruments in the prophet's unauthorised plan of campaign.'[1]

A defence of Te Ua is that he was a simple, if disorientated, religious maniac of messianic leanings who unfortunately chose

[1] Cowan.

malevolent and ruthless prophets or archpriests to propagate his message: Hepanaia Kapewhiti, Matene te Rangi-tauira, Patara Raukatauri, Kereopa te Rau and Horomona; all these, except Patara, a chief of the Oakura and Kaitake area who was reasonably moderate, were to meet violent and bloody ends, either by the bullet or the rope. But the parading of the *Pakeha* heads was a recruiting campaign for the Pai-Marire religion which, having embraced all the Maoris in North Island, would then drive the *Pakeha* into the sea. Te Ua cannot be dismissed as a mere religious dreamer whose political naivety was seized on by desperate King-ites, such as Tawhiao and Rewi, or the dispossessed landless such as Wiremu Kingi.

Certainly, one of the more reassuring tenets that Te Ua preached to his simple co-religionists had a very direct military bearing: they would be invulnerable in battle if they held up their right hand level with the face, palm towards the enemy and intoned: 'Hapa! Hapa! Pai-Marire, Hau!' This solemn invocation was designed to cause the bullets of their enemies to pass over them. When the first casualty lists indicated that all was not quite well with this particular dogma, Te Ua explained that those who received bullets very directly were lacking in faith.

The new movement soon grew aggressive and threatening. The fall of Kaitake *pa* had quietened the south but the threat now re-appeared to the north of New Plymouth. Two hundred picked warriors converted to the Hauhau faith, mainly from the tribes of Taranaki, Ngatiawa and Ngatiruanui, with some Ngarauru from Waitotara and Wanganui men, under the prophet, Hepanaia Kapewhiti, assembled to attack the British redoubt on a round hill, called by the British, Sentry Hill and the Maoris, Te Morere, and garrisoned by forty soldiers of the 57th under Captain Shortt; one and a half miles away, at the old battlefield of Mahoetahi, was another blockhouse of the 57th commanded by Major Butler. Te Kahu-pukoro, a Ngatiruanui who was to die at a venerable age in 1920, recounts his experience at the attack on Sentry Hill as a strong, tall lad of twelve years in his first battle. His father and uncle were to die and he received two wounds.

'Now, had we followed the advice of our prophet, Hepanaia, we might have succeeded in our assault on the soldiers' fort. Hepanaia proposed that the *ope* should make a sudden attack on the rear of the fort, but Hare te Hokai, a chief of the Te Atiawa, insisted that the force should boldly attack the place in front, and this met with the support of most of the other chiefs. Another unfortunate thing was that, as we were marching from Manutahi, one of our men discharged his gun in order to give warning to any Atiawa people who might chance to be in or near the redoubt, for some of the tribe were serving on the *pakeha* side. This gave the soldiers warning of our approach. It was about perhaps 8 o'clock in the morning when we attacked the redoubt. Hepanaia led us on. He was a fine man, with a great love for his country and his people. In appearance, he was tall and lean; he was stripped except for a short *piupiu* of flax about his waist, and was armed with a gun. We went into battle loudly chanting our Pai-Marire service. Fern, about waist-high, and bushes of *tu-tu* clothed the plain and the lower slopes of Morere Hill, and through this we marched after coming out of the forest. We passed near the spot where the railway station now stands, and then began the ascent of the gentle slope which led to the mound on which the soldiers' redoubt was built. It was a strong, high earthwork surrounded by a trench; within were the barracks of the soldiers. We did not stoop or crawl as we advanced on the redoubt; we marched on upright and as we neared the fort we chanted steadily our Pai-Marire hymn. The soldiers, who were all hidden behind their high parapet, did not open fire on us until we were within close range. Then the bullets came thickly among us, and close as the fingers in my hand. The soldiers had their rifles pointed through the loopholes in the parapet and between the spaces on top (between bags filled with sand and earth), and thus could deliver a terrible fire upon us with perfect safety to themselves. There were two tiers of rifles blazing at us. We continued our advance, shooting and shouting our war-cries.'[1]

The warning shot had allowed Shortt to rehearse his defensive tactics thoroughly and when the Hauhau host moved forward to attack, he kept his riflemen hidden behind the parapet until the Maoris were a mere fifty yards away. He then brought his men up to their firing positions and poured volley after volley into the packed ranks. Many Hauhaus who bravely and blindly pressed forward fell into the glacis about the redoubt but under such a

[1] Cowan.

lethal fire, most broke, dragging their wounded with them. When Butler arrived with reinforcements, 35 dead Hauhau lay before the redoubt, and Te Kahu-pukoro states about 50 were killed, with many wounded. As this crushing rebel loss happened on the day after the debacle of the Gate *Pa* on the east coast, its news must have been very heartening to Sir Duncan Cameron.

Wanganui was the next objective of the Hauhaus. At Pipiriki, sixty miles up the Wanganui River, Matene Rangi-tauira was brandishing the head of Captain Lloyd. An Upper Wanganui man himself, Matene found the people of this area very susceptible to Pai-Marire, as many of their men had been lost in the battle at Katikara the previous year, and he soon raised a war party to attack Wanganui settlement. However, lower down the river, the Ngatihau not only declined to join the Hauhaus in their grand design but also refused the passage of their war canoes. The Ngatihau, joined by the Ngatipamoana and other Lower Wanganui *hapus*, told Matene that if he attempted to force his way down the river, they would fight the Hauhaus on the river island of Moutoa, 'the isle of heroes', a historic battleground of the river tribes.

Early on the morning of 14 May, about 120 hand-picked Hauhau warriors pushed off from the right bank of the river in great war canoes, to the shrill excitement of their watching women and children. Crouched half-way along the elongated island in the *manuka* and fern, waiting for the Hauhaus to land on the shingle and boulders of the upper part, were a hundred loyalist warriors under Tamehana te Aewa, while another fifty under Haimona Hiroti, a Ngatipamoana, waited in the lower end of the island. As the Hauhaus streamed in from the beach shouting their incantations, the island became wreathed in gunpowder smoke as Tamehana's men opened fire. But their heavily-charged double-barrel guns were overcharged and the opening volley went high. On came the Hauhau warriors shouting and roaring, and urged on by the shrieks of their many adherents on the far bank. The few casualties caused to the enemy panicked some of the Lower Wanganui men, remembering the so-called immunity of the Hauhaus, and they began to break under pressure, sustaining casualties as the Hauhaus fought their way forward. The courageous Tamehana, who had killed five enemy with gun, spear and tomahawk before a bullet shattered his kneecap, somehow rallied his men to hold, and then Haimona Hiroti came dashing into the fight with his reserve. The shock of this charge, and the ensuing fight with gunbutt and tomahawk, now drove the Hauhaus back relentlessly to the beach until they broke and fled into the river.

Among those to die was the prophet, Matene. Wounded, he was swimming back to the right bank when he was seen.

'Haimona Hiroti, standing on the gravel beach of Moutoa, gave his whalebone club to one of his men, Te Moro (afterwards a policeman in Wanganui), and, pointing to the shaggy black head of the struggling prophet, said, "Yonder is your fish." Te Moro dashed into the rapid river and overtook Matene just as the prophet reached the Tawhitinui side of the river and grasped an overhanging shrub in an effort to drag himself out of the water. The *kupapa* warrior, seizing him by his long hair, killed him with a smashing blow of his patu on the side of the head. Te Moro returned to the island, hauling the dead priest of Pai-Marire by his hair, and, dragging the body ashore where Haimona stood watching, said to his chief, "Ina to ika!" (Here is your fish).'[1]

The Hauhaus lost about 50 killed as well as many wounded, and the Lower Wanganui 15 killed, including three chiefs, and 30 wounded; the doughty Tamehana had his leg amputated. One European lost his life, Lay Brother Euloge of the nearby Catholic mission who was shot commanding a party of Maoris on the left bank of the river opposite the upper part of Moutoa, the island. Moutoa was not only both a drastic local setback to the Hauhaus who retreated disconsolately upriver, but Hiroti and Tamehana and their warriors prevented a general conflagration of the Wanganui *hapus* and the sixteen fallen fully deserved the monument erected in their memory by the grateful citizens of Wanganui Town.

As the winter rained and blew its course over the troubled North Island, the British began to entertain hopes of a final peace. Rewi had been defeated in the Waikato, the east coast restored by the victory at Te Ranga and the new Hauhau terror had been checked at Sentry Hill and Moutoa. Intense political

[1] Cowan.

activity, not without controversy, now ensued to reap the rewards of victory and to the Colonial Ministers, this clearly meant the confiscation of Maori lands as punishment for insurrection.

Sir George Grey was against this severe penalty and opposed his Ministers in long arguments. Perhaps he remembered old Kawiti's words long ago in 1845: 'Man is perishable, but the land is enduring.' Apart from any moral reservations, he knew the Maori's attachment to his land and was apprehensive of the long-standing feuds that stemmed from land disputes. In a despatch dated 26 April, 1864, the Colonial Secretary, Edward Cardwell, fully agreed from Whitehall with the Governor's misgivings and said so succinctly:

'To confiscate for European use the most valuable land, and drive the original owners to forest and morass, would convert the Maori into desperate banditti.'

Yet the New Zealand Ministers, in their own light, were acting from a firm moral base: it was a war custom of the Maori himself, if successful in battle, to seize land from his defeated enemy, and if vanquished himself, to expect to lose land. The colonial Ministers of the time, drawn from the merchant and professional class of a smalltown colonial society, are often accused of being petty men of limited vision and a certain commercial outlook, and perhaps some were, but they were all patriots imbued with the vision of nationhood for their young country. Their determination to open up the interior to European development tended to distort their view and from being somewhat frightened men when the full tide of native rebellion lapped about most of North Island, they were now feeling vengeful and adamant on settling the rebel question thoroughly. As politicians, they were also acutely conscious of feeling in the European communities, especially those who had been exposed to the terror of native attack and had suffered injury and loss of property. This public pressure ensured that they were not too sensitive to the finer moral issue of the native problem.

To compound the political issue were the attitudes of both the Imperial Government and the British Army serving in New Zealand. The viewpoint of the Colonial and War Offices can be shortly summed up: an anxiety to be rid of a commitment that demanded 10,000 troops and a sizeable naval presence, aggravated by a growing mistrust of local motives that seemed to wish to prolong the war. This may appear to be a dilettantish view from a Whitehall oblivious to local conditions, but in New Zealand itself a certain disenchantment had set in between 'the Military' and the colonists. The Army suspected that the real *raison d'être* for its presence was to grab Maori land while the side-issue of Army contracts for cattle, sheep and other provisions, billeting, road haulage and sea transport was a lucrative asset to the creaky colonial economy. This critical view was confined to the senior ranks, but certainly at regimental level respect and even cameraderie had grown up for the Maori warrior, and admiration for leaders like Te Oriori, Rewi and Rawiri Puhirake. A strong sympathy arose for these proud fighting men who 'fought straight', and whom they pressed back, through superior organisation and equipment, deeper and deeper into the forest. The British soldier was perfectly content when protecting the families and property of isolated settlers, but the political machinations and profiteering in the towns, where plans were laid for the Maori land he had overrun, left him cynical and unenthusiastic.

That dour, unyielding Scot, Lieutenant-General Sir Duncan Cameron, was naturally the spokesman for Army feelings and he was becoming somewhat terse in his views on confiscation. Relations between the Ministers on the one hand and the Governor and the General on the other were also exacerbated by the treatment meted out to the prisoners from Rangiriri, including Te Oriori, who languished in a prison hulk in Auckland harbour for many months. After repeated intercession by the Governor, spurred on by the Army, the prisoners were belatedly transferred, in August, 1864, to the isle of Kawau, Grey's own property in the Hauraki Gulf. However, this act of clemency rebounded on Grey as one month later, the whole 200 made a mass escape to the mainland and a furious Press outcry arose. The Ngapuhi gave food and shelter to the fugitives, who promised to disperse quietly if no troops were sent against them and this was sensibly, if grudgingly, agreed by the Government.

138

The next phase of the war suggests that if the colonial Government had not had the Hauhaus as a readymade casus belli, it would have had to invent them or some similar threat. For the next military task given to the Lieutenant-General Commanding was to open up the territory between New Plymouth and Wanganui. Admittedly, the tribes of the south-west had always been dangerous, as the unpleasant record of ambush and settler murders indicates, but the deeper intent was to wrest control of the land along this attractive littoral.

The end of the Waikato campaign that winter had caused a certain military re-deployment, and the coming pacification of Wanganui and Taranaki accelerated the movement. The 40th Regiment remained in the Waikato, with the 12th also stationed at Ngaruawahia, Te Awamutu, Rangiriri and the Queen's Redoubt until December when the Regiment marched to Auckland to embark in HMS *Esk* for Napier. An early departure from the Waikato was the 70th, who moved in May to Taranaki, and also in December, the 50th, after being encamped in the Maungatautari ranges until August, embarked from Onehunga for Wanganui.

Beyond the Waikato, other Regiments were also soon to be on the move. In August, the 43rd left Tauranga for Auckland and that November, four companies under Lieutenant-Colonel Synge sailed for New Plymouth and Taranaki. Even the 68th had to interrupt its cricket at Tauranga to despatch four companies as reinforcements for the west coast in January, 1865. The 14th Regiment, like the 70th, had been taken out of the Waikato in May for the various stations of Napier, Wellington, Waikato Heads and Mokau Heads, but was back in Auckland by November, except the two companies at Wellington who rejoined in February, and in March, 1865, sailed under Lieutenant-Colonel Trevor in HMS *Brisk* to Wanganui. The 18th, after three months in the Auckland Garrison as a pleasant change from their upcountry detachments, embarked seven companies under Major Rocke in January in HMS *Falcon* and *Eclipse* for Wanganui.

By the end of 1864, the long-service guardians of the Taranaki, the 57th Regiment, also left for Wanganui under Lieutenant-

Colonel Logan, though Colonel Warre remained in New Plymouth as the senior military officer. After three years of setpiece actions, ambushes and emergency turn-outs, the 57th were sorry to go and were especially appreciative of the support and co-operation they had had from the local Volunteers and militia and the civilian community—Captain Frank Mace's Volunteer horsemen who efficiently performed escort and courier duties and who had excelled themselves in their recovery of the wounded at Poutoko, also the companies of Bush Rangers and even the drivers of the impressed bullock carts, who under escort, cheerfully supplied the outposts, exposed to ambush many times.

Considerable changes were also occurring in the political scene. In October, Sir George Grey requested Frederick Weld, the Member for Wairau and Minister of Native Affairs, to form a Ministry and a major re-casting of war policy was introduced. Weld, who had accompanied Governor Gore Browne to Te Arei *pa* to deliver terms to the Ngatiawa, accepted on condition that his 'self-reliant' policy was followed:

'I should propose to ask the Home Government to take away all the soldiers, and reduce our forces to about two thousand men, whom I should arm with the best rifles procurable: these I would have trained to bush-work, and employ a part of them on the roads when not required to fight. With regard to the natives, I should not disarm them—it would be equivalent to a war of extermination to insist upon doing so. Their pride would be hurt as well as their fears aroused, and we should only succeed with the loyal tribes, who would thus be at the mercy of their enemies. I should pardon all offenders except those convicted of murder, and I should confiscate only enough land to show that they lost by going to war; and, in order to secure the peace of the country, I should start armed settlements where they are required. But I should leave even the most turbulent tribes more land than they could ever require, which would then be of treble its value. I should offer every inducement to the defeated tribes to settle down quietly, and enforce their submission by making roads through the most disturbed parts of the country—by force, if necessary. At the same time I should stop the lavish presents and bribing the natives to keep quiet. By the policy I have sketched out I believe the expense of the colony might be reduced by one-half.'

THE MENACE OF THE HAUHAUS

Frederick Weld's proposals had much good sense. He recognised that the war was moving into a guerrilla phase and saw the need to come to terms with bush warfare, and his Maori policy was intelligent and just. His sweeping decision to dispense with the ten Regiments of the Line had the powerful recommendation that it was completely in harmony with the mounting anxiety of the Imperial Government on the same theme, and Governor Grey agreed, though clearly with reluctance and considerable reservations. He realised that the Waikato campaign had broken the main effort of Maori intransigence but he distrusted the practicability of self-reliance at this stage of the Colony's evolution. He was probably also worried whether, in view of the rapidly spreading Hauhau cult, the Colony was really moving to a condition where peace between the two races was more than a flickering glimmer of hope. Certainly, the coming year, 1865, did little to reassure him.

CHAPTER 13

War comes to Wanganui

'At early dawn on a peculiarly brilliant morning in the beginning of the year 1865, the quiet settlement of Wanganui was startled from its slumbers by the booming of a gun, announcing the arrival of the first of seven regiments despatched to crush the Maori rebellion in that district. The township of Wanganui is situated half-way between Wellington and Taranaki, and is surrounded by the finest agricultural land in New Zealand. It derives its name from the noble river which waters it, and is navigable for steamers up to Pipiriki, a native settlement sixty miles from its mouth. As the troops landed, all was bustle and commotion, and the quiet agricultural village suddenly became a centre of importance. I was soon on the wharf, and I shall never forget the martial bearing of Colonel Logan as he marched up the beach in command of the 57th Regiment—as fine a body of men as ever had the honour of serving their country.'

THOMAS GUDGEON set down this vivid impression in his *Reminiscences of the War in New Zealand*. Then a militiaman, about to become a veteran of much active service, Gudgeon was blessed with a dry sense of humour. He went on to write:

'I also had the honour to receive Her Majesty's commission as lieutenant and quartermaster, after having for months served as a full private, doing picket duty on alternate nights, subject to the orders of my son-in-law, who was captain and adjutant, and of my own son, who was a lieutenant. Such was then the fortune of war in New Zealand.'

On 20 January, 1865, Lieutenant-General Sir Duncan Cameron himself arrived at Wanganui, after calling in at New Plymouth to confer with Colonel Warre. Before he left Auckland, Cameron had written to Sir George Grey about his task of bringing war to Wanganui to open up the country along the fertile coast to New Plymouth and to enforce confiscation. Clearly the old soldier's heart was not in his work:

> 'he thought he should not be wrong in informing Earl de Grey that there is no prospect of early reduction of the force or the military expenditure; indeed he thought that they ought at once to apply for reinforcements.'

However, four days after the General's arrival the expeditionary force of 1,200 soldiers, mainly of the 18th, 50th and 57th Regiments, under Brigadier-General Waddy marched out from their encampments about Wanganui Town and Alexander's Farm towards the Kai-iwi River, leaving the headquarters and three companies of the 57th for the local defence of the township. The departure of the 57th's other companies, drawn up before the Rutland Hotel, was not without drama. A wild bullock escaped from a nearby stockyard and charged the mounted Major Chauncey at the rear of the column, uprooting horse and rider. When the maddened beast return for his second assault, fifty bayonets of the 57th summarily disposed of it.

The route of the advancing brigade led initially through pleasant settlers' farms, lush with cloverfields, then crossed the Kai-iwi where settler Captain James Hewitt had recently been murdered by Hauhaus, his heart torn out and his head stuck on the *niu* pole. Keeping close to the coastline, the column arrived after fifteen hot and dusty miles at Nukumaru lake, in the heart of the Waitotara block. This block, like Waitara and Tatarai-maka in Taranaki, was another emotive piece of land to both *Pakeha* and Maori; it had been sold to the Crown but was now contested by the Hauhau-ridden Ngatiruanui who manned a strong *pa* at nearby Weraroa. The clearance of the Waitotara block was one of the important side-issues of the expedition and the local Ngatiruanui anticipated this by summoning fighting men from Taranaki, Waikato and Ngatimaniapoto. Some 2,000 Hauhaus gathered on the Waitotara to bar Cameron's path.

As the afternoon was late, the order was given at Nukumaru

to pitch camp on a plain inland of the coastal foothills, with high *toe-toe* grass extending to the bush only half a mile away. While the tents were being off-loaded and erected, Major Witchell of the Military Train, which acted as cavalry, rode up to Cameron and drew the General's attention to the dangerous proximity of the bush.

'General Cameron replied, "Do you imagine, Major Witchell, that any body of natives would dare attack 2,000 of Her Majesty's troops?" '

Meanwhile, the picquets had gone out and the detachment detailed from the 18th Regiment was under the command of Captain Hugh Shaw. As the Irish soldiers advanced in skirmishing order towards the scrubline, they suddenly came under heavy fire. With some coolness, Shaw got his men back to a ditch he remembered having crossed and as they settled down into fire positions after a breathless rush back, he saw that one of his soldiers was lying badly wounded in the open ground. With volunteers Shaw dashed out to the wounded man and carried him back; despite the concerted fire brought to bear on them, no one was hit. Meanwhile, the sound of the firing brought the suspicious Witchell and his horsemen up, for after his abortive discussion with Cameron, he prudently ordered his troopers to remain saddled, and also Major Rocke and a company of the 18th came hotfoot to the scene. Their coming into action drove off the marauders to the haven of Wereroa *pa*. Shaw was later awarded the Victoria Cross, while his comrades in the sortie, Privates James Kearnes, George Clampitt and John Brandon, each received the Distinguished Conduct Medal.

Early next morning Captain Noblett, also 18th Regiment, led up a relieving force of 75 men of his own Regiment and 25 soldiers from the 50th. He posted the 18th detachment to watch Nukumaru village while away on their left the men of the 50th observed the dangerous covered approach offered by a deep watercourse with its banks overgrown by wild flax; another picquet of the 50th, not under his command, was sited on the other side of this re-entrant. During the hot forenoon nothing stirred in the undergrowth and straggling scrub to their front.

But at 2 pm that same drowsy scene, shimmering in the summer heat, erupted into violent activity as several hundreds of Hauhaus, led by the chief of the Ngatihine *hapu*, Patohe, rose out of the cover and went for the picquets, rapidly enveloping the 50th detachments about the re-entrant and engaging the 18th. The sheer weight and force of the attack threatened to sweep the picquets into disorder, with the general confusion and alarm cleverly heightened by the Hauhaus setting fire to the long, dry grass to mask their movements. The 18th and 50th detachments fought their way back desperately, with men dropping as casualties, as Noblett tried to stem the onrush with a coherent firing line, but its fury now carried it to the point of bursting through to the main camp.

As the picquet line wavered on the brink of being completely overwhelmed, succour came from Captain Daubeny's company of the 18th and the new volume of sustained fire checked the onslaught, though several daring warriors penetrated into the camp lines; Lieutenant Johnson, of the Staff, was shot dead by his tent. The whole camp had stood to arms as soon as the opening volleys of the attack were heard and now the disciplined reaction of the field force began to tell; shells from the two 6-pounder Armstrong guns crashed into the Hauhau attack and the Military Train charged in support of the infantry. After an exciting and confused action that lasted two hours and threatened the existence of the British camp, Patohe and his chiefs called off the attack and melted back into the bush to Weraroa, abandoning twenty-two dead and two wounded and carrying away about seventy dead and wounded.

This 'near-run thing' for the field force cost the 18th Regiment three killed and twelve wounded, one of whom died later, and the 50th, eleven killed and twenty wounded, including both officers of their outlying picquets, Lieutenant Wilson and Ensign Grant. However, the disturbing feature of the Nukumaru attack was the startling departure from the time-worn Maori tactics of defending a well-constructed *pa* where they could not only be pounded at will by artillery but, also, inevitably were cut off from water, food, ammunition and reinforcements. Though Hepanaia's attack on the Sentry Hill redoubt, instigated by Hauhau fanaticism and

K

arrogance, was ill-chosen, these new tactics of hitting out in the open at places and times carefully selected could have had a profound effect on the war. An intelligent guerrilla warfare, waged against the inviting targets of civilian communities about the coastlines of North Island, would have extended the Army so much that the insurgent Maoris could have at least negotiated a peace from a position of strength, if unable to win the war.

The full-blooded Hauhau aggression of 25 January chastened Cameron considerably. Aghast that Maoris had the audacity to attack British regulars in the open field, he nevertheless shifted his camp away from the *toetoe* reeds and *tutu* bushes towards the sea into the comparative security of the open vista of sandhills. The expeditionary force remained in the new camp until early February and the campaign deteriorated into two notable features: the extreme slowness of Cameron's advance and the rise of acrimonious correspondence between the General and the Governor. On 28 January, Cameron wrote to Grey to say that he now had made enquiries about the purchase of the Waitotara block and had reason to believe 'that it is a more iniquitous job than the Waitara block'. That month the controversial question of confiscation was very much in the air, as the Government issued a proclamation that the confiscated native lands in mid-Taranaki were now open for settlement, and this, with lands already taken by conquest in the Waikato and at Tauranga and, later, in the South Taranaki and Wanganui districts, amounted to 8,000,000 acres, though later reduced to 3,000,000. Sir Duncan Cameron and certain of his officers clearly felt they were being used as the tools for a systematic land plunder.

The fate of Weraroa pa, a few miles up the Waitotara river, was also the subject of much friction. Cameron refused to attack it, claiming in the letter to the Governor of 28 January that his force was insufficient both to take the *pa* and open up the road to New Plymouth; he would need to increase his present force from 1,100 to 2,000. The Governor replied that the Lower Wanganui Maoris, fresh from another triumph that February against the Upper Wanganui Hauhaus at Otoutahi, five miles below Pipiriki, under their leading fighting chief, Hone Hipango, were eager to undertake the reduction of Weraroa. Cameron wrote back to dismiss this friendly native zeal as 'all bounce'.

Yet another inflammatory issue between the two men was the proposed withdrawal of five Regiments from the Colony. Whitehall had left discretion on the crucial aspect of timing to Cameron and when he wrote to ask Grey his views, the Governor, not unnaturally resentful at being ignored by the Imperial Government, replied acidly that 'I should not think it right to interfere with the large discretion left to you'. It is significant that, during February, Cameron wrote to resign his command on the grounds of ill-health. Worn out by physical fatigue and mental anxiety, the general, now 56 years old, had probably lost confidence in himself as well as being disillusioned with the course of the war, with the one consequence that he was determined to husband the lives of his soldiers. The task of having to assault Weraroa *Pa*, defended by many frenzied Hauhaus, probably conjured up for him the ghosts of Rangiriri and the Gate *Pa*.

On the night of 4 February the next phase of Cameron's advance got ponderously under way. With the main body of the brigade, Brigadier-General Waddy crossed the Waitotara river over a floating bridge constructed by the Royal Engineer detachment, while Col Weare, 50th Regiment, remained at the Nukumaru camp with a smaller column, consisting mainly of four companies of the 70th who had just arrived by sea from Taranaki.

The usual redoubt for 150 men and two guns was built at the Waitotara and on 15 February Waddy marched on to the Patea River, leaving Major Rocke and four companies of the 18th to guard the precious bridge of casks while the rest of the battalion, now rejoined by Lieutenant-Colonel Chapman and the three companies from Auckland, moved with the main column. Weare then broke camp at Nukumaru and closed up to the Waitotara, while soon other reinforcements came marching along the track and over Rocke's bridge to join the forward troops on the Patea. On 20 February four companies of the 68th under Lieutenant-Colonel Morant had disembarked at Wanganui and five days later marched out bravely behind the Band of the 18th to

Alexander's Farm. The next day the 68th were encamped on the Waitotara and another twenty-four hours saw them in the General's advanced camp.

At the Patea River, Waddy took a week to construct a redoubt for 200 men, then crossed over to the other bank to dig entrenched lines and make a camp and stores depot to hold at least 600 men. In the deliberate leapfrog fashion of Cameron's movements, Weare's force came up to the Patea on 9 March and there he received orders to march up the right bank of the river the next day with 1,400 men of the 50th, 57th and 68th Regiments, fifty Volunteer cavalry and two guns. But torrential rain, followed by a gale, disrupted all preparations for the operation which eventually started on 13 March.

The column had moved only two miles over flat fernland when the mounted scouts came under fire from Hauhaus posted along a ridge on their right flank. The advanced guard, composed of the 57th under Major Henry Butler, came up in extended order, changed direction right and went for the ridgeline. The enemy, about 200 Ngatiruanui warriors, were driven from it after a gallant fight but walked, refusing disdainfully to run, as they retreated and in crossing a swamp in their rear many were shot down. The action degenerated into a massacre, for some 80 rebels were killed in this uneven fight where a brave, heavily outnumbered few, armed with ancient shotguns and tomahawks, faced well-equipped British soldiers.

> 'In the field hospital afterwards, General Cameron asked a badly-wounded warrior, "Why did you resist our advance? Could you not see that we were in overwhelming force?" The Maori replied, "What would you have us do? This is our village; these are our plantations. Men are not fit to live if they are not brave enough to defend their own homes." '[1]

The British pushed on to the village of Kakaramea where pigs and fowls were seized for the cooking pots, and spent the night there. This severe Hauhau defeat had caused only one soldier of the 57th killed and three wounded, and a soldier of the 68th and another of the Military Train wounded. The column marched on the next day, leaving a detachment to construct a

[1] Cowan.

148

redoubt, and without opposition took Manutahi with its large foodstocks, including a vast store of potatoes, three miles from Manawapou on the mouth of the Ingahape river. At Mana-wapou, whose sandy shoreline seemed to offer possibilities to land stores over the surf, a redoubt was set up and the advance then thrust along the coast to the mouth of the Wai-ngongoro, which had similar open port opportunities. Here, on 31 March, the construction of a large camp was started, with redoubts on both sides of the river mouth, and to ease the exhausting supply line struggling over very difficult country in early April a small steamer landed stores over the beach at both the Wai-ngongoro and Manawapou. Surf boats operated as this supply system became routine, but capsizings were frequent, with several tragic drownings.

Manawapou is notable in that it was here that the notorious Kimble Bent, a half-breed American Indian, deserted from the 57th after a flogging for insubordination and joined the Hauhaus. In a similar but unsought incident, another private of the 57th, Hennessy, was taken as a slave of the Hauhaus when he was captured foraging for potatoes near Manawapou. He escaped after a year and at his subsequent court-martial was acquitted and awarded the back pay for the period of his captivity.

With the approach of winter, Cameron suspended his desultory operations and withdrew most of his force to Patea, mainly Colonel Weare and the 50th; one company of the 50th remained upcountry at Manawapou with a company of the 57th, while another two 57th companies garrisoned the redoubts at the mouth of the Wai-ngongoro. In May the four companies of the 70th left to return to the Taranaki and the four companies of the 68th marched back to Wanganui to a routine of several dull months of uneventful patrolling. However, on 2 June, Colonel Weare took a column of his 50th along the coast from Patea to effect a juncture with Colonel Warre's troops from Taranaki who had reached Opunake, twenty-four miles from Patea. Contact was made without incident and Weare returned to Patea on 13 June.

At the end of April Sir Duncan Cameron left the field and sailed back to Auckland where he set caustic pen to paper,

149

writing to the War Office to say how much he disagreed with the motives of the present campaign. His relations with Grey had now deteriorated to the point of acrimony. The Governor, not only angered by Cameron criticising the political direction of the war direct to Whitehall, was exasperated by the dilatory progress of operations, particularly that Weraroa *pa*, that symbol of Hauhau power poised on the Waitotara to strike at the coastal communications, was still intact. Even the local Maoris were now calling Cameron 'the Lame Seagull'.

While Cameron wrote his despatches in Auckland, Grey demonstrated his genius as a colonial Governor: he returned to his old military calling and took the field himself against Weraroa *pa*. By the middle of July he had assembled a force of 470 men: two companies of Forest Rangers, including von Tempsky's, the Wanganui Yeomanry Cavalry composed of settlers and their sons, and about 200 Lower Wanganui Maoris under Capt Thomas McDonnell, a veteran of the Waikato campaign and an excellent Maori linguist. When peace overtures to the Hauhaus failed, he took offensive action. He persuaded a diffident Brigadier-General Waddy at nearby Nukumaru camp, unsure whether he was being seduced from his General's orders, to position a company of the 14th and another of the 18th ostentatiously in front of the *pa*, siting posts and acting as a show of force, with another 400 troops not far away in support. Then on the morning of 20 July the Volunteer force under Major Rookes, an ex-Imperial officer with West African service, set off in heavy rain on a long and arduous march through the bush to the rear of Weraroa and by nightfall were in position overlooking the adjacent Hauhau village of Arei-ahi. At dawn the village was silently surrounded and surprised, with sixty Hauhau prisoners taken, including twenty luckless Ngatipukeho who had just arrived from the Bay of Plenty. The column then ascended a track from the village up to the high ground overlooking the *pa*, and when a long-range plunging fire was opened into it the ferocious defenders of this impressive Hauhau stronghold, that Duncan Cameron required 2,000 troops to attack, panicked and fled without firing a shot, swarming down the steep cliff face that ringed most of the *pa*'s perimeter.

This considerable tactical coup by Sir George Grey, due entirely to his audacious spirit and brilliant reading of the ground, appears to have cost the elated Volunteers no casualties at all, but it inflicted a deep wound on the General Officer Commanding. He immediately penned another bitter despatch to the War Office, complaining of the Governor's presumptuous military initiative. When the Duke of Cambridge received this latest missive, the Royal Commander-in-Chief expressed surprise at the Governor's behaviour and a mild shock wave disturbed the stately corridors of the Colonial and War Offices. The terse official ruling came back that while the Vice-regal representative was the local Commander-in-Chief and, in this case, had also held an Army commission, he was not entitled to direct military operations in person.

Meanwhile, after their splendid success at Weraroa, the Wanganui Volunteers went on to fresh glory. In late April, Pipiriki, on the upper reaches of the Wanganui River, had been occupied by 8 and 9 companies, Taranaki Military Settlers, a company of the Patea Rangers and sixty Lower Wanganui Maoris under the excellent Kepa Te Rangihiwinui, commanded by Major Willoughby Brassey, another ex-Regular who had served in the Afghan War. Later, the Wanganui Native Contingent was withdrawn for the Weraroa operation, leaving three redoubts on the west bank of the river manned by about 200 Volunteers. This garrison at Pipiriki was too much of a challenge to the Hauhaus who began assembling in force from the Upper Wanganui *hapus* and from the Ngatimaniapoto, Ngatiraukawa and Ngatitu-wharetoa, about 600 strong under the paramount chief of the Upper Wanganui, Topia Turoa. The Hauhaus built two large *pas*, one on the east bank and another two miles upriver on the west bank, each with a dominating *Pai-Marire* pole of worship 60 to 70 feet high, complete with yard and halliards from which the Hauhau war flags of black, red and white flew.

On the morning of 19 July the Hauhaus closed in about the British redoubts and when their initial assaults failed, a rather desultory siege developed. Possibly Topia Turoa, a *rangatira* of great prestige, was a lukewarm adherent of the new cult; also, he had been personally captured, and later released, in a defeat

151

inflicted by Lower Wanganui warriors under the brave Hone Wiremu Hipango, who was mortally wounded and buried with military honours at Otoutahi five months earlier; in any case, he certainly did not press the siege with much enthusiasm or vigour. Nevertheless, the surrounding woods were well served with Hauhau snipers and water replenishment from the river was hazardous. As the days wore on, foodstocks ran down to quarter-rations of biscuit and saltmeat but Brassey's main worry was his dwindling ammunition. He resorted to writing messages in Latin and French, sealing these in bottles with a feather in the cork to attract attention and throwing the bottles in the river to drift the long journey to Wanganui Town. Two of these messages survived the rapids and were picked up, one by a friendly Maori the other by Mr G. F. Allen, and handed in to Militia head-quarters in the township where, in those robust days of Empire, a classical scholar was found to translate the two appeals: 'Omnes sunt recti. Mitte res belli statim' and 'Sumus sine rebus belli satis'.

Finally, Brassey sent off two volunteers, Sergeant Constable and Private A. Edgecombe of the Patea Rangers, in a canoe during the night of 30 July. They slipped through the enemy cordon and soon met an imposing flotilla of war canoes paddled by the Lower Wanganui Maoris and bearing a relief force. Many, like Major Rookes, the commander, Kepa and Thomas McDonnell were fresh from the superbly-executed operation at Weraroa.

Meanwhile, the Pipiriki garrison had spent another anxious night, wondering if the Hauhau host would co-ordinate for a major attack. A false peace hope had been raised when the Hauhaus hoisted a white flag and Lieutenant Newland performed an extremely brave deed by journeying to the main Hauhau *pa* to negotiate, but the Hauhau hard core prevailed over the moderation of the older leaders. At least, however, the intrepid young Newland returned safely, which says much for the old Maori chivalry personified by Topia Turoa.

The feelings of the beleaguered Volunteers can be imagined when this memorable scene of old New Zealand was enacted before their eyes as they manned their parapets and trenches:

'Next morning the canoes of the relief expedition were sighted poling up the bend below Pipiriki, and the river gorge rang with the canoe choruses of the toiling crews. The force that raised the siege was composed of a company of Forest Rangers under Major F. Nelson George, a company of the Wanganui Rangers under Captain Jones, and Kepa's Native Contingent, in all 300 strong, together with several hundreds of the Lower Wanganui friendly tribes.'

Thomas Gudgeon, who was in the relief force, recounts the scene on the river that morning after a bitterly cold night. The force had come up the river in the steamer *Gundagai* as far as Raorakia and then transferred to canoes to get through the rapids.

'As the sun was rising, the warlike canoe song of the Wanganui could be heard, and in a few moments the river was alive with canoes, each one trying to outstrip the other in the race for Pipiriki. Our men had a good start, and expected to win easily, but just before we reached the landing place, Haimona with fifty men of the Ngatipamoana in a big war canoe passed us as if we had been standing still. The first thing that met our eyes on landing was the dead body of a Taupo chief, Mikaera; he was lying in a small stream and must have been shot during the first days of the fight, for the rats had been hard at work.'

After raising the siege, Rookes moved up the banks of the river but the Hauhaus had dispersed before his show of force. Six enemy bodies were found and buried, but their fatal casualties were probably about thirteen, while the Volunteers only had two wounded; the *pas*, with the malevolent *niu* poles, were destroyed. That August the Military Settlers were relieved entirely at Pipiriki by two companies of the 57th Regiment under Brevet-Major Shortt, and moved to the East Coast.

In nearby Taranaki also, the middle of 1865 saw a resurgence of Hauhau violence. On 12 June Colonel Warre took a column of the 43rd, 70th and Taranaki Bush Rangers out from Opunake over sixteen miles of very wet and swampy going to chasten the troublesome *hapus* of the Taranaki in the Warea district and he destroyed four villages. However, on 28 July, a strong patrol of the 43rd from Warea Redoubt ran into an ambush and its commander, Captain Close, and Private John Hallohan were both mortally wounded before the enemy were cleared at the point of the bayonet.

This tragic incident drew yet another punitive expedition which marched out the next day from New Plymouth, 220 strong under Brevet Lieutenant-Colonel Colville of the 43rd. On 2 August his column fought a brisk action in the bush and scrub country between Warea and the Tataraimaka block near the Hauhau village of Okea. As he approached the village, Colville divided his force, with one wing composed of 70th soldiers under the overall command of Major Russell of the 57th, holding frontally while he took the other half on a flank march to the rear. Inevitably, the time calculated for the flanking approach march over the broken bush country was optimistic and in the meantime, Russell's force came into premature contact with the Hauhaus.

Near Okea Russell had occupied four hillocks that gave good all-round observation and sent on Captain Cay and sixty men of the 70th to reconnoitre. Cay soon came on some Hauhau rifle pits and *whares* which he promptly charged and in his surprise attack killed thirteen with the bayonet. He then fell back on Russell, but now the Taranaki warriors had rallied and began to close dangerously on the detachment. Russell withdrew in a direction that he hoped would rejoin Colville, but the serious harrying by the Maoris moving swiftly through the bush caused him to halt and make several stands to fight them off. Before he made contact with Colville, Russell lost Lieutenant Henry Bally and three soldiers of the 70th and one of the 43rd killed, and Lieutenant Charles Tylden, who had been one of the first to enter the Hauhau trenches at Okea at the head of his men, severely wounded, with five soldiers of the 70th. All the British casualties were caused by musket balls, so the fire discipline of the soldiers at least kept the numerous pursuing Hauhaus at a distance.

Finally, in October, again in turbulent Taranaki and at almost the last action the 43rd Regiment was to fight in New Zealand, Colville was severely wounded in a company-sized ambush he mounted in the Warea district, where the 43rd also lost a sergeant and a soldier, and another sergeant was dangerously wounded. In the same month Captain Mace, with three comrades of the

Taranaki Mounted Corps, rode into an ambush staged by seventy Hauhaus between the Warea and the Hangatahua. Though the opening volley missed, the Hauhaus came dashing out of the flax and the fern firing from the hip and one trooper, lying along the neck of his horse, became dazed from a bullet that cut through his scalp and rode about in circles, aimlessly firing his revolver. Frank Mace returned to the killing zone of the ambush, got hold of the horse's bridle and, though hit in the leg and with the bullets whipping about him, galloped the wounded man away; Mace's own horse was hit and later dropped.

But as the winter of 1865 developed into spring, the overall operational and political situation in North Island, despite the latest Taranaki outbursts, again gave rise to some optimism. On 28 May at Tauranga, Wiremu Tamihana, the king-maker of the Waikato, and other chiefs came to make submission to the Queen. Brigadier-General Carey came forward to meet Tamihana who dismounted from his horse, advanced towards Carey uncovered and grounded his *taiaha* and shook hands. Elsewhere on the East Coast the Hauhau poison was spreading, but on the West, whatever the criticisms of Cameron's snail-like progress the Wanganui littoral had been cleared with appreciable Hauhau casualties and two British Colonels, coming from different directions, had shaken hands on the New Plymouth-Wanganui track. Though the coastline was still only controlled within rifle shot of Imperial or colonial forces, this symbolic meeting was an important fillip to the morale of the adjacent European communities.

Consequently in September Sir George Grey took a calculated gamble: he issued a Proclamation declaring that the war was now officially at an end, that he considered that the warring tribes in being soundly defeated had suffered enough and that there would be no witch-hunt or prosecutions except for some notorious murders, and more important no more confiscations of land would ensue from the recent campaign. The vituperative William Fox labels this endeavour by the Governor 'a paper tiger', holding the Government up to ridicule in the eyes of the hard-line Hauhaus and King-ites, but it was a statesmanlike and worthwhile gesture. Unfortunately the canker of *Pai-Marire* and

155

the deep-ingrained suspicion of the white man now prevalent among the hostile tribes caused it to have a disappointing impact, as Fox predicted.

While Grey prepared his proclamation Lieutenant-General Sir Duncan Cameron departed from the shores of New Zealand. On 25 August he sailed for England to assume finally the honorific appointment for an elderly General Officer of Governor of the Royal Military College, Sandhurst. It is a pity that this gallant, if stereotyped, old Scottish officer left the Colony in such a low key and in an unhappy atmosphere of strained relations with the Governor and his Ministers. Within his limitations he had conducted a series of difficult campaigns over primitive and unmapped terrain where supply problems were always paramount as, unlike other native adversaries in Africa or Asia, his mobile and elusive enemy had no cattle. Whatever the sneers of his detractors, it was Duncan Cameron's Waikato campaign that shattered the hopes of co-ordinated Maori resistance to the onward march of *Pakeha* domination, as the ultimate submission of a discerning, intelligent leader as Wiremu Tamihana shows. It was his Regiments that gave some security and confidence to the scattered European communities living hazardously about the shallow settled periphery of North Island.

CHAPTER 14
Terror on the East Coast

WHEN the schooner *Eclipse* sailed into Opotiki harbour, Bay of Plenty, on 1 March, 1865, the feelings of two clergymen on board as they gazed at familiar landmarks can be imagined. The Rev Carl Volkner, a German Lutheran whose church was in the large Whakatohea village, had been warned not to return because of the local Hauhau menace, and his companion, the Rev Thomas Grace, came from a mission station inland at Lake Taupo that he had been forced to abandon.

Volkner and Grace could not have been borne into a more rabid Hauhau trap. After the deaths of Hepanaia and Matene in 1864 Te Ua despatched two other minor prophets, Patara Ruakatauri, a Taranaki Chief, and Kereopa Te Rau, an Arawa, to carry the message of *Pai-Marire* to the tribes of the East Coast and they were now in the Opotiki area. Patara had led the defence of Kaitake against the 57th Regiment and the Taranaki Volunteers in late '63 and despite his addiction to Te Ua's cult, was inherently a moderate man. Unfortunately for Volkner he was away from Opotiki when the *Eclipse* made her landfall and a hysterical mob had been whipped up by Kereopa.

This bloodthirsty savage, who had fought in the Waikato campaign, had seized on Hauhauism, apart from the dubious greatness it thrust on him, to revert to the darkest practices of Maori barbarism. He and Patara journeyed to the East Coast in early 1865 attended by another degraded deserter, Louis Baker, a stoker from HMS *Rosario*; extraordinarily, Baker, like Kimble

Bent, had American Indian blood in him; he was a French-Canadian half-breed. Baker's task was to bear the smoke-dried head of Captain Lloyd.

The grisly mission proceeded first to Taupo, where Patara stole the absent Grace's double-barrelled English shotgun, then to Te Whaiti to meet a concourse of the fierce Urewera mountain tribe. Lloyd's head was placed at the foot of the *niu* pole, attended by the wretched Baker, while scenes of frenzied hate were worked up in the Hauhau rituals that ensued. The blatant psychological attack of the emissaries of Te Ua, who had piously abjured them to non-violence, was hatred of the white man; 'the widows of Ohakau' was an emotive phrase that never lost its appeal.

Kereopa was clearly after the blood of a Christian missionary to sacrifice to the gods of *Pai-Marire*. At Whakatane he had demanded the Catholic priest of the district but as the priest was both absent and a Frenchman he moved on to Opotiki accompanied by many new devotees, including Mokomoko, a leading chief. At Opotiki the conversion of the Whakatohea tribe was completed and when the *Eclipse* sailed into the river the sinister *niu* pole, with Lloyd's head at its base, was waiting.

Both missionaries were immediately seized and the schooner looted; but as Captain Levy and his brother were Jews they were spared in the confused theology of *Pai-Marire* as co-religionists. After a night awaiting his fate, Volkner was marched into his own church under escort where Kereopa stood by the altar. He was sentenced to death by Kereopa, who promptly divested him of his coat and waistcoat and the final act of the tragedy was enacted by a large willow tree a hundred yards away, where a ship's block and tackle lay over a branch. Volkner knelt and prayed, rose and shook hands with erstwhile parishioners nearby and was then barbarously hauled up and down; possibly and mercifully he was also shot by Kereopa, unable to restrain his bloodlust. The body was then taken away towards the church and beheaded, with the crowd fighting to catch the blood pumping out. Kereopa filled the white metal communion cup with blood and took the head into the church where he mounted the pulpit with it. He then gouged out Volkner's eyes which he swallowed, not without a certain amount of difficulty as he needed a drink of water to get the second one down. He finally ended this obscene ceremony by passing the blood-filled chalice among his congregation.

Thomas Grace was saved by the return of Patara who was so infuriated at Kereopa's atrocity that he publicly castigated him before the Whakatohea, warning them that Kereopa, as an Arawa, was a hereditary enemy of their tribe and that he was wreaking his revenge by bringing down the wrath of the *Pakeha* on them. He saved Grace by offering to exchange him for Hori Tupaea, a Hauhau high chief of the Ngaiterangi, who had been captured by an Arawa war party when he tried to cross their country to join Te Ua's ambassadors. Hori Tupaea, a venerable chief who had rather naïvely swallowed the new cult, ended up in Tauranga Gaol, but in the ensuing days of negotiation Grace escaped. A more powerful *Eclipse*, the man-o'-war commanded by Captain E. Fremantle, hove in sight, sent to investigate reports of Volkner's murder, and Grace, by taking a long walk from his loose house arrest, joined one of two cutters Fremantle sent in.

On board HMS *Eclipse* was James Fulloon, a half-Maori surveyor and the well-connected son of an East Coast chieftainess who was now working for the Government as an interpreter and native agent. When the warship worked down the coast, landing armed parties at Hicks Bay and other points to intercept Kereopa and Patara who had rapidly left Opotiki on the appearance of *Eclipse*, he transferred to the trading lugger *Kate* to proceed to Whakatane to make enquiries there. While the lugger lay overnight at the harbour bar for high water twenty Hauhaus urged by the other Taranaki archpriest, Horomona, stole on board and murdered Fulloon and two Europeans.

Meanwhile, Volkner's smoke-dried head, borne on a tray by Baker, accompanied Kereopa as he moved inland with his adherents to Tauroa, on the Rangitaiki river, to convert the Urewera and Ngatiwhare. Government reprisals for the murders of Volkner and Fulloon were slow in coming, even allowing for the fact that much of the Army was engaged in the Wanganui campaign and pinned down by restive Taranaki. A muddled military direction was now arising from initial enforcement of the Self-Reliant Policy. For months the fight against the triumphant progress of the Hauhau prophets was left to Maoris antagonistic to *Pai-Marire*, and when Government forces did take the field they were entirely Volunteer.

Immediately after Opotiki both Kereopa and Patara moved east from their successful mission in the Bay of Plenty to the tribes of the *Tai-Rawhiti*, the Coast of the Rising Sun. Patara preached to the Ngatiporou from Hicks Bay to the Waiapu river while Kereopa went to the Turanganui plain, well settled with Rongowhakaata farms and orchards and soon so contaminated this district, prosperous with a flourishing schooner trade to Auckland, that Bishop Williams had to flee from his mission station at Waerenga.

The growing subversion of the Ngatiporou, however, was to be sharply checked, mainly by the energy and military genius of a minor chief who rose to great status in the coming battles, Ropata Wahawaha. He was among his people at the opening of a new church at Popoti, near the base of Hikurangi mountain, when he heard that a large number of Hauhaus had arrived at Pukemaire, in the lower Waiapu valley. A war party of forty fighting men, armed with one rifle, seven muskets and their native weapons, set off; though they lost six men in the battle, Ropata's reputation, which was to make him the hammer of the Hauhaus on the East Coast, was initially made at this fight.

In May, when Kereopa and Horomona sought to leave the East Coast backed by many Urewera followers to carry their religion to the Waikato, another band of forty warriors from the small Ngatimanawa tribe barred their way across the Tapiri track. In a hastily-erected redoubt this epic band, which included a chief who had been wounded at Orakau fighting the *Pakeha*, held out for five weeks, losing five killed. As they withdrew, pursued by the Urewera, Major William Mair, now a native Resident Magistrate, appeared with a relieving force of Arawas. Kereopa and Horomona melted away but the bodies of three Ngatimanawa dead found among the fern had been decapitated. Kereopa again had swallowed eyes while bloodstained revelry went on about the *niu* pole where the Manawa heads joined Lloyd's; Volkner's head had been left at Tauroa.

In the Hawke's Bay district the loyal chiefs appealed to Donald

McLean at Napier for arms and ammunition, which he sent. Also, on 5 July, a company of Military Settlers and some Hawke's Bay Volunteers, about 100 men under Major James Fraser, late 73rd Highlanders, landed from HMS *Eclipse* at the mouth of the Waiapu to reinforce the *pa* of the Ngatiporou chief, Mokena Kohere, who was being hard-pressed by local Hauhaus, and *Eclipse* had the satisfaction of bombarding enemy positions beyond the *pa* with 110 lb shells. Fraser and Biggs promptly took their men out skirmishing and for several days desultory bush fighting occurred, with Ropata winning a salutary minor victory at Te Horo when he feigned retreat and killed several Hauhaus in his ambush. On 2 August Fraser took his force, guided by Ngatiporou, in two columns up the Waiapu valley to attack the Hauhau at Pa-kairomiromi at first light. Though the main assault received a heavy but wild volley from enemy who had been sleeping in the fire trenches, Fraser gained the gateway with many of his men while Biggs and Lieutenant Gascoygne swarmed over the palisade with their detachments from other directions. Brisk hand-to-hand fighting developed before the Hauhaus broke and fled into the bush, leaving 25 killed and 30 prisoners. Eight of the European volunteers were wounded.

In August another gallant defence was made at Te Mawhai headland *pa* by five loyal Ngatiporou, three old European whalers and the women when local Hauhaus, smarting from their rough handling by Fraser, Biggs and Ropata, sought an easy victory when the chief, Henare Potae, and almost all his fighting men were away. With old muzzle-loaders and hurling stones the defenders beat off the attack and Potae returned to find thirteen enemy bodies lying among the rocks, with only two wounded within the *pa*, including the whaler John Henderson who died later in Auckland hospital. Ropata then came along with his warriors to join Potae and the two chiefs forced the abandonment of two nearby Hauhau *pas*, Tautini and Pukepapa, with Ropata dealing out grim justice to eleven Hauhau prisoners from his own *hapu*, the Aowera.

'Calling them out, he briefly told them that they were about to die, and said, "I do not kill you because you have fought against me, but because I told you not to join the Hauhaus, and

L   161 you have disobeyed me. So saying, he shot them one by one with his revolver."[1]

Ropata and Potae scoured the bush between Tokomaru and Tolaga bays that month with many close and fleeting encounters before returning to the Waiapu valley where three miles inland stood the Pukemaire hill with two Hauhau *pas* connected by a covered trench. Here Fraser, reinforced by fifty Forest Rangers under Captain Westrup landed from HMS *Brisk*, assembled a force of 380 and on 3 October marched on Pukemaire. But though he breached the outer palisade with a sap and nine Hauhaus were killed, the bitter cold and pouring rain induced him to call off the attack after two of his men had died, one shot, the other from sickness. He resumed the operation on the 8th, with Westrup getting round the rear while the main assault went in frontally, but on entry the *pa* was found deserted. In appalling weather a pursuit was mounted through rugged country towards the Kawakawa river where after twenty miles the fugitives were cornered *en masse* in a hill *pa* at Hungahungatoroa ('Down of the Albatross'). Though the *pa* was encased by steep cliffs, Biggs and Ropata scaled a dominating height nearby with twenty European and Maori marksmen and shot into the *pa* with deadly effect, killing twenty and wounding many.

Under this heavy, morale-breaking sniping the *pa* surrendered and on Mokena Kohere's specific request to Ropata the Ngatiporou *hapus* were this time called out to be spared. The stranger Hauhaus waiting in the *pa*, Whakatohea, Ngatiawa, Whanui-a-Apanui, Aitanga-a-Mahaki and Taranaki, realised only too clearly what their fate was and a concerted blind rush over the palisades, down the cliffs and into the bush got many of them away. Fraser and Biggs were as ruthless as Ropata in this savage bush warfare and Biggs shot in cold blood Pita Tamaturi, a Hauhau chief of the Aitanga-a-Mahaki, caught by Ropata. Hungahungatoroa was a major Government victory, not only because 500 prisoners and 300 weapons were taken but because it broke the Hauhau grip on the Ngatiporou who became invaluable allies.

Meanwhile, in the Bay of Plenty, William Mair and his

[1] Cowan.

162

Arawas had also been active in August, hunting down many of the accessories to the murders of Volkner and Fulloon through the swamps and lagoons of the lower Rangitaiki about Matata settlement. He had cleared the coastal area of Hauhau marauders when, in October, at his base at Matata, he heard that a concentration had entrenched themselves twenty-five miles up the Rangitaiki at Te Teko. Mair collected a strong force of 450 Arawas and moved up the river by canoe and foot to invest the *pa*, held by 170 Hauhau fighting men. He decided that it was too formidable to assault and proceeded to make a number of saps to it, allotting a sap to each of the Arawa *hapus* to dig competitively. As the converging saps reached the *pa* and all was ready for the attack, the Hauhaus surrendered, filing out dejectedly while the Arawas danced an exultant *haka* about them. Among the captured was Horomona, the instigator of Fulloon's murder. He was hanged in Auckland Gaol seven months later.

In August, also, Kereopa, complete with his Ngatimanawa heads, returned to the Opotiki area after his abortive attempt to reach the Waikato and it was now time for the so-called Opotiki Expeditionary Force, ponderously mounted from Wanganui, to land and seek retribution for the murder of Carl Volkner. The Force, some 500 men under Major Willoughby Brassey, the defender of Pipiriki, was composed of the two companies of Military Settlers withdrawn from Pipiriki, three companies of Bush Rangers, the Wanganui Native Contingent under Kepa and Thomas McDonnell and the dismounted Wanganui Yeoman Cavalry.

Its departure from Wanganui, the ensuing voyage and landing were hardly propitious. At Wanganui the Maori wives got on board the troop steamer carrying their husbands and refused to leave, placing the whole expedition in jeopardy as their men were also far from keen on the prospect of a long sea voyage, but McDonnell acted decisively to eject the ladies into their canoes and the little convoy of the *Ladybird*, *Stormbird* and *Ahuriri* sailed hurriedly before mass desertion set in. At Wellington the Contingent urged on by Meti Kingi, a difficult senior chief, demanded their arrears of pay of only a fortnight to have a spree and the Government quickly paid up. Finally, at Hicks

Bay on 7 September the convoy met HMS *Brisk* and the tender *Huntress* and the Patea Rangers, 8 and 10 Companies of the Taranaki Military Settlers transferred to the *Huntress*, with Captain Levy of the ill-fated schooner *Eclipse* at the wheel, both as pilot and interpreter, ready for landing at Opotiki at dawn. The troubles of the amateur amphibious force, however, were just beginning.

'The tender crossed the bar safely, but found a heavy freshet in the river, against which she was powerless; a rush was made against the freshet, which carried them some distance up the river, but only to be swept back and lodged on a sandpit in the middle of the stream, where they could not land, for the tender had no boats, and there was deep water on either side—as the tide receded the little steamer heeled over on her side, and in this perilous position, her decks crowded with men, she offered the Hauhaus as fair a target as they could wish; but, fortunately for the force, the beach offered no cover, and the enemy, not caring to expose themselves, fired at such long range that but little damage was done. Ensign Northcroft was hit on the buckle of his belt, and one of the men had a bullet pass through between his foot and the sole of his boot.'[1]

A Hauhau fanatic then advanced slowly over the sandflats to the edge of the river not fifty yards from the stranded *Huntress*, mouthing his incantations and waving his hands, but his mystic performance was cut short abruptly when no less than eighteen bullets fired almost simultaneously from the infuriated Rangers and Settlers knocked him flying.

The rain was now lashing down in torrents and eventually at low water the *Huntress*'s unhappy human cargo, drenched, cold and hungry, waded ashore to the river bank. Their ordeal was far from over, as the wind was rising rapidly to gale force, whipping the sand dunes into a scourging sandstorm, and *Brisk* had to desert them to run before the gale all night. Next day she came in briefly to float a keg of rum and cask of biscuits to the famished men ashore before retiring to the shelter of Whale Island. On the following day the storm had abated and *Brisk* anchored off Opotiki, lowering her boats crammed with the Native Contingent. Hauhaus came running down the sandhills

[1] Gudgeon.

to engage the landing but the Wanganui under Kepa and McDonnell who had his cartridge box shot away, drove them inland for several miles, killing six. The force crossed the river and cleared through the large prosperous village, taking possession of Volkner's church where many of the Europeans slept, thankful to get refuge from the bitter weather. Next day camp stores and baggage were landed and the Rangers and Settlers set about fortifying a camp around the church, while the Wanganui foraged happily about the locality for pigs, poultry and horses.

On 14 October the Native Contingent, supported by Captain George's Rangers, followed up an enemy sortie from the Hauhaus' *pa* at Te Pua with an attack on the *pa*, but the co-ordination went badly and the operation was called off, with little achieved and Captain Percy of the Cavalry badly wounded in the hip. Some inaction now set in, with the Expeditionary Force doing little more than scout and forage and it seems some friction was being generated among the officers by Brassey's command, with McDonnell particularly chafing under the lack of initiative.

However, it was McDonnell's aggressive patrolling tactics that brought about a spirited action at the new Hauhau *pa* of Te Tarata in the lee of Te Pua only one mile distant. In pursuit of enemy scouts who had fired on his patrol, he quickly came upon Te Tarata and the resultant noise of firing reached Opotiki four miles away, bringing about an involuntary turn-out of the not-very-orthodox Volunteers. That veteran and hard-marching lot, the Patea Rangers, were first on the track but were soon overtaken by the Wanganui Yeoman Cavalry galloping by on their looted Maori horses. Te Tarata was surrounded on three sides, as the steep bank of the Waioeka River dropped away on the final side, and briskly and furiously engaged. An old 6-pounder gun from the *Huntress*, brought by the Military Settlers, even found its way to this field of action and was sited in position, loaded with chain shot and old iron.

As the day wore on the onlookers from Te Pua *pa* could bear their impotence no longer and a war party of forty warriors began to descend the hill to Te Tarata. One of the very few

165

cavalry charges of the Maori Wars made by the redoubtable Wanganui Yeomanry then dramatically ensued:

> 'The order was given to mount and charge the Maori reinforcements. There was a slight dip in the ground between us and the Hauhaus, and they did not see us until we were pretty close on them. With drawn swords we galloped into them and caught them in the short fern, and we killed or severely wounded twenty—nearly a Maori apiece for us. One of our big troopers, Hogan, gave them the point of his sword and ran through three in succession. Others cut at them with the sabre, but the point was best . . . A fine big warrior with a great bushy beard who was lying wounded in the fern made an attempt to rise to fire the second barrel of his *tupara*, but a trooper—Maxwell, I think—reached it first and shot the owner dead with it. We were amongst those Maoris for a few crowded moments, swords slashing and thrusting, and guns and revolvers popping. The Maoris dodged in all directions. One daring fellow grappled one of our men and nearly pulled him off his horse . . . It was wonderful to see the way the Maoris parried the sword-thrusts and cuts. We found one gun afterwards which was hacked across the stock and up the middle of the heel of the butt; the man who had used it had parried two sword-cuts in quick succession. Our troops could have done more execution if we had wheeled about at once after the charge and gone through the Maoris again, but we were not quick enough. Just after a fight I saw a Maori lying wounded in the field, and I went to a waterhole and brought him some water in my forage cap, and I handed him over to the Wanganui Maoris who took care of him.'[1]

With this severe repulse of the relief force the investment of Te Tarata was resumed with heavy firing by both besiegers and defenders until dusk. A moonlit night set in and at about 8 pm the Rangers, dug in very close to the *pa*, heard the hacking and cutting of the lashings binding the palisade. Then a great crash came as part of the palisade suddenly fell and with a shout a concerted rush of Hauhaus poured out, firing and brandishing tomahawks as they charged and leapt over the heads of the astonished, entrenched besiegers. The Rangers had no time to use their carbines but their quick-firing Dean & Adams revolvers did much despatch at these close quarters. Carbine butts and tomahawks were wielded with fury and determination and to

[1] Cowan.

increase the din of the confused mêlée the *Huntress*'s gun on the other side of the *pa* fired, its conglomeration of old bits of iron screeching horribly overhead. As it discharged its awful contents it somersaulted backwards, scattering its amateur crew wildly.

Sixteen dead Hauhau resulted from this desperate break for freedom and the whole day cost the enemy 35 killed; three Government men were killed. Next day Major Brassey arrived from Opotiki to assume command against Te Pua, and a certain change of emphasis in tactics occurred, as eye-witness Thomas Gudgeon states bluntly:

> 'The men were formed in close column of companies, a formation admirably adapted to wholesale murder, and advanced towards the *pa*.'[1]

Fortunately for Brassey's Napoleonic columns Te Pua, after a feint by the Hauhaus of rushing to man their outside rifle pits, was found to be abandoned.

McDonnell's operations had a sobering effect and the Ngatirua *hapu* of the Whakatohea soon submitted to the Government, casting off their Hauhau affiliations. More active raiding columns into Hauhau-ridden country under the energetic McDonnell, aided by Captain Newland, mainly after information had been laid where the infamous Kereopa could be taken, produced similar valuable effects. Though these forays missed Kereopa, they had their excitements, as at Koingo, on the Waimana river, where McDonnell's scouts encountered Kereopa and his bodyguard on a narrow bush track. The Eye-eater escaped into the bush but three of his Urewera bodyguard were killed and prisoners were taken. Another forced march up the Waimana valley saw the wounding of a young Hauhau Urewera named Te Whiu Maraki; five years later Te Whiu came over to the Government side and was to gain enduring fame by capturing the elusive Eye-eater. These harassing operations induced the surrender of many Hauhaus, including the chief, Mokomoko, also to be hanged in Auckland Gaol for the Volkner murder.

In November orders came for the irrepressible Wanganui

[1] Gudgeon.

167

Native Contingent to return to the West Coast to join a fresh campaign there under the new General Officer Commanding, and the *Stormbird* arrived off Opotiki on the 17th to embark the Wanganui. The Patea Rangers and the Military Settlers remained in the Opotiki district another nine months before the Rangers returned to Wanganui in May, 1866, to be disbanded by a hard-hearted Government after a dispute over their terms of service.

While the Bay of Plenty and its interior were being brought back under Government control, operations were being simultaneously mounted at Poverty Bay where *Pai-Marire* now had a powerful hold. A strong Hauhau *pa* had been erected at Waerenga-a-Hika near Bishop Williams' abandoned Mission house while another two lay a few miles inland at Pukeamionga and Kohanga-Karearea ('The Sparrowhawk's Nest'). In late October, 1865, Donald McLean enlisted 300 Ngatiporou under Ropata and Mokena and HMS *Brisk* landed the Hawke's Bay Cavalry under Captain La Serre and some Military Settlers led by Lieutenant Wilson. At the same time Major Fraser and Captain Biggs were ordered to march with their East Cape column on Poverty Bay.

Donald McLean then arrived officially as Superintendent of Hawke's Bay Province and at his summons the chiefs of the Hauhau faction came to speak with him. To avert bloodshed he gave them three days to come to their senses but all that came of this parley was that the Hauhau chiefs insulted Mokena and only the Europeans closing about them prevented the Ngatiporou falling on them. McLean waited three fruitless days then left for Napier, turning the situation over to his military commander, Major James Fraser.

The Government forces marched to attack Pukeamionga but, as many Hauhaus were seen slipping away from Waerenga to reinforce the threatened *pa*, Fraser backtracked and suddenly appeared before Waerenga. The Military Settlers and dismounted Defence Force Cavalry dug in behind a straggling hedge that conveniently ran 300 yards out from two faces of the *pa* and Captain Westrup's Forest Rangers were sited to cover the lagoon at its rear. On the roof of the Bishop's house an elite band of marksmen took up position and, at 300 yards range, began to exact steady and effective execution throughout the days of the siege. Waerenga was a unique operation in that some 500 fighting men, according to a Hauhau eye-witness, were defending the *pa* against an inferior force of 110 Europeans and 250 friendly Maoris.

After three days of heavy but not very damaging exchanges of fire, Lieutenant Wilson was ordered to take thirty of his Military Settlers off to the northern face of the *pa* and drive a flying sap through the easy digging ground there close enough to allow a rope to be thrown over the palisade when the combined strength of husky characters would heave and collapse a section and bugle calls of varying significance would set an assault in motion. While the Settlers were digging two Maoris with them observed a large body of Hauhaus, arriving from Pukeamionga, coming in on their rear. Wilson could only give the order to fix bayonets and cut their way out, but as their retreat lay across the front of the *pa*, his loss was heavy, with six men killed and five wounded.

> 'Sergeant Doonan, who was slightly wounded, was overtaken and speared to death, but the remainder, covered by the heavy fire of their comrades at the thorn hedge, made their escape, the wounded were brought off, but the dead lay too near the *pa* to attempt it, and the Hauhaus were seen stripping them.'[1]

This heady success exhilarated the Hauhaus who threw themselves elatedly into a night of wild celebration. Their *tohungas*, who in this instance had clearly received the wrong heavenly message, predicted that if an attack was made on the morrow, Sunday, it was bound to succeed as all the *Pakehas* would be at their devotions. The more earth-bound Thomas Gudgeon knew otherwise:

> 'Fortunately, the Hauhaus knew little of the godless Forest Rangers' class; their experience of *Pakehas* was confined to the Church Mission and its followers, and they made a woeful mistake, for morning broke and found us in the trenches, rifle in hand and not a prayer book in sight. About 10 am the oracle began to work, several hundred men were seen to leave the *pa*, form up in two wedge-shaped masses, one a little behind the

[1] Gudgeon.

169

other, and advance upon our position under the thorn hedge; the enemy carried large flags that appeared to be white, and this caused Major Fraser to mistake their character, and call out to the men not to fire upon flags of truce. Luckily Biggs was present; he knew they were fighting flags, and before the mistake could lead to serious consequences, ordered the men to fire. By this time the leading wedge-shaped phalanx was close to our line under the thorn hedge, our men fired a deadly volley into them, but failed to stop them in the rush, for the next moment they lined the opposite side of the hedge, firing through into our rifle pits. The camp, now thoroughly aroused, opened a terrific cross-fire on the second column which broke at once; some of the enemy rushed back to the *pa* while others, less bold, threw themselves on the ground and feigned death. The enemy under the thorn bush were completely at our mercy; the flanking pits were manned, and they were annihilated; it did not take long, for the whole affair was over in flfteen minutes, and sixty-three of the enemy lay dead on the flat. Our loss was one man wounded."[1]

Gradually, those Hauhaus who feigned death realised that there was little future in lying under a canopy of bullets that whistled inches overhead in both directions and individually began to make a dash back to the *pa*, 'with very indifferent success', as Thomas Gudgeon relates, as many marksmen were watching them.

After another two days, the bodies of the dead lying in the open ground smelt so badly that Fraser proposed a truce of one hour to bury the corpses, providing the Hauhaus brought Wilson's dead forward. The truce was agreed, but as the Hauhaus usefully occupied the time carrying water from the lagoon and collecting spare ammunition from the dead, a sharp volley from the irate Volunteers and Ngatiporou ended this one-sided arrangement. On the evening of the seventh day, a 6-pounder gun from the *Sturt* arrived but its first keen but novice gunner had the same degree of success as the *Huntress*'s at Te Tarata; each of his firings caused the gun to do a dangerous back somersault. A more proficient gunner emerged from the unlikely ranks of the Defence Force Cavalry, probably an ex-Royal Artilleryman, and his two opening shots could not have been more resounding: they crashed through the palisade very directly and

[1] Gudgeon.

170

before he could get away a third round, a white flag flew over Waerenga-a-Hika.

A splendid capture of 400 Hauhaus marched out to surrender their arms as prisoners-of-war. Another 100 had died, either as battle casualties or as the many wounded who were trapped among the burning *whares* fired by some unknown fanatic. Though the Government loss was not light, with 11 killed and 20 wounded, Waerenga was a crushing Government victory, underlining the local military virtue of surrounding a *pa* and waiting for the enemy to try to break out. It is also memorable for one incident which was to have great implications. During the siege, a loyal chief of the Rongowhakaata, Paora Parau, was seen leading away a man of his tribe with a revolver at the prisoner's head, accusing him of communicating with the enemy and only firing blanks. The arrested man was held for several days then released, as no real proof could be sustained against him. However, when the worst of the Aitangi-a-Mahaki and Rongowhakaata prisoners from Waerenga had been screened for transportation to the Chatham Islands, this suspect from the siege lines was re-arrested on other charges and included in the shipment of enforced exiles.

Whatever the merits of the early allegation in action, it is probable that the charges that had him transported were convenient to many in the rich and fertile valley of the Turanganui. He was then thirty-five years old, a Maori of some education who had been to a Mission school, and a man of some parts, a proficient horseman and seaman with some knowledge of the wider world as he had served as a supercargo on a schooner plying regularly to Auckland. It is also clear he was a local hard case, an envied Don Juan and a difficult character who shaded his way carefully on just the right side of the law.

His name, soon to be infamous in the final phase of the Maori Wars, was Te Kooti.

171

CHAPTER 15
The Red Tribe Departs

THE *Stormbird*, bearing the turbulent Wanganui Native Contingent, arrived off Wanganui on 25 November, 1865, and local dignitaries, such as Doctor Featherston, the Superintendent of Wellington Province, Walter Buller, the Resident Magistrate, and old comrades-in-arms, such as Gustavus von Tempsky, went on board to greet the homecoming warriors. The return voyage, however, had not been without drama, starting at Opotiki harbour.

'McDonnell issued orders for the men to prepare for embarkation, but ordered them not to attempt to cross the bar in canoes. This prohibition was particularly hard upon the Wanganui, for they had accumulated quantities of loot, and were tolerably certain that room would not be found for it all in the boats. Under these circumstances they promptly disobeyed. Two canoes, heavily laden, attempted to cross the bar and, as McDonnell had foreseen, were capsized and lost everything except themselves. Maoris are not born to be drowned, unless they wish it; only one man was drowned, and he did wish it. It was the prophet Pitau, who unfortunately had prophesied his own death. The oracle spoke as follows: "You will be successful in all things, O Wanganui: only one man will die, and that will be Pitau." Now this was rough on the prophet. At Kiorekino he sought death, and found it not: his character was at stake; it really appeared as though he would be found out; but here was a chance not to be lost—rather death than lose his fame as a prophet, so out of pure cantankerousness he threw up his arms and died . . . He was much regretted by his tribe, for the Wanganui are not great in prophets . . ."

[1] Gudgeon.

172

Then in Wellington harbour, the *Stormbird*'s mate, demonstrating his knowledge of gunnery, caused an accident with a cannon that injured him and two of his Wanganui onlookers. For the Wanganui, this tragedy could only be alleviated by a two day spree in the town to ward off the ill-omen, but just then the ship was being made ready to sail and so an infuriated *haka* was danced around the capstan. The burly Wirihana solved the crisis abruptly by picking up the ringleader and attempting to throw him overboard, only to be thwarted by the combined strength of several of the man's relatives.

Among the important personalities at Wanganui who awaited the return of the contingent with more than usual interest was the new General Officer Commanding, Major-General Trevor Chute, the former Commanding Officer of the 70th Regiment who had inquired into Murray's conduct at Waireka in '60. A forceful and decisive forty-nine-year-old who had arrived from Australia on 25 August, Trevor Chute had taken his Regiment out to India in 1849 and served in command there for twelve years. When the Mutiny broke out, he acted with vigour against the mutineers of the 55th Native Infantry at Fort Koti-Mardan, rescuing their British officers, and for the next eighteen months, commanded a brigade in the Lucknow district. In February, 1861, back in command of the 70th, he took his Regiment to New Zealand and after a period on half-pay, was promoted Brigadier-General in March, 1863, and appointed to the Australian colonies.

That same August, when he landed back in New Zealand, his old Regiment, the 70th, left the Taranaki for Napier, as fear of the Hauhaus gripped the East Coast. Of his other Imperial regiments, the 12th, the 40th and 65th were holding down the Waikato and the approaches to Auckland, the 68th were in Tauranga with three companies still detached to Wanganui, the 43rd were deployed over Taranaki, while remaining in the districts of Wanganui were the 14th, 18th, 50th and 57th. However, this formidable array was mainly scattered about in company detachments to give security to the sorely-tried rural communities. Also, the drastic change of policy regarding the prosecution of the war now made the end of the tour of duty for a number of the Imperial Regiments seem certain in the near future. The Imperial Government was adamant that five regiments must be offered up by the New Zealand Government for redeployment throughout the Empire and open knowledge of this demand, plus the Self-Reliant Policy, led the Imperial forces into a more passive role, as the Opotiki expedition reflected.

But the energetic new Commander was not of a passive disposition. When Sir George Grey directed him to act against the recalcitrant Ngatiruanui and Ngarauru tribes, guilty in early October of the murder of Charles Broughton, a Government interpreter, who had been lured treacherously into a Hauhau *pa* on the Patea and executed, and of the ambush of five troopers of the Military Train near Manawapou, in which one man was tomahawked to death, he waited impatiently to take the field. But the return of the veteran Wanganui did not help his preparations as he had hoped. Soon after landing, the temperamental Meti Kingi announced that he was withdrawing his men from the Contingent and within days its active strength had shrunk from 120 to 30. But Kepa and Wirihana prevailed upon the warriors, as did Dr Featherston, who had much influence with the tribe, and their counter-advice had effect:

'The old hands began to ask themselves the very pertinent question whether it was not better to serve the Government than Meti Kingi; and one impudent scoundrel asked the chief whether he would give him 2s 6d per diem and rations.'[1]

On 30 December Chute marched out from Wanganui to Weraroa, where reinforcements joined him. His field force consisted of two companies of the 14th under Lieutenant-Colonel Trevor, a strong company of the 18th under the ubiquitous Major Rocke, a 50th detachment commanded by Captain Johnstone, a Royal Artillery detachment under Lieutenant Carre, 300 Wanganui Native Contingent under Thomas McDonnell, Kepa and Wirihana, 45 Forest Rangers under von Tempsky and finally, a Transport Corps of 45 settlers each driving a two-horse dray.

The field force marched out from the Waitotara towards the Patea on 3 January, 1866, keeping well inland under the brow of the mountain ranges. That evening the village of Okotuku was

[1] Gudgeon.

fired because of sniping and next day a detachment that had set off at first light to destroy nearby large plantations of potatoes and corn to deny food to the enemy ran into heavy fire from a temporary Hauhau *pa* while in hot pursuit of some enemy scouts. Lieutenant Keogh's company of the 14th and the Native Contingent came quickly to the sound of the firing and attacked. Keogh and six of his soldiers were wounded, one of whom died later, while three Hauhaus were killed when the *pa* was entered at several points and the enemy fled. The Wanganui, aided and abetted by the Forest Rangers, set off in pursuit through tangled country and returned to camp late that evening with one prisoner, reporting three more enemy dead and one wounded.

After this disturbed day, the morrow saw the valuable crops belatedly destroyed and the column marched on to the Whenua-kura river, by the Patea, where camp was pitched at noon on an opposite ridge to Te Putahi, a Ngarauru Hauhau *pa* sited in a position of great natural strength on the spur of a plateau over-looking the river. Chute wanted to attack at once but the bush-wise McDonnell, aware that the Hauhaus were observing every move, dissuaded him, to everybody's relief, until the early hours of the following morning.

At 2 am 7 January, the whole column set off in the darkness on a tortuous flanking march to shun the open approach spurs, where obvious enemy ambushes lay, and after a mile or so, began the climb up the steep slopes. The first streaks of daylight were threading through the sky when the Forest Rangers reached the summit and already the Hauhaus were assembling for their strange devotions about the *niu* pole in blissful ignorance that their enemy was filtering through the bush about them. Chute directed the Imperial troops to an assault position while he sent the Wanganui to a cut-off role in rear of the pa, but his whole plan was ruined by a burst of unauthorised fire by the *kupapas*, and as the startled Hauhaus abandoned their dawn service to race to their rifle pits, a great tactical chance was lost.

The soldiers now had to attack an alerted enemy. As the 50th company formed up on the left, the 14th in the centre and the 18th on the right, the Hauhaus kept up their spirits with war dances. The assault went in and after a sharp fight, Te Putahi was taken, with the defenders leaving fourteen dead and Private Michael Coffey of the 14th hauling down the Hauhau flag to present to his Colonel. British losses were two killed and twelve wounded, including the usually lucky McDonnell who on this occasion received a bullet in his foot; however he insisted on accompanying the expedition, as he feared trouble with the Native Contingent if he was not there. As the enemy fled from Putahi, one of several ambushes laid by the 50th sent up from Patea by Colonel Weare killed one Hauhau and captured another on the far side of the river.

Next day the column rested and the company of the 18th under Major Rocke marched back to Patea as the action at Putahi had decisively cleared the country south of the river. Chute then forded the Whenuakura and continued his advance over the Patea to Kakaramea redoubt were two sergeants and fifteen gunners of the Royal Artillery with two 6-pounders joined, and on 11 January, as the column approached the Tangahoe river, Brevet-Lieutenant-Colonel Jason Hassard and 130 men of the 57th Regiment marched in. The advance was now deep in the Ngatiruanui territory and moving on their strongest *pa*, Otapawa, high above thickly-forested and precipitous gorges that fell away into a loop of the Tangahoe. En route Chute burned the village of Taiporohenui where cooked dinners of beef, boiled potatoes and native cabbage, with well-tended cattle, horses and pigs nearby, indicated a hasty evacuation. He encamped five miles south-west of Otapawa on the Tawiti river and here more reinforcements, another detachment of the 57th under Lieutenant-Colonel Butler, arrived.

After a reconnaissance by Ensign William McDonnell and Wanganui scouts, Chute decided to attack without delay along a track they had found. Before first light on 14 January, while the three guns of the Royal Artillery were moved to adjacent high ground within range, the storming force of 200 men of the 14th, 180 of the 57th, 36 Forest Rangers and 200 Native Contingent began a silent approach march along the darkened and steepening bush track.

After a slow and exhausting ascent, the force gradually assembled on the plateau where the broad base of wedge-shaped

17. *The Engagement at Te Ranga, June, 1864 – from a sketch by Gustavus von Tempsky.*

18. *General Sir Trevor Chute, K.C.B.*

19. *Sir George Grey, Governor of New Zealand 1845–53 and 1861–7.*

20. *The death of Gustavus von Tempsky at Te Ngutu-o-te-manu, September, 1867.*

Otapawa *pa* faced them over open ground, its flanks protected by the sheer drop to the river gorge. Three shells from the Armstrong guns crashed into the *pa*, setting some *whares* on fire, but a strange and unusual silence enveloped it and Chute began to think it was deserted. He had sent off the Native Contingent to take up position for their usual waiting role in the rear to catch any escaping enemy but he was too impatient to wait for them and determined to attack at once. He had worked out his own drill for this inevitable facet of New Zealand warfare:

'General Chute's "ready" mode of attacking *pas* was this. There was usually an open space in front of the *pas*; he brought up his men there to the edge of the bush, and when his line and supports and natives in reserve were all ready, he made his bugler sound a single G; the men advanced from under cover, and on the double G being given, a rush was made at the *pa*, hatchets were drawn from the belts of the men, the withes of the outer fence were suddenly cut, the palisading broken through, and the *pa* stormed with cheering "in the smoke" '[1]

Chute ordered the assault: '57th, advance! Rangers, clear the bush!'

The attacking lines of soldiers moved forward from out of the bush, advancing steadily with the imperturbable discipline of British regulars towards the silent *pa*, but two hundred yards away, Butler, leading his Regiment, saw that the rifle pits under and behind the raised bottom of the palisading were dense with black heads. Fifty yards out, a storm of fire roared out from the waiting Hauhaus, shaking even the veteran 57th to a staggering halt until Butler's voice roared out: 'Go on, Diehards!' and the 57th broke into a charge and went for their objective. Though well-supported by the 14th who extended to their left, casualties also fell from a telling crossfire by Hauhau marksmen on platforms in trees on the flanks. Von Tempsky's Rangers surged through the bush, at the cost of two wounded, to take out the snipers but their numbers were too few to clear the menace quickly enough.

Under this well-planned enemy reception, Chute's assault was a bloody one. Though the *pa* was carried, Jason Hassard, a

[1] *Bush Fighting* by Major General Sir James Alexander.

Crimean veteran, fell mortally wounded and nine soldiers, seven from the 57th, also died, while Lieutenant Swanson, 14th, and fourteen men were wounded. Thirty Hauhau bodies were found in the *pa* or on the line of retreat but many fugitives escaped, plummeting down through the scrub into the gorge, as the Wanganui were still struggling to get fully into position. Officers used to Cameron's more deliberate tactics had tried to persuade Chute from rushing prematurely to the assault but he would not listen. When Lieutenant Carre, his gunner, offered his congratulations after the operation, he regretted his impetuosity:

> 'He shook his head. "Lost too many brave poor boys! Nearly lost myself," he said, pointing to his jumper, from the breast of which a bullet had torn the braid.'

Butler and the 57th were angry about their casualties as they had not been allowed to send flanking parties to clear the bush as they advanced and it had been heavy enfilade fire that had caused Hassard and part of the 57th to wheel left and go for the hidden enemy in the bush. Their remorse was also aggravated by soldier gossip that Kimble Bent, the 57th deserter, had been present in the *pa* and it was his bullet that pierced the lung of his old officer, Jason Hassard. This was a fallacious rumour, for though Kimble Bent was a slave of the Ngatiruanui, he was then several miles away. However, Te Ua, the illustrious high priest of *Pai-Marire*, had been at Otapawa a few days previously but had ridden off before the attack. Though the fall of Otapawa could have been achieved less bloodily, its loss had a profound effect as the *pa* had an aura of impregnability dating from the old native wars.

After Otapawa, the gallant 57th detachment marched away to rejoin their Regiment at stations throughout Wanganui, while Chute continued his determined advance well inland from the coast. On 15 January, he descended on the stockaded village of Ketemarae, at the junction of several historic war-tracks, where ten Hauhaus were killed, and thence across the Waihi and Wai-Ngongoro where the Wanganui were superb, skirmishing under the leadership of Kepa-te-Rangihiwinui. With the Wanganui littoral cleared, Chute now decided on a rather startling departure from his axis of advance: he would move behind Mount Egmont to emerge on the Waitara river in Taranaki.

The immediate military advantage of such an arduous thrust through the hinterland was obscure, but its conception was typical of the bustling Mutiny veteran. In the waiting period before the campaign, while his field force built up and the warm, dry weather approached, he doubtless had to listen to gibes from the colonial society that the Imperial troops were only fitted for the open field, to lay siege and storm *pas*, but shirked bush fighting. He was now determined to show the Colony the fallacy of this allegation by leading an Imperial column along an ancient war-track, opened up twenty years ago by New Zealand Company working parties to a bridle path but now badly overgrown, to the famous, but distant, Waitara block.

The unfortunate marchers for this marathon of endurance were three companies of the 14th Regiment, von Tempsky's company of Forest Rangers and eighty 'picked' warriors of the Native Contingent. These Wanganui rather selected themselves out of loyalty to their venerable chief, Hori Kingi te Anaua, who had accompanied Sir George Grey dangerously close to Weraroa *pa* last winter to call on its surrender. The Contingent, almost en masse, and probably with good judgement about the ordeal that lay ahead, refused to march so far away from home. Neither Thomas McDonnell nor Dr Featherston could shake their decision, so in desperation, as the wholesale withdrawal of the Wanganui could wreck the expedition, they called on the tent of Hori Kingi. The grand old warrior listened to them, drew himself up and went out to berate his tribesmen, threatening never to live again in Wanganui if they disgraced him.

At first light 17 January, the column moved out. Each soldier carried a waterproof sheet, a greatcoat, blanket and two days supply of biscuit, backed by 67 packhorses with their drivers; 24 saddlehorses carried the General, Dr Featherston, the Staff and regimental officers. The Staff of this enterprise of insoluble supply problems included Colonel Carey as Deputy Adjutant-General, Lieutenant-Colonel Gamble, an experienced Deputy Quartermaster-General, and as head of the Commissariat, Deputy Commissary-General Strickland. On the packhorses Strickland carried five days' supply of hard rations, except for the Native Contingent who insisted on having all their rations in advance and then promptly proceeded to eat the lot prematurely. James Cowan graphically describes the eight days of physical challenge that awaited the brave venture:

'As the column advanced across the lower spurs of the mountain the country became more and more difficult; the forest undergrowth was dense and matted, and gullies and watercourses continually intersected the line of march. The Forest Rangers in the advance did excellent work as pioneers, cutting the track and bridging creeks and swampy gullies with the trunks of fern-trees, which gave good footing for the horses. Half-way through the forest heavy rain set in, and the rest of the march was slow and toilsome in the extreme. The Rangers were now so exhausted by the heavy labour of pioneer duty that working parties of the 14th, under Colonel Carey, were sent to the front.

On Sunday, the 21st, the force marched only four miles, crossing four rapid streams and fifteen gullies, and went into bivouac early in wet and gloomy weather. That evening it became necessary to kill one of the horses for a meat ration; all the provisions but a little biscuit had been exhausted. On the night of the 20th Mr Price, of the Commissariat, Captain Leach and Ensign McDonnell with some Maoris had set out on a forced march for Mataitawa to get supplies for the troops. The rain fell in torrents, and the struggle through the roadless bush became so exhausting that Mr Price had to be left under a tree while his companions pushed on to Mataitawa. Reaching the British post at last they obtained provisions, and on the evening of the 22nd, Captain Leach returned from Mataitawa with a party of the 43rd and 68th carrying supplies for the half-starved troops. Meanwhile, the Native Contingent and some of the Rangers had hurried on in advance to the open country. A second horse was killed on the 22nd before the arrival of the party with food. The weather continued wet, and progress through the gully-dissected forest country was slow and toilsome. At last, on the 25th, after a bush march of sixty miles, the column gladly halted in the Mataitawa Valley, and the sun shone once more.'

After a much-needed day of rest and drying-out of sodden clothes and blankets, the leg-weary and aching column fell in again with the resignation of old soldiers and moved on to New Plymouth which they entered triumphantly amid much cheering.

[1] Cowan.

The Superintendent of Taranaki Province, Mr H. S. Richmond, read a congratulatory address to the General and the soldiers were entertained to a bumper dinner by the townsfolk and settlers.

But the restless Chute did not allow his field force to rest for long. At first light on 1 February he marched out to return to Wanganui by the coastal route and complete the circumnavigation of Mount Egmont. His force was now joined by two companies of the 43rd under Captains Livesay and Horan, Captain Mace's Taranaki Mounted Corps and a company of Taranaki Bush Rangers under Captain Corbett, as some sharp action was expected with the Hauhaus in the Warea district. Between Opunake and Warea, the column came upon a *pa*, about five miles inland, called Waikoko, where Taranaki Hauhaus made a determined stand. The Wanganui actually entered the *pa* in the van of the assault but got rapidly out of the way as the attacking lines of troops, with the 43rd left, Rangers centre and 14th right, surged in; hard experience had taught them that soldiers storming a *pa* did not make too fine a distinction between Maoris, friendly or hostile. One soldier of the 14th was killed, and a Rangers sergeant and two Wanganui wounded, while four Hauhaus bodies were found after the enemy had fled.

Waikoko was the last action of Chute's brisk campaign. After shedding the Taranaki attachments, he marched on to Patea where the field force was disbanded and dispersed to its various stations on 6 February, with a Special Order of the Day:

'The Major-General begs to thank the officers, non-commissioned officers and men of the 14th Regiment, the Detachment R.A. and the Native Contingent comprising the field force, now about to be broken up, for the cheerfulness with which they have undergone the hardships of a short but arduous campaign in the Wanganui-Taranaki districts and through the forests east of Mount Egmont; also for the gallantry displayed on all occasions when they have had the good fortune to encounter the enemy. The discipline and good conduct invariably evinced by the regulars reflects great credit on officers commanding corps.'

Chute's hectic five weeks of operations, a veritable lightning campaign compared to the measured tread of Duncan Cameron, coupled with the offensive activities during January of Lieutenant-Colonel Butler with detachments of the 50th and 57th up the Wai-Ngongoro, supported by the rump of the reluctant Wanganui under Wirihana, were the last major operations by Imperial troops in New Zealand. For during 1866 embarkation for England or Australia was very much in the air for at least five Regiments.

Fittingly, the long-tried 65th were the first to go. Though under promise of relief for several years, the dictates of the hard-pressed situation, as each new regiment arrived, demanded that the 65th could not be spared. In late August, 1865, the 40th were ordered to take over the 65th's detached posts in the Waikato and that October, after a distinguished nineteen years in the Colony, 'the Hickety Pip' embarked at Auckland for England.

In December the 70th, Chute's old Regiment, also concentrated in Auckland and sailed for Dover in January, 1866, after seventeen years overseas in India and New Zealand. Next to embark were the 68th Light Infantry, with the four companies from Wanganui moving to New Plymouth in mid-December, then sailing in February to Auckland where the other half of the battalion joined from Tauranga. They sailed for Portsmouth in March.

Hard on the heels of the 68th were the 43rd Light Infantry, who also sailed in March and were met at Anglesea Barracks, Portsmouth, by their depot companies from Winchester under command of Brevet Major Smith, the Te Ranga VC. Then, in May, the 40th Regiment came out of the Waikato and embarked at Auckland, also for Portsmouth. A lull in embarkations ensued until October when the 14th sailed for Melbourne, detaching three companies to Hobart Town and two for Adelaide. That same month, the 50th Regiment also partly sailed for the Australian colonies; in February, 1866, the Regiment had moved up the coast from Patea to occupy redoubts along the south Taranaki shoreline, and now six months later, headquarters and five companies arrived in Auckland in readiness to sail to New South Wales; Colonel Weare and four companies went to Sydney while the fifth went to Brisbane. Three and a half Imperial Regiments of the Line now remained in New Zealand.

'They were pretty formidable men, these New Zealand veterans, who had lived roughly for several years in detachments remote from refining influences. A subaltern who joined another regiment recently returned from New Zealand found there was nothing these hairy old soldiers "did not know of fording rivers and storming palisades"—also, a bottle of wine was apt to turn into a dead marine in a brace of shakes whenever it dared to cross their path.'[1]

That newly-commissioned subaltern who served a short while with the 12th Regiment in Ireland after their return from New Zealand, before he went on to his true Regiment, the 92nd Highlanders, was to become General Sir Ian Hamilton, commander at Gallipoli in 1915 when his Anzacs, the citizen soldiers of Australia and New Zealand, almost made that great enterprise a glorious victory instead of one of the tragic near-misses of history.

[1] Gretton.

CHAPTER 16
Taking the Strain

$\mathbf{D}$ESPITE the activity of such energetic and courageous leaders as McDonnell, Kepa, Fraser, Biggs and Ropata, the East Coast was still disturbed by *Pai-Marire* as 1865 drew to a close. The Volunteer forces had done sound work in dampening down violent upsurges and Ropata and Mokena Kohere had cauterised the infection from their own tribe literally by fire and sword but, apart from a localised area about Tauranga, the East Coast had not been subjected to heavy and concerted military pressure as had the Waikato, Taranaki and Wanganui, and the delusions of *Pai-Marire* still bred a *folie de grandeur* among tribes who had not yet endured the violence of retribution it brought. Undeterred by the severe experience of the Poverty Bay Rongowhakaata at Waerenga, certain factions of the Ngatikahungunu under the leadership of chief Te Waru Tamatea, another embittered Orakau veteran, now exhibited all the symptoms of Hauhau fever.

Donald McLean again promptly sent arms to the loyal chiefs while in early December, Major James Fraser landed at Wairoa with 100 Hawke's Bay and Taranaki Military Settlers to join 100 loyal Ngatikahungunu under chiefs Kopu Parapara and Ihaka Whanga. On Christmas Day, the allies fought a sharp action against the Hauhaus at Omaruhakeke, killing twelve enemy, but Captain Hussey of the Taranaki Military Settlers and two friendly Ngatikahungunu were also fatal casualties. Meanwhile McLean had enlisted Ropata and 150 Ngatiporou, at the princely pay of three shillings a day, and on 4 January, they also landed at Wairoa.

The Hauhaus retreated to the southern side of Lake Waikare-moana but a column of loyal Ngatikahungunu under Kopu and Ihaka and the Ngatiporou led by Ropata, with Fraser and a small group of European officers, came on them dramatically when the Ngatikahungunu advanced guard walked into an ambush. Twelve fell killed or mortally wounded but Ihaka Whanga, though twice wounded, rushed up to rally his shattered men while Ropata fired the fern which an accommodating strong breeze drove up the slopes of the defile and covered his successful attack through its smoke. The pursuit after the fleeing Hauhaus found their camp and many prisoners were taken. Ropata in his usual way proposed that any local Ngatikahungunu Hauhaus should be spared but any foreigners, such as Ngatiporou, Urewera or Rongowha-kaata, should be executed to spread despondency in their areas. But Kopu and his other chiefs insisted that their defectors should also be killed and so some sixty Hauhaus died in this encounter which effectively purged *Pai-Marire* from the Wairoa district. Fourteen friendly Maoris had been killed and about thirty wounded, almost all in the ambush, so tempers were running high.

In mid-December, the 12th Regiment, withdrawn from its stations in the Waikato, arrived at Napier in HMS *Esk* and *Eclipse* to relieve the homeward-bound 70th. On 31 January, 1866, they sent a detachment as a stabilizing factor to Wairoa, and in mid-February, another to Tauranga but as more obvious turbulence seemed to be building up in the Bay of Plenty, Battalion Headquarters soon followed and by the end of August, almost all the Regiment was at Tauranga. Due to the departing Regiments, the dispositions of the 57th Regiment were also affected. In March, 1866, the Diehards left Wanganui for the Waikato to relieve the 40th, just as the Sergeants were being issued with the new short rifle, sword bayonet and scabbard.

Donald McLean devoted the rest of 1866 ensuring the support of the *Rangatiras* of the Ngatikahungunu but in October, a threat developed against Napier itself, now without Imperial troops, not from this numerous tribe but from the small but war-like Ngatihineuru whose villages were astride the mountain track to the Taupo country. Their leading chief, Te Rangihiroa, had become attached to the new faith, personified by a resident pro-phet, Panapa, but the menace of the Ngatihineuru lay in the possibility that a successful descent on Napier would bring the savage Urewera out of their mountains into the plains; it also had sinister overtones in that the venture was encouraged by such a distant, brooding Kingite as Rewi Maniapoto. With Te Rangihiroa and his warriors were some tough and wild spirits from far afield, such as a powerful and bloodthirsty Ngatitu-wharetoa from Lake Taupo named Te Rangitahau whose favourite way of despatching prisoners was to hurl his sharp-edged club of hard black stone from an impressive distance and kill with an unerring blow on the temple. A typical restless Ngatimaniapoto in the war party was Peita Kotuku who had fought in Taranaki in 1860 and latterly at Orakau.

The Ngatihineuru moved down on Napier in early October, 1866, with about 130 fighting men, including 25 horsemen under Te Rangihiroa. Their plan was that Te Rangihiroa and his motley cavalry would make a night attack through Petane, a settle-ment on the north side of the town, by the sea, while the main body under Panapa, Nikora and other chiefs mopped up outlying homesteads and joined in a pincer movement with the mounted foray to sack Napier.

Meanwhile, the citizens of the township mustered their forces. The local Militia were called out, about 130 strong, under Major Lambert, and Captain Buchanan's Napier Rifle Volunteers, a more military body numbering 45, also prepared to take the field; Napier also raised its 25 horsemen, too, under Captain Gordon. From Wairoa on 11 October, came the experienced Fraser with 40 of his Military Settlers and Kopu and Ihaka, now recovered from his wounds, with 30 Ngatikahungunu. The whole command devolved on Colonel George Whitmore, a former Regular soldier who had settled in Hawke's Bay after the Waikato war. Fraser and his veterans were at once detached to block the approach of Te Rangihiroa while that night Whitmore led his citizen soldiers and friendly Maoris out from Napier to confront the Hauhaus, under Panapa, who had occupied Omarunui village.

By first light, as Panapa began to conduct his services around the *niu* pole, the Napier men were firmly about Omarunui. After a surrender demand was met with sullen indifference, the Militia, led by Major Lambert, waded across the shingle bed of the river before the village and were allowed to gain the far bank without coming under fire. On mounting the bank, they were confronted with a solid phalanx of Hauhaus on the edge of the village who, if they had charged, would probably have swept away the none-too-organised Militiamen straggling out of the water. However, a heavy crossfire was at once opened on the Hauhaus who seemed to be suffering from indecision and lack of leadership, and many began to fall. Their charge never got under way and they broke away into the village to take up fire positions. Some of Lambert's men got by the outskirts of the w*hares* but a heavy return fire made them falter and Whitmore withdrew all the Militia back to fire positions along the river bank. A telling enfilade fire from the Rifle Volunteers gradually wore down the resistance of the cornered and outnumbered Ngatihineuru and finally Nikora came forward with a white flag; Panapa, who was no war leader, had already been shot dead. Some tried to escape to the rear but were rounded up, mainly by the Napier horsemen. The Hauhaus lost 21 killed and 30 wounded at Omarunui, with 58 prisoners taken, while Whitmore's force had only one Militiaman and one Ngatikahungunu killed, though nine Militiamen and five friendly Maoris were wounded.

That same morning James Fraser and his men, joined by Captain Carr, a former Royal Artillery officer and other local settlers, ambushed and trapped in a defile Te Rangihiroa and his horsemen. The tough old chief fought it out, with the dire result that he and eleven of his warriors died, one was wounded and three captured. Only Sergeant Fletcher among the ambushers was wounded. If Te Rangihiroa had been at Omarunui, the conduct of the defence might have been intelligent and forceful as well as courageous.

The ambitious Ngatihineuru dream of rampaging through Napier, brought on by the fantasy of *Pai-Marire*, had ended in

187

disastrous fiasco. More severely, it brought about the ruination of this small tribe, for those who survived, including recovered wounded, were shipped off to the Chatham Islands to join the prisoners from Waerenga of a year ago.

1866 was also a disturbed year in Wanganui. After Chute's campaign, a lull ensued but with the surveying and clearing of 50,000 acres of confiscated land south of the Wai-Ngongoro for paid-off military settlers to occupy, the tribes began to grow restive and the Ngatiruanui plainly indicated that they would resist confiscation. As the inevitable sniping and ambushing of surveyors and working parties set in, the Patea Rangers, 8 and 10 Coys Taranaki Military Settlers and the Wanganui Yeomanry Cavalry were recalled from the East Coast and encamped at Patea. Here, in June, the Wanganui Native Contingent, released from garrisoning Pipiriki as peace had been made with Topia Turoa and the Upper Wanganui, joined their old comrades-in-arms from the Opotiki Expedition.

Major Thomas McDonnell took command and moved the force to Manawapou to be better placed to protect the survey work. However, an ambush on 16 June of Octavius Carrington, the Chief Surveyor of Taranaki, Percy Smith, who was to become Surveyor General of the Colony, and Wirihana, from which they all miraculously escaped by the keen-eyed Wanganui detecting movement in the fern ahead, enraged him to the extent of sending a false peace offering to the offending Ngatitupaea *hapu* of a cartridge, a percussion cap, a bottle of rum and a white handkerchief, asking which they would accept. They took the handkerchief, as signifying peace. On 1 August, however, McDonnell came on their village at Pokaikai at dawn with 200 men and charged with the bayonet. The surprised Ngatitupaea fled from their *whares*, leaving some thirty firearms; but two men and women were killed, while one girl had four bayonet wounds and one young European named Spain was shot dead. Pokaikai was a sordid affair which reflected badly on McDonnell, and a subsequent Government Commission of Inquiry stated this plainly. However, soon after Pokaikai, many of the Tangahoe and Pakakohi *hapus* surrendered and swore allegiance.

But McDonnell's treacherous stroke could only breed *utu* from the Ngatitupaea and other intransigent Ngatiruanui, and on 23 September, a ration cart bound for the new Waihi redoubt, escorted by only three troopers of the Wanganui Yeomanry Cavalry, was ambushed. The opening volley dropped the horse of Trooper Haggerty and as he crashed to the ground, he was rushed and tomahawked to death. The shaft horse in the cart team was also shot and the unarmed driver fled for his life, but the other two troopers, Wallace and Noonan, bravely extricated an invalided Patea Ranger in the cart, Michael Emerson, who was an old 65th soldier. Though he could not mount a horse, he hobbled between their horses as they kept the Hauhaus away with their carbines, until Captain Newland and some of his men from Waihi came along. Haggerty's death was avenged soon afterwards through a clever ruse by a patrol under Ensign Northcroft and J. R. Rushton, a former sergeant of the Patea Rangers now serving as a volunteer, pretending to be surveyors. Little Winiata, the Wanganui, shot a Hauhau from the band that crept up on them. 'This is *utu* for my friend, Haggerty,' cried Winiata, as he ran up to tomahawk the fallen Hauhau.

McDonnell, ever offensively-minded, now determined to attack Te Pungarehu, a village of the recalcitrant Ngaruahine *hapu*, and a night march on 1 October brought his column of 110 men in position by dawn. An accidental discharge caused them to rush the village at once, and Sergeant-Major Duff of the Wanganui Yeomanry fell mortally wounded, with two other men; another four were to survive their wounds. In the heat of the exchange, Ensign Northcroft rushed out into the open to carry the dying Duff away. Five of the *whares* were fortified and strongly defended and the Volunteers had to get on the roofs to scrape off the earth protection, tear up the slabs and fire down into the occupants. In half an hour, the village was taken and fired, with several casks of gunpowder exploding in the flames, but as the column drew away, carrying their dying and wounded in blankets, they came under increasing fire from the bush as the Hauhaus were reinforced and started to close about them. However, McDonnell conducted his withdrawal well and beat off the pursuers to close the day with a well-won victory. About 30 Hauhaus had been killed, certainly 21 bodies were counted, others died in the *whares*, and nine prisoners were escorted away.

McDonnell kept up the tempo of his raids and forced the hostile Ngatiruanui deeper into the forest. However, the Hauhaus could still be cheered by some minor successes; on 18 October, a dawn advance along a bush track at Te Popoia brought the Volunteers up against felled trees and a well-concealed enemy who forced a retirement, with Captain William McDonnell severely wounded in the hip. Sir George Grey had now arrived at Patea and warned the 18th Royal Irish, under Major Rocke, to be prepared to take the field if his peace talks at Wai-ngongoro failed. When the Governor's endeavours duly did fail, Rocke took a detachment of the 18th against Te Popoia, stormed the tree barricades and burned the village without loss, killing two Hauhaus. The 18th, accompanied by the excellent dismounted Wanganui Yeomanry, ranged through the bush for three weeks, surrounding and searching other hostile villages and then returned to Wai-ngongoro. This was the last time the 18th actively took the field and, apart from a non-active support the 12th Regiment gave the Volunteers in the Tauranga area the following January, the last occasion Imperial troops took the field against the Maori.

As 1866 waned, with the approach of hot summer, Sir George Grey can only have reflected on the virtues of the Self-Reliant Policy and Confiscation, both of which he had had forced on him, despite his grave doubts, by two powerful interested factions, the Imperial Government and the Colonial Government. For unrest was festering again on the East Coast, in the hinterland by Tauranga, and it was this threat that had drawn the 12th Regiment up to the Bay of Plenty from Napier before the Ngatihineuru challenge appeared. Survey parties working in the confiscated lands on the upper reaches of the Waipa and Waimapa rivers were being harassed, mainly by the Hauhau-converted Piri-Rakau tribe who inhabited the northern bushland about Tauranga harbour and who were now also attracting malcontents from other tribes, such as Ngaiterangi seeking to avenge the casualties of Te Ranga, and some Ngatiraukawa and Waikato.

The interference with the surveyors deteriorated into the murder of a settler named Campbell near Waimapu and in January, 1867, the 1st Waikato Militia had a sergeant-major killed in a skirmish. Several days later, a punitive expedition of the 1st Waikato under Lieutenant-Colonel Harrington, supported by part of the 12th Regiment led by Lieutenant-Colonel Hamilton, crossed the Wairoa river and climbed into the rugged hill country searching for the Hauhaus. Gilbert Mair was loaned from the 12th to the Military Settlers as interpreter and had a narrow escape leading skirmishers against snipers in a village when his horse was shot dead and pinned him to the ground. As several Hauhaus rushed out to tomahawk him, he kept snapping his revolver, wet from swimming in a river, futilely at them until one cartridge at last decided to fire and he dropped the leading assailant. He was rescued with the peak of his cap, his sleeve and saddle cut by bullets.

Meanwhile, his brother William, Resident Magistrate at Maketu, had raised 200 Arawa at three shillings a day, and February saw concerted action by his warriors, with companies of the 1st Waikato and an excellent small company of Volunteer Engineers, the same harried surveyors who by dint of their profession had become sound bushmen, against the Piri-Rakau and their foreign allies. Some of the enemy were fine men, such as Pene Taka who had sited the Gate *Pa* lines and was now intent on *utu* for his gallant cousin, Rawiri Puhirake, slain at Te Ranga, and Raumati, a Piri-Rakau chief and a young veteran of the Waikato war and the Gate *Pa*, who was now to fall mortally wounded. Almost all the fighting was done by William Mair's fleet-footed Arawa who drove on against the retreating Hauhaus, despite the great ravines that seared the entangled Piri-Rakau country.

While many of the Arawa fighting men were away on this campaign, danger threatened their own lands. With the long memory of the Maori, the Waikato nursed hatred against the Arawa for preventing many East Coast reinforcements from reaching them in '64. In March, 1867, reports filtered down to the coast that 300 to 500 Waikato, Ngatiraukawa and Ngatihaua had appeared in the vicinity of Lake Rotorua, clearly with the blessing of King Tawhiao, and war parties were striking out to raid Arawa territory.

The invaders were tackled in dashing style by Gilbert Mair and some of his Arawa on 17 March. Coming up on the lakeshore, he sighted a line of burning villages in the distance and hurried by forced march to the action. With his fittest young men, he reached a ridge from which he saw a Hauhau *taua* advancing steadily towards the earthworks of an old abandoned *pa* called Te Koutu. The war party was unusual because it was led by a woman, a Waikato chieftainess who also had great prestige as a sorceress and prophetess. A classical old-style Maori battle, with Gilbert Mair as the sole *pakeha* participant, set in:

> 'He had now thirty-nine men, a small body to join issue with the strong and evidently well-equipped invading warriors as they came marching at a steady walk over the plain, stripped to the waist and armed with guns and tomahawks, with numerous cartouche boxes strapped about them. Mair's men had not a rifle among them. His own weapon was a double-barrel gun; his Arawa were armed with similar pieces and with single barrel guns and old fashioned Tower Flintlock muskets.'[1]

The Arawa knew the country well; they forded a stream, rushing into the lake with their muskets and cartridge boxes held high, the water swirling about their waists, they raced through the *manuka* scrub, pitted in this area with boiling springs and bubbling mudholes, and just beat the advancing enemy to the other half of the old *pa*'s trenches.

> 'The enemy were led by Pare Turanga, the chieftainess . . . a handsome young woman, tattooed on chin and lips, attired in beautiful native garments of finely dressed flax—a *huaki* with its double flounce of *taniko* pattern about the shoulders, leaving the right arm bare, and a *korcwai* of white flax with dangling black dyed thrums around the waist. *Huia* feathers adorned her luxuriant black hair. She wielded a long spear-headed *taiaha*, and this she handled in true warrior fashion as she came running on at the head of her warriors, perfectly indifferent to danger. Yelling their *Pai-Marire* battle-cries, the Waikato Hauhaus made desperate endeavours to wrest the opposite trenches of the *pa* from the Arawa.'[2]

[1] Cowan.
[2] ibid.

21. *A dramatic picture of Volunteers in action at Te Ngutu.*

22. *Te Kooti in tribal dress.*

After a sharp firefight, Gilbert Mair's cool leadership, with his development of outflanking movements, out-generalled the beautiful Amazon and Waikato retreated. The Arawa lost a dashing young warrior of chiefly descent named Werimana who, after shooting a Hauhau, sprang forward with his clubbed musket crying 'Mine is the first fish', only to fall himself, mortally wounded with a bullet in the lungs.

'The last to leave the battlefield—as she had been the first to enter it—was the fearless chieftainess, brandishing her red feathered *taiaha*, and rolling her eyes in the warrior grimace of the *pukana* until the shelter of the thickets was reached.[1]

The Waikato left seven dead lying about the Te Koutu *pa* and in the relentless pursuit by the Arawa four more were shot dead, though the Waikato bore away the bodies. The Arawa, apart from Werimana's death, sustained only five wounded in this encounter.

In the meantime, the main Waikato Hauhau invasion force had settled down to build a *pa* at Puraku on the high wooded range that overlooked the whole Rotorua valley. To Puraku filtered back Hauhaus who had been fighting in the unsuccessful Piri-Rakau upheaval and they joined in the digging, hewing and erecting. But another, though unseen, visitor was Gilbert Mair who, with rare courage, climbed a spur of the lofty Ngongotaha mountain—called 'the Altar of God' and famous in Arawa folklore—to observe the enemy. At the end of March, a Government column composed of the 1st Waikato Regiment under Lieutenant-Colonel St John and 100 Arawa under Gilbert Mair assembled at Maketu and marched into the interior to check this growing threat to Rotorua, so well reported by Mair's intelligence activities. The appearance of 500 rifles, under the overall command of Lieutenant-Colonel Thomas McDonnell summoned from the West Coast, was too much for the Puraku Hauhaus, despite their imposing *pa*, and though in the attack plan Gilbert Mair had been allowed only two hours to get his Arawa to the rear cut-off positions when he had asked for four, the enemy fled after only token resistance. Even so, they lost eleven dead and many

[1] Cowan.

wounded, including their leader, Kihuti, who, shot through the hips, was borne away by his tribesmen to die a year later.

In the south of the Bay of Plenty during 1866, the Opotiki district was also subject to Hauhau marauding, with the Patea and Wanganui Rangers under Captain W. Newland well to the fore in several clashes. The leading character in these depredations was Eru Tamaikowha, an Urewera of the Ngatitama *hapu* who had fought at Maketu in 1864 and an oldtime savage with a liking for mutilation and cannibalism. To get *utu* for a success Newland and his Rangers had gained in March, 1866, at Kairakau *pa* up the Waioeka Gorge where they killed four Hauhaus and recovered much looted settler property, Tamaikowha embarked on a series of murderous ambushes. His first victim was Wi Popata, an Arawa mailman whose heart was cut out and eaten, then a settler, Bennett White, whose head was cut off and set on a rock by the Whakatane-Opotiki track and parts of his body removed for a cannibal feast. Finally, in May, 1867, he struck at four isolated military settlers at the mouth of Waioeka Gorge and though two escaped, the others were shot down, tomahawked and their hearts and livers cut out.

To meet the menace of Eru Tamaikowha and kindred desperadoes, local settlers with military experience formed the Opotiki Volunteer Rangers, well-armed with breech-loading carbines and revolvers, with Henry Mair, the third of the Mair brothers, as captain and J. R. Rushton and David White, two discharged veteran comrades from the Patea Rangers, as lieutenant and ensign. The Opotiki Rangers were a valuable reinforcement to the extended Militia under Lieutenant-Colonel St John, who led several expeditions in 1866 and 1867 against the wild Urewera country but though he inflicted some casualties in that difficult terrain, Tamaikowha held his ground and even made counter-forays towards the coast.

Meanwhile, in Wellington, Sir George Grey viewed with misgiving the departure during 1867 of all the remaining Imperial troops except the 18th Royal Irish. He was now steadily in conflict with Whitehall, as he reiterated that New Zealand's native wars were of Imperial concern, not to be foist on pioneer settlers and townsfolk. He was also at loggerheads with his own Ministers, though now, even the more virulent members of the war faction of 1860–63 were beginning to realise that Confiscation was an expensive policy.

In March and April, 1867, the 57th embarked at Auckland for England. In May, the 12th left the Bay of Plenty and sailed for home, but they left one tangible memory in New Zealand: the soldiers of the Regiment who took their discharge in the Colony, as many time-expired men of all the Regiments did, named the township they founded as military settlers on the Waikato river after their old Commanding Officer, Hamilton.

In June and July, the final five companies of the 50th sailed for Australia, two companies joining Headquarters at Sydney while the other three under Brevet Lieutenant-Colonel F. G. Hamley went to Adelaide. Soon after the 50th, Major-General Sir Trevor Chute, created a KCB after his epic Mount Egmont campaign, also departed from New Zealand to assume command of his full Australasian responsibilities at his normal headquarters in Sydney.

Only the 18th Royal Irish remained in New Zealand. In March, 1867, the Regiment was withdrawn from its redoubts throughout Wanganui and south Taranaki, and was concentrated in Wanganui Town until December when Headquarters and six companies moved to Auckland, with two companies each at Taranaki and Napier. During 1868, when an issue of modern Snider breech-loading rifles replaced muzzle-loading Enfields, the Headquarters remained at Auckland while the rest of the Regiment was:

'scattered throughout the Colony in small detachments after the fashion dear to nervous civilians but so detestable to Commanding Officers.'[1]

[1] *History of the British Army*, Vol. 13, Sir John Fortescue.

CHAPTER 17
Titokowaru

Eighteen hundred and sixty-seven was a quiet year and in April, the Colonial Office opportunely chose the lull to remind Sir George Grey that his tour of duty was soon to expire and thought now had to be given to the nomination of his successor. This heavy hint materialised into fact on 5 February, 1868, when Sir George Bowen, formerly Governor of Queensland, arrived in Wellington to relieve him.

Grey retired, Cincinnattus-like, to Kawau Island for several months, then left for England. His departure may well have pleased some members of the Colonial Government but doubtless it gave a greater convenience to Whitehall. The Imperial Government, harried by a parsimonious Parliament, was desperately seeking relief from its many overseas defence burdens; even the ceding of the Ionian Islands to Greece in 1863 had been avidly seized on as the saving of a garrison. By 1866, a severe recruiting crisis had assailed the British Army and Parliament took the momentous step of raising the daily pay of an Infantry private from 13 pence ($8\frac{1}{2}$ pence deducted for rations, $3\frac{1}{2}$ pence barrack damages and laundry, 1 penny for beer money) to 15 pence. Aware of this hardened attitude, the New Zealand Government even asked in 1866 for Sikhs, whose reputation after the Indian Mutiny was so high, to fight the hostile Maoris.

The new Governor was soon made aware of the crises of early New Zealand colonial life. Portents of trouble still simmered on the West Coast despite the uneasy calm, with inevitable interference to the survey of confiscated land in south Taranaki. In May, 1868, a mild but clear warning of impending strife was given when Mr Booth, Resident Magistrate at Patea, went to Te Ngutu-o-te-manu village to inquire about stolen horses and the chiefs were truculent and defiant. Clearer signs were soon to come. On 19 June three settlers felling timber on confiscated land by the Wai-ngongoro were murdered and on the following day a ration convoy was ambushed near Waihi redoubt, with two of the eleven escorting troopers wounded, for two Hauhaus killed. The climax came with the shooting and tomahawking of Trooper Smith while looking for a strayed horse near Waihi. His body was hacked in half and the upper portion taken away to Te Ngutu-o-te-manu ('The Parrot's Beak') to be eaten. Then a chilling message from the leader of the swelling numbers of warriors flocking to Te Ngutu was delivered to a neutral chief with the clear aim of promulgation to the *Pakeha*:

> 'Cease entirely travelling on the roads that lead to Mangamanga (Waihi camp) lest ye be left upon the roads as food for the birds of the air and beasts of the field, or for me. For I have eaten man—I have begun to eat the flesh of the white man; I have eaten him like the flesh of the cow, cooked in the pot; all have eaten him, even the women and children. My throat is continually open for the eating of human flesh by day and night.'[1]

The utterer of this awful warning was Titokowaru, a Ngaruahine chief who had lost an eye at Sentry Hill in '64. Despite the Biblical phraseology, he was also steeped in the old lore and he cleverly exploited the ancient beliefs that many Maoris were now groping back to in their bewilderment. As a terror weapon he encouraged cannibalism among the older warriors, but it is improbable that he ever ate human flesh himself as this would have tainted his personal *mana tapu*. With him at Te Ngutu was Kimble Bent, now the resourceful armourer and cartridge maker of the Ngatiruanui.

Seven miles away from Te Ngutu was an old dilapidated redoubt of Turuturu-Mokai, built by the 18th Regiment in '66. After the murder of the timber-cutters it was re-occupied by a garrison of 25 Armed Constabulary and volunteer military

[1] Cowan.

settlers under Captain George Ross, but they had little time to repair the neglected defences. Before dawn on 15 July a war party of sixty picked Hauhau warriors struck. Very swiftly, Ross, armed with sword and revolver, and the canteen-keeper, Lennon, were cut down by the gateway; incredibly, in this hostile country, they lived outside the redoubt in *whares*. The modest garrison, mostly Irishmen and including three old soldiers from the 57th and 65th, tumbled out to man the five-foot parapet, protected by a wide ditch and set about an epic defence. Three men did behave abominably, jumping from the parapet and fleeing for their lives, but one was caught and despatched by the tribesmen. Within two hours ten defenders had died and another six were wounded, including George Tuffin of the Wanganui Rangers who was to endure five wounds. Among the Hauhaus was yet another white renegade, Charles Kane, a deserter from the 18th, and it is thought that a shot from him killed the younger of the two Beamish brothers in the redoubt. He was to die violently himself later, tomahawked by the Ngatiruanui on suspicion of planning the murder of Titokowaru to gain a pardon.

As the battle raged the desperate defenders wondered when relief would arrive from Waihi a mere 2½ miles away. There the firing was heard and von Tempsky, the senior officer, called out his own 5 Company, Armed Constabulary, but left abruptly without giving orders to others of his command, such as the Volunteer Cavalry. He set off on a circuitous route which took him a long time to reach the gory shambles of Turuturu, arriving at 7 am; possibly he was apprehensive of running into ambushes if he took the direct track. However, bitter later recriminations turned not on the dilatory relief, which could be laid against von Tempsky, but on the mounted men's savage accusations against their own commander, Major William Hunter, who told his waiting troopers, straining to ride to the relief of their comrades, to unsaddle. Clearly, if the horsemen had been launched, valuable lives would have been saved. A subsequent court-martial acquitted Hunter, but the stigma bit deeply.

The attack on Turuturu could only mean a demand for *utu* from Thomas McDonnell. He waited impatiently until the newly-enlisted Wellington Rangers and Wellington Rifles, 150 strong, joined him, but finally at dawn on 21 August he mustered a force of 350, consisting of detachments of 2, 3, 5 Companies, Armed Constabulary, totalling 110 men, the Wellington new-chums, 32 Taranaki Volunteer Militia, 18 Patea Yeomanry Cavalry and a number of unenlisted hard cases who had come along for the fight. The punitive expedition set off in two columns, one commanded by von Tempsky and the other by William Hunter, accompanied by a French Catholic Priest, Father Jean Baptiste Roland (whose bush trek map had been of paramount importance in Duncan Cameron's Wanganui campaign), crossed the swollen Wai-Ngongoro and marched on Te Ngutu-o-te-manu.

However, McDonnell's direct, though cautious, approach through the bush was detected and the final rush found a deserted village with only one unfortunate Hauhau trapped inside a *whare*. But as McDonnell's men burned the *whares* and blew up gunpowder casks and muskets the many warriors who had faded into the bush began regrouping. The hazards of deep penetration into close forest began to bear down on the expedition as con-certed and menacing fire came against the column, moving sinisterly along its flanks. A running fight developed to extricate the operation and the heavy, fast-flowing Wai-Ngongoro did not help. McDonnell's casualties were four killed and eight wounded, for possibly seven Hauhau dead, and though he had penetrated to Te Ngutu, he had hit air and crisis had rebounded on him as the day lengthened.

With typical determination, he mounted another operation to destroy Titokowaru on 7 September. Again from Waihi he led 360 men out at midnight in bitter weather in three columns: the first under von Tempsky, consisting of 75 men of 2 and 5 Divi-sions AC., 14 Patea Rifle Volunteers, 45 Wellington Rifles, 26 Taranaki Rifle Volunteers and 2 gallant characters euphemis-tically called Waihi volunteers; the second, under Major William Hunter, composed of 32 men of 3 Division A.C., 65 Wellington Rangers and 11 Patea Cavalry (dismounted), while the third was the welcome return of 110 warriors of the Wanganui Native Contingent under Kepa and Captain William McDonnell.

To gain surprise, the plan of attack was much more ambitious.

The approach march would go deep into the forest and then swing around on Te Ngutu to take it from the rear. It was an imaginative and courageous concept, but by the afternoon the wide flanking march was deeply embedded in a great *rata* forest. Then a track was met and Kepa sent one of his Wanganui up a tall tree from where he sighted smoke from a village. Though in this march no one was certain where they were, they were in fact exactly in rear of their objective, and further down the track they overran a sentry *whare*, where a warrior who rushed out was shot. So, tragically, were two children, though another was saved and was carried safely on a broad Wanganui back for the rest of the hard day yet to come.

The sound of gunfire reverberating through the forest alerted Titokowaru who sent the women and children, accompanied by his armourer, Kimble Bent, to refuge in the bush while he despatched his warriors to engage the approaching enemy. Soon von Tempsky's men and part of Hunter's division came under heavy fire from Hauhaus well concealed behind logs and trees and in the undergrowth. After Kepa had confirmed that they were almost on Te Ngutu, a strange malaise seems to have gripped McDonnell. Casualties were falling fast, some of the indifferent Wellington recruits were breaking to the rear, but now, the time for emphatic action, nothing came from him. A forceful order to storm would have had a salutary effect on men beginning to look over their shoulders for lack of orders, but McDonnell had lost control. Captain Buck, a former officer of the 14th Regiment now commanding the Wellington Rangers, 'Buck's Bruisers,' asked: 'Where are the axes? Why don't we charge the *pa*?'

Meanwhile von Tempsky paced up and down, waiting impatiently with William Hunter for the permission to attack they had both requested. But McDonnell was obsessed by the number of his casualties and could only think of extricating his men. Disaster now piled on disaster. Von Tempsky, as he chafed at the indecision, grew careless in his anger and was stalked and shot dead, as were another eight of his men. They were finished off with a tomahawk charge led by Katene Tu-whakararu, whose children had been killed by the Wanganui that day. They took the curved sword, cap, watch and revolver of this well-known *Pakeha* warrior. Meanwhile within Te Ngutu, the ferocious one-eyed Titokowaru breathed more fire to his warriors, crying, 'Kill them! Eat them!'

McDonnell's second attack on Te Ngutu degenerated into a major Hauhau victory. He decided on retreat to Waihi by the most direct compass route which led through wild and terrible country. Exultant Hauhaus were now cutting out the hearts of the fallen enemy, while some forty men of the untrained Wellington Rangers were already well on their way back to Waihi, which they reached several hours in advance of those who had fought. As disintegration of the force set in, one heroic figure stood out as the despair and misery of defeat closed about bewildered men. He was Captain J. M. Roberts, a veteran of the Forest Rangers in the Waikato campaign with von Tempsky. He gave James Cowan what is probably the only eye-witness account of a confused and tragic day:

> 'To this day, I do not know precisely why Colonel McDonnell decided to retire as he did, leaving the rest of us without definite orders. We could have taken the *pa*, I believe. We were handicapped, however, by the presence of some unfit men, particularly the Wellington Rangers; their officers were very good, but the men should not have been sent into the bush . . . The new men crowded together, and in consequence made easy targets for the Maoris.'[1]

As the indefatigable Roberts struggled about the bush, endeavouring to find out what was happening, McDonnell had already ordered out the wounded, while he followed with a main party of eighty. Father Roland, with several bullet holes torn through his hat, did splendid work with the surgeons, and Kepa and some of his best men fought nobly in the hard-pressed rearguard as the triumphant Hauhaus closed around the broken column. Roberts resumes his story: he had set off to contact von Tempsky:

> 'I went along the flank two or three chains towards the creek that ran in rear of the *pa*. I saw nothing of von Tempsky, but he must have been lying close by. It was all dense bush here, with

[1] Cowan.

201

some very large *mahoe* trees—the biggest I had ever seen—and some *rata*. At last I turned to come back, and just as I did so a bullet buried itself in a sapling behind me. I made my way towards the place where I had left Captain Buck a quarter of an hour previously, and I found him lying on his back, dead. I got together all the men I could find and disposed them as well as I could to resist the Hauhaus, who were pressing us hard, yelling "Surround them, surround them!" in Maori. I formed the men into a rough half-moon front, and instructed them to fire volleys—"Blaze away as hard as you can, boys, blaze away!" We fired a number of volleys, and this had a great effect on the Hauhaus, who kept a greater distance after that.

By this time it was getting quite dusk in the bush, under the close, dense foliage. I came to the conclusion that I had better try to make my way out to camp with the wounded. I had heard firing on my right and knew it must be McDonnell fighting his way back to Waihi. There were eleven wounded, but most of them could walk. My total strength now was fifty-eight men. Sergeant Russell fell shot through the hip; he was a fine, brave fellow. We had to leave him lying there propped up against a tree, with a loaded revolver in his hand. We had some faint hopes of rescuing him later, but the Hauhaus got him, after he stood them off at first with his revolver . . .

I kept my men together as well as I could in the bush, and got my wounded along; we went very slowly, occasionally turning to fire. I don't think we were travelling more than half a mile in the hour. All of us now were very exhausted, and I ordered the men to sit down in the bush undergrowth for a rest, waiting till the moon rose, so that I could fix my course . . . We were still within cooee of the *pa*; in fact, we could hear the Hauhaus' yells and warsongs all night, we were that close. About 2 o'clock in the morning the moon rose over the treetops, and now I had an idea of the points of the compass, I made a start again."[1]

Roberts led his gallant remnants into Waihi about 8 am, after coming on the track to the Wai-ngongoro at dawn and meeting soon afterwards a delighted Kepa who had gone back with 60 Wanganui to look for him. He had a worthy compliment paid to him by his friend, Captain Brown, when that officer rushed out to shake his hand: 'Some of them said you were all killed, Roberts, but I knew you'd turn up because you know the bush.'

On the day after the fight, Hauhau exultation at their con-

[1] Cowan.

siderable victory reached fever pitch at Te Ngutu. Bodies of twenty white men had been brought in from the forest, including von Tempsky's, before the brooding figure of Titokowaru, who ordered their destruction in a great pyre outside the *pa*. As the logs were piled about the bodies Titokowaru delivered an oration to the fallen warrior, von Tempsky (called *Manu-rau*, or 'Many Birds', from his guerrilla prowess), against the barbaric setting of this Antipodean Viking's Funeral:

'In the days of the past you fought here and you fought there, and you boasted that you would always emerge safely from your battles to the bright life of the world. But when you encountered me, your eyes were closed in their last sleep. It could not be helped; you sought death at my hands. And now you sleep for ever.'[1]

Titokowaru's homily in the poetical and chivalrous vein of the old Maori warrior was reported by Kimble Bent who also stated that one body was reserved for eating.

The repercussions of defeat at Te Ngutu were far-reaching. A Press outcry demanded the dismissal of McDonnell and the crisis rocked the Stafford Ministry. From Hawke's Bay, however, Colonel George Whitmore, the victor over Te Rangihiroa and a Member of the Legislative Assembly, wrote to defend McDonnell and advised the despatch of the experienced 1 Division A.C. from the East Coast to reinforce the shattered forces in south Taranaki. He also offered to accompany the Defence Minister, Colonel Haultain, on his proposed visit to the front and even to serve there under McDonnell, his junior.

When Haultain arrived at Waihi he found conditions appalling. The small hospital was crowded with sick and wounded, the treatment was inadequate and even the staunch Wanganui were dispirited by Titokowaru's *mana*. Haultain, in consultation with McDonnell, ordered the abandonment of Waihi and a drastic withdrawal along the coast to Patea. But even this operation had its tragedies: two Government parties fired on each other in the bush, killing Captain Smith, another von Tempsky veteran, and one outlying military settler, Sandy McCulloch, driving in his sheep, was cut off by Hauhaus near Kakaramea and mur-

[1] Cowan.

dered, his bones being found later in a swamp. The Wanganui returned disconsolately to their homes and handed their arms in to store.

Thomas McDonnell, disgusted by his failure before Te Ngutu, resigned and Whitmore assumed command. This wiry and energetic former Regular officer was offensively minded, too, but he was also a strict disciplinarian who immediately set about reorganizing the demoralized force at Patea. The mutinous 5 Division was disbanded and the ill-trained and ineffective levies from Wellington and Nelson sent packing with their discharges. He exorcised the effects of the Demon Drink from the depressed Volunteers by loading stocks of confiscated liquor on board the steamer *Sturt* for Wanganui, and endeavoured to restore discipline and morale in Patea, now crowded with refugee settlers and their stock.

Meanwhile, Titokowaru left Te Ngutu and advanced boldly south to the Patea river, gathering Pakakohe and Ngatihine recruits as he moved. In early November Whitmore heard with some alarm that he had reached the Waitotara. Consequently, Whitmore shifted his base to Wairoa to prevent raids into the rich, settled areas south of the Waitotara. Titokowaru began to fortify a camp at Moturoa, several miles inland and below Okotuku, one of Chute's actions in '66, and Whitmore determined to attack him before he became too strong. When the new 6 Division of the Armed Constabulary, composed of young, hardy men enlisted from Auckland and the Thames goldfields, marched into camp on 6 November under the hero of Te Ngutu, Captain John Roberts, Whitmore was so cheered by their purposeful appearance that he decided to attack the next day.

At midnight, in misty, showery weather, the column marched out from Wairoa, 250 men drawn from 1, 2, 3 and 6 Divisions A.C., the Patea Cavalry (dismounted), some Patea Rifles and Wairoa Militia and also 300 recently-returned Wanganui under Kepa. Before dawn Whitmore halted three miles out to form a firm base for his reserve ammunition, medical stores and personal haversacks, guarded by his Wairoa Militia under an experienced local man, Captain Hawes, and as dawn came the rest of the force threaded its way along a bullock cart track towards Moturoa. The Hauhau *pa* was built across a neck of land between a deep wooded gully and a large level expanse of forest, with the high, timbered tableland of Okotuku about a mile away in rear, but though well sited it was only partially built. Only the front fence of the stockade, about twelve feet high, with three wooden redoubts capable of holding about twenty men, had been finished, running across the cleared ground and then jutting off in a short arm to the gully. The tragedy of Moturoa was that Whitmore did not conduct a proper reconnaissance to discover this false front.

As the attackers slipped silently along the skirting of the bush not a sound or movement came from the *pa*, no dogs barked, no women appeared to gather firewood, and it was obvious to the old hands that this unusual and eerie silence meant that they were expected. One of Whitmore's lesser gifts was his handling of his native allies, as he had no comprehension of their minds or understanding of their language as McDonnell did, and in this instance only Kepa and some 80 Wanganui were used in the action, due to umbrage being taken by most of the Native Contingent. Whitmore sent most of 1 Division A.C. and Kepa's men to the timber on the right flank and prepared to assault frontally with 3 Division and the Patea men under Major William Hunter. 6 Division under Roberts, nicknamed 'the Young Division', were to follow the stormers in close support.

Whitmore gave the signal for the assault and Hunter led his men in a fierce rush across the stump-strewn, fern-covered ground for the *pa*. The Hauhaus, lining their trenches behind the palisade and the parapets of the three redoubts, watched in grim silence until the leading wave of attackers was a mere fifteen yards away. Then a veritable sheet of fire spewed from the whole length of the stockade wall and the stormers were shattered. The gallant Hunter, with a death wish from the allegations of neglect of duty at the relief of Turuturu-Mokai, ran along the whole length of the wall seeking an entry point and was shot dead. 6 Division came doubling up, moving towards the right flank where a fierce firefight was developing, skirmishing behind logs and stumps, but a large enemy party had also worked its way into the timber preventing Kepa and his men from moving around to the false rear of the stockade. Whitmore, shaken by the decimation of his assault, now ordered his bugler to sound the retire. Gradually the embattled firing lines worked their way back to their start point, carrying the bodies of the dead and wounded, except for four dead men who lay too dangerously close to the palisade, and the exultant Hauhaus began jumping the palisade to follow up. Fierce volleys from the Young Division checked them, and the only known Hauhau casualty of the day, an old naked tattooed savage, was killed then.

Meanwhile, a detachment of 2 Division had been engaged in picqueting the deep gully on the left of the *pa* against infiltration around that flank and were soon hotly engaged, holding their rim of the gully for some time after the retreat began. The commander of this detachment was Corporal Talty, an Irish veteran of the 57th with Indian Mutiny and Crimean service, who had also been at Te Ngutu as a colonial volunteer, and William Wallace, one of his men, paid tribute to him to James Cowan:

'Corporal Talty handled us as coolly as if he was on parade. We retired by sections, each one in turn keeping the enemy engaged while the other reloaded and retired a certain distance.'

Outside the *pa* the victorious Hauhaus cut the heart out of one of the bodies left, set fire to it and as the wind blew the smoke in the direction of the retreat, followed up howling with bloodlust to repeat the rout of Te Ngutu. But 1 and 6 Divisions covering the retreat moved with complete steadiness, like Cpl Talty's admirable detachment, alternating between taking up a stand and passing through the other division, which was then in a fire position. The Hauhaus followed the retreat past Hawes' temporary entrenchments almost to Wairoa redoubt and only desisted when the Armstrong guns were brought out to shell, though some daring warriors penetrated to within rifle range of the redoubt.

As the wildly excited Hauhaus streamed back to Moturoa, frenzied scenes of dancing, war songs, and waving captured uniform and equipment were enacted. The abandoned bodies were dragged onto a triumphant funeral pyre and again one was eaten.

Profound gloom once more settled over the Government's military fortunes. Among the tired and baffled men at Wairoa, this was aggravated by again having left bodies in the field. Moturoa certainly was the worst military reverse in Wanganui, for the casualty list was 19 killed, 20 wounded. Much of the bitter taste came from opinion that George Whitmore, normally full of bounce and aggression, had lost his nerve before the day was far from lost. James Cowan recounts the testimony of an officer who was in the rearguard:

'I could never understand why we left the Maori position at Moturoa so soon. We had the day before us. We should have surrounded it and stayed there. Losing a few men was no reason for retreating; we should have stuck to it. It was bad management—you couldn't blame the men; they all behaved well. I don't know to this day why we retreated. We could not have had a better fighting ground. We were only three and a half miles from our base; we had a good force and plenty of ammunition. It was easy country, mostly level and open and only a little bush. Te Ngutu-o-te-manu was different; there we were far from our base in dense bush. Guns could easily have been taken in along the bullock-track through the belt of bush right up to the Moturoa clearing.'[1]

Whitmore now fell back behind the Waitotara, leaving Fraser and 1 Division with local men to garrison Patea. Wairoa redoubt, rationed with one month's supplies, and its surroundings were crowded with refugee settlers. Whitmore, conscious that he commanded the Colony's only field force, though two companies of the 18th Regiment were stationed in Wanganui Town, re-occupied Nukumaru entrenched camp while inland the victorious Titokowaru marched almost in parallel to begin work on an elaborate fortified position at Tauranga-ika. Colonel Haultain, the Defence Minister, visited Wanganui and agreed with Whitmore's request for yet another withdrawal: the evacuation of 50 Wanganui Militia from exposed Weraroa. After his summary defeat Whitmore offered the Minister his resignation, which was refused.

At Nukumaru recruits and reinforcements, including 7 Division under Captain Brown, poured in and the ration strength

[1] Cowan.

rose to 350. However, from the Governor and Haultain, who were both now in Wanganui, startling orders came to Whitmore: he was to give up even more ground and retire behind the Kai-iwi. No reason was given but Whitmore obeyed at once, helping settlers on the Waitotara to remove their stock. The only territory between the Wai-ngongoro and the Kai-iwi now commanded by the Government was within rifle-shot range of the Patea and Wairoa redoubts, with communication kept open to these outposts by two local cavalry troops composed of farmers and their sons.

Whitmore then received even more dramatic instructions. Wanganui was to be left to a holding operation by local forces under Lieutenant Colonels William Lyon and Thomas McDonnell, while he sailed with 200 Armed Constabulary on 2 December for the East Coast. A terrible massacre had occurred at Poverty Bay where 70 men, women and children had been murdered by hostile Maoris. The instigator of this outrage was an escaped Chatham Island convict whom Whitmore had fought before—Te Kooti.

CHAPTER 18

Te Kooti

A<small>T</small> dusk, 10 July, 1868, the schooner *Rifleman* slipped into Whareongaonga cove south of Poverty Bay and began disgorging 163 Maoris with their women and children. That well-known local character, Te Kooti, had achieved a brilliant mass escape from the scandalously-run convict settlement at the Chatham Islands. With him came many Hauhaus, loaded with captured arms, ammunition, provisions, liquor and £500 in cash. By the power of his shrewd intellect and driving nature Te Kooti had gained complete ascendancy over his fellow exiles and true to the fashion of the day had even founded a new religion to cement his influence, a careful amalgam of *Pai-Marire* and the Bible. Among the desperadoes who scrambled off the seized *Rifleman* were Te Rangitahau and Nikora, the Ngatihineuru chief, who had both been captured at Omarunui in '66.

Two days elapsed before Major Biggs, Resident Magistrate at Poverty Bay, heard this astonishing news. The European skipper of the *Rifleman* when released by his dangerous consignment had incomprehensibly sailed for Auckland without stopping to give the alarm. Biggs at once sent messages to Wairoa and Napier for reinforcements, called out the local Mounted Rifles commanded by ex-Forest Ranger Captain Westrup, and despatched a Rongowhakaata chief to Te Kooti to ask for his surrender. Te Kooti refused, protesting blandly that he only wished for peaceful passage to the Waikato, and on 15 July marched inland

o   209 for the immediate sanctuary of the Urewera mountains. Biggs decided to intercept the escapees at Paparatu.

His plan was to prove a dismal failure. On 20 July Biggs had to leave Westrup's column of 50 Europeans and 30 friendly Rongowhakaata under chief Henare Kakapango to hurry up an urgently needed ration party. He had barely gone when Te Kooti and his well-armed host, moving very slowly with all their loot from the schooner, came straggling through the bush towards Paparatu. Action was soon joined and went on intermittently all day, but by nightfall Westrup's force, with only 30 rounds per rifle, had lost two killed and six wounded. He was now cut off from the reserve ammunition in the valley below and the half-starving, inexperienced men were demoralized and tired. During the night many of the friendly Maoris decamped and retreat was the only prospect. Led by Henare Kakapango in a nightmare journey through swamps and creeks and over hillsides in the inky darkness, the exhausted and famished men carrying two of the wounded reached Westrup's own outstation at Tapatoho at dawn.

As the 40 men rested, Colonel Whitmore came in with 20 Napier Volunteers and 40 Ngatikahungunu. The enthusiastic Whitmore exhorted the drained-out Poverty Bay men to join him at once in the pursuit and the blunt refusal he received shocked him to launching into a savage castigation of the Paparatu survivors that rankled for a long time. But greater damage had been done at Paparatu than the soured relations between Whitmore and the Poverty Bay men. Te Kooti's early and salutary little victory, mainly executed by Te Rangitahau and Nikora, gained him much *mana* as well as the booty of abandoned horses, weapons and ammunition.

Whitmore also had trouble with his own Napier men and, after conducting a court-martial of doubtful legality, with the President using a biscuit tin to write his proceedings on, he had the ringleaders marched away under escort to Turanganui and shipped back to Napier. With this disaffection among his Volunteers, Whitmore judiciously waited until Major James Fraser's 1 Division A.C. came up and until Biggs and Westrup had re-organised the Poverty Bay force. Meanwhile, a gallant attempt by

Captain Richardson and Lieutenant Preece, with a mixed Volunteer and Maori contingent from Wairoa, to check Te Kooti's march failed dismally at Te Koneke on 24 July through scarcity of ammunition and a marked lack of enthusiasm by the Wairoa natives.

Eventually, on 31 July, Whitmore moved out of the Te Arai valley with a force of 200 and began a relentless pursuit of the slow-moving Te Kooti by a direct line over rugged terrain, hampered by snow showers and rain-swollen streams. On 5 August the column had reached the Hangaroa River, having come across the body of Paku Brown, a well-connected half-caste mailman, who had been murdered by Te Kooti, with the carcass of his dog thrown across his body as an insult; this had a depressing effect on the Poverty Bay Maoris. The Poverty Bay Europeans now confronted Whitmore with the fact that as the expedition was moving out of their district they would have to leave, and the furious Whitmore let them go, consoling himself with remembered lines from *Henry V*: 'He which hath no stomach to this fight, Let him depart.' Some stouter members of this contingent stayed, including the only doctor, and Whitmore left these to protect a base camp with the horses and heavy stores, then pushed on, passing through old camp sites Te Kooti had used until his remaining worn and hungry men were also coming to the verge of mutiny. On 8 August, just as the rations were about to run out, in the gorge of the Ruakituri a reconnaissance party under Captain Carr, the ex-Regular who had fought at Omarunui, and Mr Davis Canning, both Hawke's Bay settlers, came dramatically on Te Kooti's camp.

This news infused fresh spirit into the hard-tried expedition and the column set out in single file along the river gorge for several miles, but when they reached the bend where the track led out of the defile rifle fire from a strong picquet swept into them. The column tried to fight its way through the icy stream, dodging behind boulders, but the steep banks denied any exit except the track commanded by Te Kooti's men. A furious exchange of fire developed between the frustrated and pinned-down Government forces and the Hauhaus, who were now being reinforced in strength by their main body. It was soon reported

211

to Whitmore that both Carr and Canning, in the van, had been killed, and Captain Tuke, who was trying to organise a charge to break out of the riverbed, had been wounded. Whitmore could only now retreat, as he had sustained five killed and five wounded and the weight of the Hauhau strength was beginning to tell. But the enemy were also disconcerted as Te Kooti had been wounded in the foot and, with eight dead and two others wounded, withdrawal was in the air there, too. It took all the ebbing strength of Whitmore's men to get their wounded over the torrent and march back through the night to their primitive base.

Despite his wound Te Kooti spread the word of yet another humiliation for the *Pakeha* and many believed him. He moved to nearby Puketapu where he rested and planned, secure in the knowledge that he was temporarily safe and attracted many recruits to his leadership. Whitmore and his forlorn force returned disconsolately to Poverty Bay, except Fraser's 1 Division which went to Wairoa, but even he permitted himself a stony smile when he entered the township and saw the walls daubed with: 'The Gravedigger has arrived', a resentful illusion to his celebrated aside at the bush court-martial of the truculent Napier men: 'Sergeant-major, are those men ready with the spades yet?'

Whitmore left for the West Coast and his first encounter with Titokowaru. An uneasy quiet settled over the disturbed districts inland from Wairoa and Poverty Bay until October, when two young chiefs of the Ngatikahungunu were murdered with two of their men as they slept at Whataroa while scouting up the Wairoa.

Donald McLean was acutely aware of the menace Te Kooti posed and that month he arranged for 200 Ngatiporou under Ropata to come down to Wairoa. A large column under a recovered Captain Tuke, consisting of Ropata's warriors, many Ngatikahungunu led by Tareha and Henare Tomoana and forty Armed Constabulary under Lieutenants Ferguson and Preece, set out for Puketapu but moving up the Waiapu valley Tuke was overtaken by Lieutenant-Colonel Lambert, newly appointed to command Wairoa District. At deserted Whataroa the bodies of the four murdered scouts were dug up and an old man and woman left in the village warned Lambert that Te Kooti had left Puketapu and was moving on Poverty Bay. Ropata and the European officers urged Lambert to follow hard in pursuit but the new commander was apprehensive of moving into ambushes and losing heavily. He ordered a return to Wairoa, despite Ropata's acid remark: 'We do not expect to return with the same number of men with which we started.'

Te Kooti was indeed moving on Poverty Bay. He had long been convinced that he had been unjustly transported by local Europeans jealous of his trading success and he was now going to exact a terrible revenge. Rumour had been strong for some time that he intended to attack the two settlements of Turanganui and Matawhero and Biggs and his local militia were tense and vigilant. However, during the night of 9 November Te Kooti led his murderous band, all mounted and well-armed, along an old overgrown war-track that Biggs, usually so prudent, had told Lieutenant Gascoygne not to waste any of his limited scouts watching. Before midnight Biggs and his whole family were dead, butchered by the terror that descended suddenly and silently out of the night, as were 33 other European men, women and children and 37 friendly Maoris.

The marauders had split up into various parties to murder, loot and burn over the whole locality, which was soon lit up by the blaze of fired homesteads. Terrified farmers and citizens fled into the haven of the bush or made their way to the bay to find a boat. Gascoygne dashed in with his few men from his abortive vigil but he was quickly outnumbered and cut off and had to abandon his horses to escape, also by boat, across the water.

Te Kooti gathered up his plunder from among the devastation and with his prisoners, captured arms, ammunition and horses, withdrew to the hills. Captains Westrup and Tuke came from Napier with some European volunteers and many Ngatikahungunu and cleared through the area burying the dead, while the horror of the massacre sent a grim shudder through the whole of North Island as the news spread. With news of military disaster coming from the West Coast and now the rise of an evil star on the East, fresh outcries were soon heard against the Self-

Reliant Policy. Anxious thoughts turned on the imminent departure of the sole remaining Imperial regiment, the 18th Royal Irish. Though constrained from taking the field by orders to remain in their garrisons, the 18th was still a symbol of solidity and security in troubled days, physically indicating commitment by the Mother Country.

The tireless Gascoygne followed up Te Kooti with 450 Ngatikahungunu under their chiefs Renata Kawepo and Karauria and on 20 November surprised the enemy rearguard at Patutahi, killing two. Two days later Gascoygne came upon Te Kooti's main body at Makaretu and after initial skirmishing both opposing forces dug in on adjacent ridgelines. The Ngatikahungunu lost four killed, including Karauria, and about 12 wounded, but the enemy had similar casualties, and Gascoygne was content to hold Te Kooti for several days as he hoped that reinforcements would soon reach after him. But the astute Te Kooti used the time brilliantly: he sent a strong raiding party, under a blood-thirsty half-caste, Peka te Makarini, rearwards to Gascoygne's base and captured 12,000 rounds of ammunition.

Meanwhile, on 25 November Donald McLean had launched a pincer movement from Wairoa of 200 Ngatiporou led by Ropata and Hotene Porourangi and 170 local Ngatikahungunu under Lieutenant Preece up the Wairoa via Te Reinga to the Hangaroa to get behind Te Kooti while the Poverty Bay Force drove forward. On the 28th the force had reached Tarewa and as no intelligence was waiting, Preece and the chiefs decided to move to Turanganui where they arrived on 1 December and were informed of the fight at Makaretu. Two days later Te Kooti's position was attacked by the Ngatiporou and Ngatika-hungunu with great zest :

' "It was a beautiful sight," wrote Gascoygne, "a line of fire and smoke a half a mile long, with both flanks thrown forward, rapidly ascending the hill." The men closed on the centre as they approached the Hauhau entrenchments, and a deadly fire was concentrated on the camp. The Hauhaus fought well until the final rush, when they dashed out of their entrenchments and across the river, leaving two score dead and dying in the captured position. A number were shot in the river immediately in rear. Among those who fell was the notorious Nama, who had been concerned in the murder of Karaitiana and his three comrades at Whataroa; he was mortally wounded by Henare Kakapango, one of Gascoygne's scouts.'

Nama's death was unpleasant; he was dragged, wounded, over a fire by the Ngatikahungunu in vengeance for the murder of their young chief. Te Kooti's force lost about sixty killed in this sharp and sorely-needed Government victory, for only one Ngatiporou killed and two Europeans wounded; Te Kooti himself had to be carried away ignominiously, as he had damaged his old foot wound in the rocky river bed. The rebels retreated six miles to the mountain fortress of Ngatapa, a dominating and historic *pa* 2,000 feet above sea level, which had been rapidly restored while the forward lines at Makaretu were held. Once safe in this formidable stronghold, flanked by precipitous gorges and with a sheer drop of several hundreds of feet at its rear, Te Kooti waited with 300 fighting men.

Preece, Ropata and Hotene soon closed about Ngatapa and on 5 December mounted the first attack. Ropata and Preece, having climbed the great bush-covered forward slope, gained some outerworks with a few men and hung on all one night, but most of the Ngatiporou and Ngaitkahungunu remained inactive in the valley below despite Preece journeying down the mountain in the night to cajole them. Three Hauhaus were known to have been killed, but shortage of ammunition forced the gallant lodgement to be abandoned and Preece could only call the operation off. As the unhappy force trailed back to Turanganui, Colonel Whitmore met them at Patutahi with 300 Armed Constabulary from the West Coast and the newly-raised 8 Division of Arawas under Captain Grundry. Whitmore, true to form, immediately called on the retiring Maoris to join him in a fresh attempt on Ngapata but the response was far from enthusiastic. Ropata told Whitmore that he was disgusted with his own tribe and wished to return to Waiapu to enlist new men. He added in a burst of temper that he would then return to attack the Ngatikahungunu who had failed to support him. Whitmore, whose abrupt manner did not usually seek or gain any *rapport* with Maoris, agreed with Ropata and so the whole expedition settled down at Makaretu for the Ngatiporou to return.

After Ropata had left, Whitmore sent scouts off to Ngatapa who came back with reports that Te Kooti was evacuating the *pa* as the hilltop was ablaze with burning *whares*. With this intelligence, Whitmore re-embarked 6 Division on the *Sturt* to return to the West Coast, but Roberts' men were soon landed again as the *Sturt* holed herself, very fortuitously, as Te Kooti's burning programme was only to clear fields of fire in front of his *pa*. To emphasise his presence, on 13 December he raided down towards Te Arai killing two Europeans and one friendly Maori; as he withdrew to Ngapata Whitmore was advancing to Patutahi again and he ran into a mounted patrol of sixteen troopers under Captain Newland, who unfortunately were too weak to attack.

By 31 December Whitmore, now rejoined by Ropata, was ready to move on Ngatapa. He approached the mountain fastness along the same high ground until a ravine halted his advance half a mile from the *pa*, and here he positioned a Coehorn mortar. He then disposed his force of 400 Armed Constabulary and 350 Ngatiporou about the wedge-shaped *pa*, whose apex merged into the razorback ridge at the summit of the hill, though many men were committed to protecting the base camp in the valley and toiling forward with ammunition, water and supplies. It was evident that much work had been done since the first attack; apart from the cleared front, three very thick parapet lines now ran across the broad bases of the wedge.

The first phase of Whitmore's assault plan next day was brilliantly successful. In a brisk attack that afternoon Captain Grundry's Arawas and Captain T. W. Porter, at the head of picked Ngatiporou, supported by 7 Division, captured a vital waterspring that served the *pa*. By nightfall Whitmore's own headquarters were established 300 yards behind this front line. James Fraser's experienced 1 Division worked their way along the flanking slopes to the razorback rear and touching in with Ngatiporou under Hotene, formed a siege line 700 yards long with Roberts' 6 Division, except for about 70 yards of sheer precipice. In front, flying saps were dug to the enemy's main front parapet as three days and nights of total investment developed with the Coehorn mortar lobbing its bombs into the *pa* from across the ravine. A steady trickle of casualties, however, began to occur among the besiegers from the well-protected marksmen in the *pa*, and Captain Brown of 7 Division was mortally wounded.

Fraser's 1 Division in the rear had an exciting time as some of his men, notably Maori Sergeant Heteraka and Constables Benjamin Biddle and Solomon Black, climbed up to fire positions among the rock terraces at the very summit of Ngatapa. This dramatic occupation caused much agitation among Ngatapa's defenders and several desperate sorties were made to dislodge the men. All were beaten off and Nikora was badly wounded leading one of the attempts.

On the afternoon of 4 January Whitmore made the preliminary moves for a main assault. Thirty men of 7 Division under Gascoygne dashed through belting rain, gale-force winds and enemy bullets to secure a position near the outer parapet, while Ropata led a picked band of fifty Ngatiporou and Arawa down into the right flank ravine to proceed along its bed and climb slowly up the cliff face so that they would come up at a close assault position where the *pa* turned along the ravine edge. Their tortuous progress was detected by Te Kooti's riflemen who crowded to that flank to shoot down at them as they crouched among the rocks. At last they surged out of their final position with a cheer, lodged under its shelter and dug furiously through with their spades to open a raking fire on the trenchwork inside, and finally scrambled through their mouseholes to seize the trenchline.

Eight enemy were killed in this smartly-managed operation and Ropata lost about the same. Night set in and Whitmore proceeded to sap to the inner lines intending to blow in the next parapet and assault through the breach at dawn. However, during the wet and windy night a woman's voice was heard calling from the *pa* at about 2 am that Te Kooti had gone. As she would not emerge the impasse lasted until dawn when the whole Government line advanced suspiciously.

Te Kooti had indeed departed, as he realised after the loss of the spring that his situation was hopeless. The defenders of Ngatapa had escaped by shinning sixty feet down *aka* or bush-vine ropes in the dark down the unguarded sheer drop to where

THE MAORI WARS

the mountain side offered a possible footing. The wounded abandoned in the *pa* were ruthlessly despatched by the Ngatiporou and Ropata suggested an immediate pursuit. Whitmore readily agreed and the Ngatiporou and Arawa set off down the mountainside into the bush, splitting into small parties as they quickly detected the fugitives had. Many prisoners were taken in the hunt and all were summarily shot, with the Europeans looking the other way; the massacre of Poverty Bay was too fresh in their minds to muster any righteous thoughts. Among those cornered and killed was Nikora, moving pitifully slowly because of his wound though protected faithfully almost to the last by his ferocious cousin from Taupo, Te Rangitahau. Total casualties suffered by Te Kooti at Ngatapa are estimated at 136 dead, of whom 120 were executed during the pursuit. Government casualties were 11 killed and 11 wounded.

These terrible losses broke Te Kooti's immediate military power. He fled through the forest with the remnants of his followers but the magic of this malevolent man's *mana* ensured a quick recovery; the Whakatohea, the Taupo people and the Urewera each invited him to take refuge in their country. He moved to the forbidding Urewera mountains and set about attracting new recruits. His remarkable durability was to be amply demonstrated by three more years in the field.

In the aftermath of Ngatapa Colonel Whitmore withdrew most of the Armed Constabulary to the West Coast where he arrived on 16 January, 1869, to confront again the threat of Titokowaru. Along the East Coast a certain satisfaction was felt by *Pakeha* and friendly Maori alike. Poverty Bay had been avenged.

CHAPTER 19

The Tide Turns against Titokowaru

'Except in a very languid way Titokowaru had not asserted himself or taken advantage of his opportunities. Some small expeditions by inconsiderable war parties had occurred, but practically he had simply held his ground at Tauranga-ika, since I fell back to the Kai-iwi, near Nukumaru, plundering and devastating the district.'[1]

So wrote Colonel Whitmore, assessing the situation on his return to Wanganui on 16 January, 1869. He now had at hand a strong force of 800 Armed Constabulary, including 4 Division from the Waikato, the Wanganui and Kai-iwi Mounted Rifles, 200 selected Wanganui, now properly sworn-in and enlisted with a uniform to prove their elite status, under Kepa te Rangihiwinui with a major's commission, and a detachment of Armstrong guns and Coehorn mortars. Recruits had arrived from the South Island and Australia and were being drilled and trained by his second-in-command, Lieutenant-Colonel William Lyon. Meanwhile, Thomas McDonnell, with some mounted Wanganui, had revisited Waihi and Ngutu-o-te-manu, reporting the countryside empty of active enemy who had presumably flocked to Tauranga-ika. Lyon had also taken out a reconnaissance in force and found the isolated garrisons of Patea and Wairoa in good heart.

The strange inertia of Titokowaru, after his success in re-occupying so much of the confiscated lands, was certainly a

[1] *The Last Maori War in New Zealand under the Self Reliant Policy* by Major-General Sir George Whitmore.

respite for the Government's battered fortunes, but he did use the time to strengthen his fortress at Tauranga-ika. A formidable *pa* had arisen on this commanding site overlooking open country sloping down to the Nukumaru lakes and the sandhills of the coast, with thick forest at its rear. It was solidly built and capacious, with a double line of stout palisades, whose forward fence was raised from the ground between its bulwark poles to allow riflemen in the trench between to shoot at ground level. Enfilading fire was cleverly sited along each flank from abutting wooden towers and inside the *pa* proper was the usual complex of connecting trenches with overhead cover and shellproof dug-outs. From several flagpoles Hauhau war flags flew defiantly, for the *pa* had already smelt powder when Lyon had moved out his Armstrong guns and fired twelve shells at it. Unchastened, Titokowaru had sent two heralds to Woodall's Redoubt on the Kai-iwi to say that he intended to drive all the *Pakeha* into the sea.

Whitmore soon moved to the offensive. On 25 January, his force moved on the Waitotara, crossing the repaired Kai-iwi bridge preceded by an elite group of mounted scouts called the Corps of Guides whom he had formed under William Lingard, a former Kai-iwi Cavalry trooper, except 6 Division who entrenched at Woodall's Redoubt on the Kai-iwi under the overall command of Lyon. The Guides were soon in action, flushing an ambush, in which an old ex-Imperial soldier from the Mutiny, Mackenzie, had his head bashed in by a tomahawk, but the Hauhaus withdrew and on 1 February, the column regained Nukumaru. The next day Whitmore established camp 800 yards from Tauranga-ika and set the Armed Constabulary digging in on a rough semi-circle about the *pa*. But it was an indifferent investment that Whitmore directed, for, though the Cavalry scouted about and two Armstrong guns were brought up to a position 500 yards away, the *pa* was not fully surrounded. Perhaps Tauranga-ika, coupled with the *mana* of Titokowaru, brought out tragic ghosts of Moturoa.

As darkness fell, some of the Armed Constabulary moved up to dig in closer to the *pa* and enlivened the long night watches with sing-songs of popular songs from the recent American Civil

War: *Oh, Susannah!* and *Marching through Georgia* which was greatly to the liking of the Hauhau defenders. 'Go on, *Pakeha*, go on,' some of them shouted, 'give us some more!' But later that night the *pa* grew silent and at dawn, after a few shells and mortar bombs had exploded on it to cover the movement by Whitmore's men to the rear, Tauranga-ika was found to be deserted. Kimble Bent, who had been in the *pa*, later explained that the reason for the abrupt abandonment of this great defensive work was that the *mana tapu* of the great war leader, Titokowaru, had been ruined by an uncovered liaison with the wife of another chief, and such an omen pointed to imminent disaster.

Whitmore ordered an immediate pursuit, pushing on the Volunteer Cavalry to Weraroa and loosing Kepa's Wanganui and Captain Porter's 8 Division of Arawa and Ngapuhi with some *Pakeha* bushmen on Titokowaru's rearguard. Kepa came upon the Hauhau on the left bank of the Waitotara but ran into an ambush, suffering some casualties. Kepa, supported by Porter, broke through and killed three Hauhaus before they dispersed, but he was enraged to find the decapitated body of his relative, chief Hori Raukawa, with heart and liver cut out. By 4 February, contact had been lost and 1, 2 and 8 Divisions camped on the Karaka plateau near Weraroa, after Lyon, who had now moved up with 200 men, had also become engaged, losing several wounded. As the whole force was becoming disorganised from the pursuit through wild country, Whitmore regrouped his force about Weraroa and Nukumaru until Titokowaru's firm trail could be re-established.

While Whitmore took off on a fleeting visit to Wellington to plead for the enlistment of Ngatiporou, who, with the Urewera, were the best bush-tracking tribe in North Island, disaster soon rebounded on the victorious Government forces. On 18 February, Sergeant Menzies led nine men of 2 Division across the Waitotara opposite Karaka camp to raid a tempting peach grove, when he was ambushed by rebels under a massive Ngarauru called Big Kereopa. Menzies was killed with six of his men, and his leg cut off to be cooked and eaten.

Meanwhile, determined deep reconnaissance by Kepa and his Wanganui, thirsting for *utu* for the dead and mutilated Hori, harried Titokowaru and his followers deep into the forest where their fortunes, in food and ammunition, sunk to a dismal ebb. Half-starving, they were forced to subsist on edible mosses, the large white grub, *huhu*, and the pith of the *mamaku* fern tree and were afraid to light fires at night. In early March, Titokowaru was at his bush camp at Otautu, ten miles up the left bank of the Patea, and by 11 March, Whitmore was back at Patea township to re-occupy positions abandoned after Moturoa the previous November. As his scouts had now located the enemy at Otautu, the following night he marched out with 400 men under his own command along the left bank of the Patea river with Lieutenant-Colonel St John with 200 on the other bank to cut off retreat across the river.

It was a very dark night as 8 Division padded silently along the track in single file, closely followed by 1 Division, and early morning brought little respite as dense fog enveloped the bush. As the leading Arawa threaded their way cautiously along the track, near their objective they came on a dozing Hauhau sentry. Benjamin Biddle, the Ngatapa hero and a fine bushman, was about to tomahawk him when he was stopped by an unknown officer who cried out that the man was an Arawa. In the confusion, the Hauhau escaped into the bush and gave the alarm, and a desperate fight followed as the Hauhau bravely tried to cover the flight of their women and children. Soon the Hauhaus, knowing the ground, began enveloping the strung-out column and Government casualties began to mount. The Hauhaus fled only when their ammunition failed, killing six Government men and wounding twelve for only one fatality. They followed their women across the river, where St John's column was too badly placed to intercept, to Whakamara, ten miles to the north-west.

Here the starving Hauhaus killed some pigs and rested. By 16 March, Kepa's scouts had discovered Whakamara, but a mounted Hauhau scout soon gave the alarm as a double movement under Whitmore and Lyon closed in. Titokowaru and his whole force fled into the bush 'racing like wild pigs before the hunter', as Kimble Bent was later to describe the evacuation, and all Whitmore's men found was a massive *niu* pole flying a fascinating variety of flags, which pathetically indicated the confusion of mind of these hostile Maoris: among the dozen or more flags flying were several pre-war Union Jacks, some bearing the words 'Kingi Tawhiao', and 'Tiriti o Waitangi', others with the popular stars and crosses emblems. In the tradition of New Zealand flagstaffs, this was promptly cut down by the occupying forces.

Titokowaru was now a broken man, but the relentless Government pursuit continued to harry him. Over most arduous country from Whakamara to Taiporohenui, a selected mobile column set out after his blood. This force was unique as its 350 men, composed of Wanganui and the Arawa-Ngapuhi 8 Division, also had 60 volunteers from the various AC Divisions under Captains Northcroft and Watts and was commanded by a Maori officer, Major Kepa. Within twenty-four hours, the first stragglers were captured and now a barbarous reversion to the old Maori warfare was ordered by Kepa, burning to avenge Hori Raukawa. All prisoners were killed and decapitated, though this was also partly due to a misinterpretation of a parting exhortation by George Whitmore, who offered £10 'a head' for a captured Hauhau chief and £5 for a warrior, and he was taken literally. Porter, saw this head-chopping in operation by the Wanganui, and suggested weakly that surely ears would do, but he was met with a hearty Wanganui admonition: 'No, Witimoa said "heads", and if he doesn't get the heads he may not pay us!' When Whitmore came up to Taiporohenui, he was horrified when Wanganui and the *pakeha*-Maoris Tom Adamson and Donald Sutherland came into his tent and emptied eleven Hauhau heads on his floor.

An Arawa veteran of the pursuit, Pirika Hohepa of Rotorua, in later years described this head-hunting to James Cowan:

'The heads of the slain Hauhaus were dried and preserved in the olden Maori fashion, and I shall describe to you what I saw. It was the Ngatihau, the Wanganui tribe, who carried out this process; we Arawa did not take part but we crowded round to watch the *tohunga,* or expert, at work. The *tohunga* who carried out the process of *papipaku-upoko* was an old man named Teoti, from the high country near Tongariro. He had dug a hole in the ground and in it made an oven (*hangi*) with stones on which he placed wood. When the wood was mostly consumed he raked the burning sticks away and left the red-hot stones. Above this glowing oven the head was placed on the end of a stick, and flax mats and other garments were heaped closely over all to retain the heat. From time to time the old man removed the coverings to smooth the skin down and wipe off the moisture. The intense heat made the skin very white (*kiritea*), like the complexion of a European, and this showed up the tattoo lines prominently. The process was repeated on the other heads and old Teoti really made a very good job of it!'

Kepa's ruthless methods, together with the mounting exhaustion of the retreating Hauhaus, were now causing mass desertions and several *hapus* broke away from Titokowaru's lost cause. Women prisoners brought in gave the intelligence that Titokowaru was moving into the great swamp area of Ngaire and Whitmore immediately sent word to the Committee of Public Safety at New Plymouth to request military co-operation from their Volunteer forces to move into the enemy rear by advancing up the Waitara. But New Plymouth replied that the native situation was far too delicate, as Ahitana, the chief of the *hapu* at Ngaire, had been promised neutrality if he remained peaceful; if this agreement was broken, the whole Taranaki tribe would rise. Whitmore was also warned by several fearful pundits that the notorious Ngaire swamp had engulfed a Waikato war party of 500 in the old native wars, and he was strongly advised to stay away from this sinister area. But the Colonel was not to be dissuaded. For three days he reconnoitred the swamp carefully and then on 24 January, well-equipped with ladders and hurdles, advanced into the legendary swamp without mishap, but his quarry had gone. Titokowaru and his few remaining faithful followers had disappeared into the trackless forests of the Upper Waitara to find refuge with the Ngatimaru, and there he vanished into oblivion.

When Whitmore realised this, he returned to Waihi where he found his requested 100 Ngatiporou, newly arrived from the East Coast as 9 Division AC. He placed these valuable reinforcements under Major Noakes, Captains Kells and Bryce, who scoured the Upper Patea for four months after scattered Ngatiruanui and Ngarauru malcontents. The steamers *Sturt* and *St Kilda* now arrived off Taranaki to take most of the Armed Constabulary back to the Bay of Plenty, and Whitmore made his dispositions for the pacified Taranaki and Wanganui districts; he posted one Division at New Plymouth, another at Patea and the Ngatiporou Division at Waihi. For the first time since 1860 it was safe to ride unarmed from Wanganui Town to New Plymouth.

George Whitmore did not go direct from South Taranaki to the East Coast that April, but marched the Divisions destined for embarkation in two columns to the coast, one to sail from Opunake, the other under Lieutenant-Colonel St John by General Chute's old track behind Mount Egmont to the mouth of the Waitara. Whitmore rode along this track also, and went into New Plymouth to discuss an urgent matter with Mr J. C. Richmond, the Native and Defence Minister. On 15 February, a ghastly massacre had occurred at Pukearuhe Redoubt, or White Cliffs, on the north Taranaki coast, when Lieutenant Gascoigne, his wife and four children, two military settlers and the Rev John Whiteley had been murdered by Ngatimaniapoto from Mokau Heads under Wetere te Rerenga and Te Oro.

The murders were tragically motiveless, unless they presaged a Ngatimaniapoto invasion of Taranaki, for Pukearuhe had originally been built in '65 to block their reinforcements reaching Taranaki from Mokau. Whitmore and Richmond duly appearing off Mokau in *Sturt* and *St Kilda*, landed some punitive boatloads of Armed Constabulary, while *Sturt* fired her modest armament of one brass gun at the *kainga*. But the fearful Wetere had fled upriver with his confederates, to be received very coolly by his King-ite fellow tribesmen, who were especially irritated about the death of the Rev Whiteley, a venerable and respected Wesleyan missionary.

Sturt's random shells were the last naval or artillery rounds to be fired in the Maori Wars. Meanwhile, another eventful development of a more fundamental nature was causing concern in New Zealand at this time. The *Regimental History* of the 18th Royal Irish recounts the situation:

'Early in 1869, the battalion was warned to be in readiness to relieve the 50th in Australia. The European population, however, strongly opposed the departure of the Royal Irish: officers and men alike were popular with all classes of society, and while on personal grounds the colonists wished to retain the regiment among them, from the political point of view they deprecated the withdrawal of the XVIIIth. As a concession the Ministry at home reluctantly postponed the departure of the battalion, but after a few months, again ordered it to Australia.'

The Governor, Sir George Bowen, fought strenuously to hold the 18th, and even forwarded Press cuttings to London, showing demands for annexation by the United States if the Mother Country so clearly showed her abdication from responsibility to solve her young Colony's military troubles by withdrawing the last Imperial regiment. But the Colonial Secretary replied that New Zealand now had a European population of 220,000 to counter the depredations of a few hundred rebels, and he refused to countermand the orders for the Royal Irish.

The man who held the Regiment was Major-General Sir Trevor Chute, who came over from Australia and, on his own responsibility, delayed their embarkation. But in early 1870, the Regiment did sail, with Headquarters and four companies going to Sydney, and two companies each to Melbourne, Adelaide and Hobart. 'The men who wear red garments' had finally left New Zealand. It was now New Zealander against New Zealander.

CHAPTER 20

Final Shots

'I had resolved to steer north or south from Waitara, according as the wind was favourable either way, and as it happened to be a south-west wind, made for Manukau, marching across to Auckland and embarking there for Tauranga. Had the wind been from the north, I should have been off Napier on the very day Te Kooti was at Mohaka, and might have landed and attacked his force while carousing at the public house they had plundered, and incapable of resistance or escape. But in two days he was gone back to the fastnesses of the Urewera and the chance was lost.'[1]

COLONEL WHITMORE could only bitterly lament his delayed departure from the West Coast, especially as he had trouble en route at Auckland with his contingent who, less dedicated than he, were all for celebrating in the town after their hard months in the bush. But as early as March, 1869, Te Kooti, flush with Urewera and Whakatohea recruits, was on the move again and raided in strength down to the coast at Whakatane against the Ngatipukeko, rich in horses, cattle and grain. A band under Te Rangitahau killed a surveyor, Mr Pitcairn, at Ohiwa while, as a preliminary before the main operation against Whakatane township, 100 warriors under Wirihana Koikoi of Taupo were loosed against the flour mill and small redoubt at Te Poronu, defended by a Frenchman, Jean Guerren, his Maori wife and sister-in-law, two Ngatipukeko and two other Maori women. This tiny band, ably led by the brave Frenchman who was a crack shot, held out for two days before they were overrun and tomahawked, though

[1] Whitmore.

227

Guerren's wife lived to be carried off, and one of the Ngatipukeko escaped. Seven of the attackers died, including Wirihana.

Te Kooti was now three miles to the south of the town before Rauporoa *pa*, which was desperately defended by the Ngatipukeko against the 400 well-armed marauders. After nearly seizing the *pa* under the guise of a flag of truce, a favourite Te Kooti stratagem, a regular siege set in, with the defenders considerably heartened by the entry under heavy fire of Hori Kawakura and twenty fighting men who had been absent at a funeral. Two days and two nights dragged by and the Ngatipukeko looked anxiously for relief. However, their well-being was in the capable hands of the three Mair brothers. Major William Mair, Resident Magistrate at Opotiki, despatched Captain Henry Mair with the Opotiki Rangers and some Armed Constabulary under Captain Travers, while Lieutenant Gilbert Mair led a force of Arawa on a forced march from Matata. As Gilbert reached the approaches to the Whakatane River, he came on fugitives from Rauporoa *pa* which had just fallen, though with only four killed; all others had escaped. His Arawa were able to beat off a mounted enemy pursuit.

Te Kooti crossed the Whakatane after the fall of Rauporoa, where he lost ten killed, and advanced on the settlement with his main body. The Urewera raided Whakatane with enthusiasm, burning houses and pillaging the local liquor store with such efficiency that they were all soon drunk. Gilbert Mair could see many of them clad in looted red Garibaldi jumpers, with their swords flashing in the sunlight as they rode about drunk, but his own Arawa were too exhausted from their march to intervene. But soon afterwards William Mair landed at Whakatane with his brother Henry, the Opotiki Rangers and 1st Waikato Militia, and Te Kooti, again laden with loot and captives, judiciously chose to retire to the mountains. The three Mair brothers followed him up but the Arawa, who had suffered many reverses in earlier days from the Urewera in the defiles and ravines of their country, were far from keen and the operation foundered.

Te Kooti struck next at Mohaka, Hawke's Bay, in early April. One force, which he sent down the Wairoa valley was repulsed with loss by the Ngatipahauwera, but his main column moved into Mohaka through the outlying homesteads and *whares* with murderous precision. Men, women and children, European and Maori, were butchered with pitiless ferocity, the children of the Lavin family being thrown up in the air to be impaled on bayonets; the leading butchers were Timoti te Kaka (Volkner's ex-deacon), Te Rangitahau and Eru Peka Makarini. The Ngatipahauwera took refuge in two *pas*, Te Huke and Hiruharama without their main strength, as some 80 to 100 men were absent, fighting against the Wairoa diversionary attack. Te Huke fell soon to a white flag deceit by Te Kooti and all its occupants were massacred. Now Hiruharama bore the full brunt of the attack.

Meanwhile, the Napier lifeboat, bearing fourteen armed men, appeared off Mohaka on 12 April, a wounded Maori having brought the news to Napier, but they came under heavy fire from mounted enemy who galloped along the beach, and as night fell, they returned to Napier. There all available local men who could be mounted were now under arms and mustered and moved to Mohaka. As the siege of Hiruharama went on, more immediate relief approached in the shape of fighting men returning from Wairoa under Ihaka Whanga. Te Kooti had anticipated this by posting men north of Mohaka on the Wairoa track and their strong position held up the force except for a handful of determined warriors who filtered through the bush to reinforce the embattled *pa*. They were led by a remarkable trooper from 1 Division, AC George Hill, who had been sent out mounted to reconnoitre Mohaka and, having sent back news of Te Kooti's presence, zestfully joined the relief force. James Cowan recounts the career of a remarkable personality:

'His fighting career was one of extraordinary variety and adventure. A native of the famous little Devonshire town of Dawlish, he joined the Royal Navy in 1851 and saw over ten years' service as a blue-jacket. He was in HMS *Leopard* at the bombardment of Sevastopol, and on returning to England from the Black Sea in 1856, he joined HMS *Shannon* and went out in her to the China Station. When the Indian Mutiny broke out in 1857, the *Shannon* was ordered to Calcutta, and Hill was in Captain Peel's famous Naval Brigade which took a battery of 32-pounders into the heart of India. He fought at the taking of

Lucknow, where he was slightly wounded, and at Delhi, and in the desperate battle at Cawnpore, under Sir Colin Campbell. In 1860 he was in the Mediterranean in HMS *Cannibal*, and with three shipmates, took French leave at Palermo and enlisted, like many other British bluejackets, in Garibaldi's Army of Liberation. After a brief campaign in Italy, where he was wounded, he rejoined his ship—the desertion was overlooked, for English sympathy with Garibaldi ran high—and afterwards served in HMS *Euryalis*. On coming to New Zealand in 1863, he joined von Tempsky's No. 2 Company of the Forest Rangers and fought in many actions in Taranaki and in the Hauhau campaign on the East Coast. Later he was in Major Fraser's No. 1 Company of the Military Settlers in Hawke's Bay, and then for several years in the Armed Constabulary."[1]

George Hill became the heart of the wearied Hiruharama defence and was not only to win, deservedly, the New Zealand Cross for his courage and leadership but romantically, there met the Maori half-caste girl who became his wife, Harata Hinerata, who had escaped with her three sisters at the last moment from doomed Te Huke *pa*, two of the women with children on their backs as they swam across the Mohaka river.

When Te Kooti heard that the Napier relief force was near, he again withdrew unhurriedly, but not before many of his men had once again got drunk on looted rum. He left behind a death roll of 7 Europeans and 57 friendly Maoris, for the loss of 12 of his own men. After Te Kooti had pulled away from Hiruharama, George Hill swam the river with his horse and rode along the beach where he soon met the advancing Napier horsemen under Colonel Lambert. Now, suddenly, the fortunes of war were about to be turned: that indefatigable Armed Constabulary scout, Ben Biddle, reported to Lambert that many of Te Kooti's men were drunk and incapable a few miles away. Though the Wairoa and Mohaka *hapus* of the Ngatikahungunu were burning for *utu* and his Napier Europeans were eager to attack, Lambert said that he would have to think about this proposal. Thus the opportunity to destroy Te Kooti passed, to the disgust of many. Ben Biddle tracked Te Kooti alone until one night he let 150 looted horses out of their corral, mostly to return to Mohaka.

[1] Cowan.

Te Kooti retired to Waikaremoana where a week of feasting and horse-racing along the lakeside was abruptly interrupted by the news that Whitmore was advancing on the Urewera mountains from the north. While the *Sturt* and *St Kilda* took 1 and 2 Divisions on to Whakatane, Whitmore marched with Roberts' 6 Division from Tauranga to Matata, which inhospitable spot, devoid of sheep or cattle, had to be the forward base for his invasion of the unmapped Urewera. He reckoned that there was little to be gained by waiting for Te Kooti to break out again where he chose; the only course was to invade the mountains, destroy his food supplies and drive him out, even if he avoided battle. His plan was to advance with two main columns, Roberts with his 6 Division and 200 Arawas, under Gilbert Mair, through Fort Galatea, up the Rangitaiki River, and St John with 1 and 2 Divisions and about 180 friendly coast Maoris. A third column under Colonel Herrick, co-ordinated by Mr Richmond, the Native and Defence Secretary, who had come from the Government to confer with Whitmore, was to come from Wairoa, cross Lake Waikaremoana, destroy all *pas* and hunt down stragglers driven in by the two northern columns advancing into the mountains by the main tracks. A fourth column of sixty mounted troopers from Wanganui was meant to proceed to Taupo to cut off fugitives heading towards the Waikato, but the savage Mohaka raid caused its diversion and it came under command of Herrick. This was just as well as Herrick was having considerable difficulty with his native allies from Wairoa, even with Ropata, who had reluctantly appeared with 170 Ngatiporou. Winter was coming, and a miserable and arduous campaign amid the high altitudes of the Urewera mountains was not to the Maori liking.

The force from Matata started two days earlier than the column from Whakatane and had dug in at Fort Galatea by 3 May, to be supplied for twelve miles up the river by boat and thence by pack horse. St John's column along the Whakatane had a simpler movement and supply problem. On the 4th and 5th, both columns marched, carrying six days provisions; a further supply of 40 lbs of bacon, or 400 rounds of reserve ammunition, was carried by native porters. Their rendezvous was the Ruatahuna valley, fifty miles up the headwaters of the Whakatane river, where the main villages of the Urewera tribe were.

Whitmore's column had a fight at Te Harema *pa* after two days out, the Arawa behaving with great dash and four Hauhaus were killed and about 45 taken prisoner. The next day, the elite Corps of Guides, a mere twelve scouts containing first-class bushmen like Sergeant Christopher Maling and the Adamson brothers, Tom and Steve, ran into an ugly ambush from which they were rescued from certain death by Gilbert Mair's Arawas, who came through the bush to the sound of firing. A veteran Taranaki scout, Hemi te Waka, better known as 'Big Jim' or 'Taranaki Jim', was mortally wounded in this affray after years of faithful and very active service; he always proudly carried a presentation revolver given to him by the officers of the 57th Regiment after the ambush at Ahuahu in '64 and wore a 43rd Regiment forage cap.

The Guides and Arawa led on, leaving the ravines and now trekking exhaustively over ridgelines through magnificent, rugged scenery. At 2 pm 8 May, they topped the great timber-covered Tahuaroa range and saw the splendid sight of the Ruatahuna valley, with its villages and cultivations, spread 1,000 feet below them. In the distance they also saw much movement, and Whitmore, despite the doubts of others, correctly guessed that it was St John's men capturing Orangikawa *pa* at Tatahoata. It took four hours to descend the precipitous slopes into the valley, but Whitmore was anxious to make contact with St John that night and he pushed on, through dangerous country, with Captain Swindley of the Guides, Lieutenant Preece and a Guides escort led by an unenthusiastic Urewera. When he reached the Whakatane ford opposite Ruatahuna, Whitmore ordered his bugle to blow the 'Officers Call'. Out of the night and the surrounding forest came an answering British bugle and a roar from St John's force. Whitmore met his subordinate commander at Orangikawa at 10 pm 8 May, and it was an historic encounter in the heart of these enemy mountains, never before penetrated in force by Europeans.

' "A great cheer went up to the heavens from our whole force when he came in," says a veteran of No. 2 Division in St John's column. "We were beginning to know the little Colonel by this time." [1]

St John's column, with Fraser and Gilbert Mair as his subordinates, had seen more action than the Matata men. Starting out with packs and equipment weighing a crushing 70 lbs, they slogged up the Whakatane river, crossing and re-crossing it many times and spending much time trudging along the river bed in the absence of any track. On 6 May, they overran Whataponga village, killing 3 men, two women and a boy; atrocities were not necessarily confined to Te Kooti or the Hauhaus, as the lad was shot by the half-Maori Captain Grundry in blatant *utu* for the death of his fourteen-year-old brother Fred in the action at Otautu, Taranaki, on 13 March. The following day, veteran Lieutenant David White, leading his scouts, was shot dead as he was about to ford the junction of the Mahaki-rua stream with the Whakatane, and heavy skirmishing occurred until a lodgement was forced against the Urewera riflemen in the scrub on the other bank. By noon on 8 May, however, St John had marched through the Ruatahuna valley and was before Orangikawa *pa*. Captain Travers was leading 4 Division on a flanking movement to gain better ground when he was also shot dead, but the Urewera evacuated the *pa* just as St John had closed up, after inflicting 5 killed and 6 wounded on the column and sustaining about the same losses themselves.

Whitmore's combined force remained in the valley until the 14th, systematically destroying potato crops and other cultivations. This task was aided by wild pigs, for whom the careful Urewera fences were taken away to allow the pigs to root and eat or expose to the frosts. Stray Urewera attempting to fend off the pigs were shot by their ruthless native enemies from the plains. As they were dispersed, a great loss of confidence ensued among the mountain tribe, whose fastnesses had never before been breached. Whitmore's brave and imaginative operation had paid off well, perhaps a little fortuitously as his opponent had occupied himself on the south side of the mountains with many Urewera fighting men. But tribute must be given to his sheer determination, for serious problems like supply and the treat-

[1] Gudgeon.

233

ment and evacuation of casualties were almost insoluble in that rugged terrain, unless the fortunes of war smiled.

Whitmore, however, was worried about Herrick's column, especially as he was due to come from Waikaremoana, where Whitmore now deduced Te Kooti must be. Consequently, on 11 May, he despatched Roberts and 100 AC and 100 Arawa under Gilbert Mair and Pokiha Taranui of Maketu, to make a reconnaissance in force through the gorge south to the Huiarau mountains and Waikaremoana to contact Herrick. This force had hardly gone two miles down the valley when they ran into Te Kooti's advance guard, which he had despatched under Eru Peka te Makarini when he heard of Whitmore's invasion. Gilbert Mair, in the point of the advance, was very nearly killed, but was enraged when he heard a bugle sounding (the big half-caste had learned all the bugle calls during his Chatham Islands sojourn and always carried a bugle) and Peka shouting through the bush that he had slain the white man. Mair dashed off with some stout Arawa spirits to outflank the ambushers, and burst on a large group being harangued in a clearing by a *tohunga* and opened fire. Fortunes were turned smartly, with the Arawa not only decapitating the fallen, but securing a hastily abandoned meal of tasty pork after another bugle call from Peka summoned a retreat. Gilbert Mair was to settle a final account with Peka in February, 1870.

With Te Kooti's own men in the field, Whitmore wanted to march his whole force to Waikaremoana, a march of twenty miles through gorge and mountain, but the Arawa now showed a distinct unenthusiasm for the snows of Huiarau and felt, perhaps not unnaturally, that they had done enough. Whitmore had to cancel the proposed operation, to universal relief, as ammunition was almost exhausted and food was scarce. Te Kooti was in fact lying in wait in force in this excellent ambush country for a main advance, and so he was denied a possible major victory that could have caused many more tribes to flock to his banner and raise him from the status of a brilliant guerrilla leader to a national hero, able to raise the numbers to encounter the *Pakeha* in the open field.

On the 14th, Whitmore led his troops back to Fort Galatea

and he himself went out of the war. Suffering from acute dysentery, then attacked by rheumatism, the rigours of his hard campaigning bore down on him and he handed over command to St John. After medical treatment in Auckland, he went to Wellington to give military advice to the Government. Shortly to become Major-General Sir George Whitmore, this erstwhile Hawke's Bay settler and colonial politician had started as a very orthodox young British officer, though service in the Kaffir Wars had given him valuable colonial experience. After passing through the infant Staff College, he came out to New Zealand as Military Secretary to Sir Duncan Cameron, and after the Waikato campaign, retired to become a sheep farmer in Hawke's Bay. From there he became a converted colonial and New Zealander, even going to the extent of referring to the Imperial regiments as 'the royal troops' in his writings. Though the curt and intolerant Regular still lurked under his new colonial militia veneer, as his early unhappy handling of Volunteers and native allies showed, his offensive spirit and sheer grit redeemed much. To balance one bad decision at Moturoa, he achieved the victories of Ngatapa and the penetration of the Urewera mountains. It was his unswerving spirit, sense of discipline and bite that the semi-amateur colonial forces needed so much and in the end, they appreciated this, as the great cheer when he walked into Orangikawa *pa* indicates.

Whitmore's last operational orders in the field were to St John to move his base between the Urewera mountains and Taupo, suggesting Opepe where the Napier road crossed the main track from Taupo to the Rangitaiki Valley, as he was sure Te Kooti 'must in a very few weeks break cover and come out in the plains'. It was not until 6 June that St John felt re-organised enough to begin this forward deployment, and promptly met with one of those sharp reverses that so redounded to Te Kooti's reputation. At Opepe, his own mounted escort, though he himself was absent, was engaged in conversation by Maoris pretending to be friendly and then savagely attacked. Nine troopers were killed, though Cornet Smith, severely wounded, his sergeant and two men managed to escape back to Galatea. Then Te Kooti, who indeed was leaving the mountains as Whitmore predicted, continued his march towards Taupo, and at Hatepe, his Urewera wantonly shot an old man called Hona. In the subtle nuances of Maori warfare, this proved later to be a grievous mistake, as Hona was a close relative of the great Wanganui *rangatira*, Topia Turoa. Ironically, Te Kooti himself had tried to protect the old man.

At Taupo, Te Kooti's *mana* was soaring and arrogantly, with 300 followers of various tribes, he decided to pay a state visit to Waikato. But at a great assembly at Tokangamutu, where he was received in the lines of Ngatimaniapoto by Rewi, he offended the proud Waikato greatly by firing a volley of ball ammunition over their heads and the enraged tribe declared battle for next day. Te Kooti wasted a week waiting for the Waikato to cool down but they ignored him: only a few Ngatimaniapoto under Rewi went back with him. King Tawhiao, however, gave his blessing to Te Kooti's enterprises.

With the passing of the winter of '69, a trial of strength built up between Te Kooti and the Government forces in the Taupo district. By September, Te Kooti had occupied Tokaanu but now concentrating in the Taupo area under the new Government commander, Lieutenant-Colonel Thomas McDonnell, was a large war party of Ngatikahungunu under Renata Kawepo and Henare Tomoana, Arawa under Lieutenant Preece, and the Armed Constabulary contingent from Wairoa commanded by Lieutenant-Colonel Herrick. After a preliminary clash on 9 September, with the Ngatikahungunu holding Tauranga-Taupo *pa* at the south end of the Lake, Te Kooti retired from Tokaanu and took up an entrenched position on the forested Te Pononga Ridge.

McDonnell followed up with his whole force and by 25 September, his scouts had fixed Te Kooti at Te Pononga. Captain St George, Preece and Henare Tomoana led a dashing attack by the Ngatikahungunu and Arawa which carried the position, leaving ten enemy dead in their trenches, including a close relative of Te Kooti's, Wi Piro, another Chatham Island escapee who was notorious for his butchery of prisoners, for the loss of two killed and four wounded. To complete McDonnell's delight, he later found Captains Northcroft and Scannell, with 2 Division AC from Napier waiting in his base camp. More relevantly, Te Pononga, where Te Kooti in person with 250 men was defeated by an almost entirely Maori force, lost Te Kooti his military *mana*. Rewi returned disillusioned to his own country, taking the promise of 600 excellent fighting men with him.

While Te Kooti's cause sickened, the Government's strengthened when, on 1 October, Kepa and 70 Wanganui, accompanied by Captain William McDonnell, also joined Thomas McDonnell's very mixed force. His difficulties were not least in keeping the peace between the tribal contingents, contending with the morning-after effect of bad dreams on otherwise brave men and balancing the vehement predictions of the various honoured tribal prophets. William Gudgeon recounts a fine scene from warring Victorian New Zealand:

'The Arawa and Napier tribes now prepared for a war dance to greet the Wanganuis, who were advancing in column, stripped naked, and rifles at the port. Renata Kawepo and the other chiefs sallied out of their *pa* naked as the day they were born and waded the river; after the usual challenge, Wanganui came on and the Napier tribes opened the performance. Only one man has ever succeeded in describing the war-dance, so I refer my readers to *Old New Zealand* for that, freely acknowledging my inability to help them. At the close of the dance, Ngatikahungunu formed front two deep, and a hoarse cry went down the ranks of "Eyes Right", with the addition of "Pai ia rewhi" (by your left), which was promptly obeyed by bringing the muzzles of their rifles to the front, capping, and after whirling the guns two or three times over their heads, snapping them off at Wanganui, who were kneeling in columns of fours, their eyes on the ground, and heads turned a little in listening attitude—in fact, they were doing it properly. The ceremony of snapping the caps (called the cap-dance) was gone through three times and was done in capital time, when again the command "Eyes Right" was heard, and they all knelt down as Wanganui sprang to their feet. Kepa, who seldom took part in a war dance, now appeared stripped to the waist, lean and gaunt from his late illness and led his men off in first rate style. At the conclusion, the renowned little fighting man, Winiata, called out to Ngatikahungunu in broken English, mixed with much bad language, "Too much you make a loose the bloody caps; my word, Colonel Gorton make you pay!" '

Anyone who has served in the Army will appreciate Winiata's concern. Colonel Gorton was the Inspector of Stores.

After another bout of prophet and prophetess trouble fore-telling imminent disaster for his tribes, McDonnell managed to move his whole force to Lake Roto-a-Ira and, on 3 October, mounted an excellent attack against Te Kooti holding two hills and an entrenched redoubt at Te Porere by instilling, with his astute knowledge of the Maori mind, a sense of rivalry between the three main tribal allies. Running with great elan through the short fern after fording the Wanganui river, the Wanganui, Ngatikahungunu and Arawa, supported by the Armed Constabu-lary and Guides containing such veterans as Northcroft, Preece, Maling and the McDonnell brothers, assailed the redoubt on three sides. But casualties tragically fell: the intrepid little Winiata was shot dead astride the parapet firing down into the enemy; in the assault earlier, so was Captain J. St George, a true colonial beau sabreur who had joined the Hawke's Bay squadron of the Colonial Defence Force Cavalry with his friend Gas-coygne in 1863 and who had just distinguished himself in the Pononga attack. As the attack swarmed over the parapet, most of the defenders, including their notorious leader who had a finger shot away, were bolting over the rear. Te Porere was the last redoubt constructed by Te Kooti and the enemy rifleman who dropped St George with a bullet in his brain, Peita Kotuku, told James Cowan in 1921 about its fall:

'Our redoubt was a massive redoubt earthwork—it is standing there today—but it had one defect, which resulted in our defeat. In making the loopholes in the sod and pumice walls, interlaid with fern, we made them straight and could not depress the muzzles of our guns to fire into the ditch. The Government troops, *pakeha* and Maori, got under the parapets, and many of them snatched up lumps of pumice and stuffed up the firing apertures with them. We therefore could not see our nearest attackers, unless we exposed ourselves over the top of the parapet.'[1]

The Wanganui, maddened by the death of Winiata, and the Arawa, who had lost a chief, gave no quarter to the enemy they

[1] Cowan.

238

trapped in the redoubt, and today, as Peita also recounts, thirty-seven enemy warriors lie under a grassy mound there. Te Kooti retired quickly into the King country where the Government had no wish to get embroiled with the Waikato and Ngatimaniapoto, and after many marches and counter-marches, McDonnell lost contact with his elusive foe. Several factors caused him to disperse his force. In a hard climate beset with intense cold, rain and fog, his supplies failed and the operation degenerated into a hunt for potato crops to stave off hunger. A final and virulent bout of prophesying drove the Ngatikahungunu home to Hawke's Bay, while Kepa was recalled urgently for consultations with Topia Turoa, the paramount chief of his tribe.

Again, a badly beaten Te Kooti was given sorely-needed respite, as the colonial war effort, now with William Fox, the former voluble critic, as Premier from 1869, was crumbling away. The Government entered into clumsy negotiations with the proud and implacable Rewi as an intermediary to reach Te Kooti, but he blandly snubbed the endeavours. Meanwhile, though Thomas McDonnell was still their titular field commander, he was poorly supported, and the Government forces retired to the coast with much hard-won ground left uncovered again. As a last straw, the Armed Constabulary, who were New Zealand's only semblance of a regular force, now became the target of a strange Government campaign for transformation into a kind of rural policemen. A Police Commissioner from Otago was appointed to change these hardy bush soldiers of such excellent material with police uniforms and regulations and by the disbandment of Divisions who had proud battle honours.

However, some good news cheered the hard-working McDonnell. Kepa had been summoned by Topia Turoa to be told that the Wanganui *rangatira* and former Hauhau was now actively joining the Government side, as the Waikato had requested his alliance to rid their lands of Te Kooti and both Kepa and Topia were marching back with 200 Upper Wanganui, Ngatihaua and even Ngarauru from Pipiriki on 13 December. When intelligence then reached McDonnell at Tokaanu in January, 1870, that Te Kooti had emerged in the Ngatiraukawa country at Matamata, he moved off along the east side of Lake Taupo, crossed the

Waikato at Taupo and before he re-crossed the great river at Whakamaru, waited for Kepa and Topia who came up on 20 January. McDonnell now had 600 Constabulary, Arawa and Wanganui and he set off into the Tokoroa and Patatere plains to to close with Te Kooti. On 24 January, he seized the Ngatirau-kawa *pa*, Tapapa, on the bush track to Rotorua, killing three enemy, but next day in dense fog, just before he was about to move out, Te Kooti attacked the Government camp, with his main weight coming against the Ngaruaru. Thomas McDonnell describes an engagement which depicts the delicate relationships of a *Pakeha*-Maori force at this stage of the wars, and yet again, another of those splendid Maori Amazons makes a dramatic appearance:

'I feared to let No 2 Division rush at the enemy, lest they mistook the Ngarauru for them, or intentionally mistook them. Our men who had been ambushed at Waitotara ten months earlier had belonged to this Division, and one of the men had come to me during our march up, and told me that the chief had the rifles which had belonged to Sgt Menzies and Cpl Horsepool, two of the men who had been tomahawked on that occasion, and I knew nothing would have pleased them better than to have a slap at them. Privately, I had no objection, but it would not have suited just then, and I had to be careful. The temptation, however, was great.

The Ngarauru fought well, but were thrown into disorder and retreated on our Europeans, to whom I now gave the order word to "Make ready". The wife of Pehimana, a Ngarauru chief, mounted a high *whata* (food platform) and regardless of the bullets that flew about her, waved her shawl, crying out at the top of her voice, "Turn, turn, O Rauru! Fight on, O tribe! Fight on! absolve yourselves from sin! Clear yourselves, fight on, fight on, fight on!"'

The exhortation to absolve themselves was referring to their having fought against the Queen, and now they were to do their best to prove their sincere sorrow for the past. The attitude of the excited woman was a perfect picture. Not one rap did she care for the bullets. Then the Ngarauru rallied, and with one wild yell charged at the enemy. Meantime I slipped round with some of the Arawa to our left and came down on the flank of the reserve of the enemy, who were kneeling at the rear of our camp, one man holding a staff with Te Kooti's flag on it. We opened fire on them, and after one volley, which knocked over three, they gave us

240

one in return, and then broke and fled into the bush, but the fog now rolled up more dense than ever, so that it was useless to follow them farther."[1]

Te Kooti lost six killed and probably twice that number wounded at Tapapa while McDonnell had one European and three Maoris killed and four wounded. The ensuing days and weeks were taken up trying to re-establish contact with the elusive guerrilla leader in the wild, ravine-dissected Mamaku Plateau and the uplands inland from Tauranga, with Kepa relentlessly to the fore. With his amazing resilience, Te Kooti soon scored a sharp counter-blow when the advance guard of Colonel James Fraser's column toiling up a bush track from Tauranga was ambushed by forty enemy, under Peka Te Makarini. Four were cut down by the fire, and their leader, veteran Sergeant Ben Biddle, received a personal bullet from Peka through his bag of pork rations.

Te Kooti's real intention was a long-cherished attack on Rotorua. In this vendetta of hatred against the Arawa tribe for their staunch adherence to the Government, he intended to fall on Ohinemutu when most of their fighting men were away in the hills with Gilbert Mair, who had been ordered by James Fraser to leave Rotorua and reinforce McDonnell in the Tapapa area, much against his own judgement. He was promptly sent back by McDonnell, and during the return, on 7 February, Te Kooti's trail was picked up, and great excitement arose as the Arawa rushed back. Mair was nearing the lake when news came that other Arawa had captured Louis Baker, the deserter from HMS *Rosario*, who gave the vital intelligence that Te Kooti was about to descend on Ohinemutu with 200 men, mostly Urewera. In an exciting forced march which was the start of a day that was remarkable for Mair's superb fitness, as well as his courage and leadership, Mair came up on Ohinemutu while some trusting Arawa elderly chiefs were talking with Te Kooti's white-flagged emissaries. Calling on all young men to join the veterans arriving after him, Mair dashed off in pursuit of Te Kooti's force which now turned rapidly to the south, hurrying their women and children before them.

[1] Cowan.

Q

241

'The black-bearded chieftain galloped about the plain in advance, shouting to his followers and waving his revolver. He wore a grey shirt, riding trousers, and high boots, and a bandit-type hat. In high contrast were his soldiery—a half-naked body of savages, whose brown skins glistened in the warm sunshine as if they had been oiled . . . each man wore cartridge belts—some had three or four—buckled around him; some were armed with revolvers as well as breech-loading rifles, carbines, or single and double-barrel shotguns.'

Te Kooti's rearguard was skilfully commanded by Peka te Makarini, making determined stands and trying to ambush. But Gilbert Mair and the fittest Arawa came relentlessly on, shooting down several stragglers until, in a sharp engagement six miles south of Rotorua at Ngapuketurua, Mair shattered the jaw of Volkner's bloody ex-deacon, Timoti te Kaka, with a well-aimed shot. The final encounter of the day came on the western slopes of Tumunui mountain where Peka and 30 of his men lay among the rock and fern waiting for Mair and his 40 Arawa in the van. When Mair came in sight, Peka fired a shot at him, leapt up and charged with clubbed rifle. As this massive savage, all 6 feet 3 inches, bore down on him, Gilbert Mair fired and dropped him with a bullet in his hip. Peka then tried to shoot him with his revolver, but this was quickly taken from him and an Arawa finished him off with a bullet through the head. Mair then pushed on against the enemy main body, but was held by their heavy fire until darkness fell. He camped with his exhausted men, but when fed, slightly rested and re-ammunitioned, moved through the night to surprise the enemy camp on the north shore of Lake Okaro, at 2 am. A volley caused the enemy to flee in confusion, leaving behind guns and food, through the Kaingaroa forest to the Urewera Mountains.

In this brilliant classic of New Zealand bush warfare, Gilbert Mair and his Arawa killed 20 enemy, for the loss of one mortally wounded and four wounded. Te Rangitahau just escaped, while the captured Timoti, the butcher who had herded captured men, women and children into a woolshed during the Mohaka raid for slaughter, was summarily executed by the Arawa. This exultant tribe then dragged Peka's body tied to a horse's tail from Tumunui mountain to the hot plain, where it was tied upright to a cabbage tree and left in the dry, burning summer heat, to desiccate into an eerie mummy. Militarily, Te Kooti was at last a spent force; he had lost 65 men over the past five months, and though he had inflicted 27 dead and 25 wounded on the Government forces, he now only had about him his Chatham Islands hard core and some Urewera. Very significantly, the war now entered a purely Maori phase, for his remorseless pursuers, who were to hunt and harry him in the ravines and hills of the Urewera country, were Ropata Wahawaha and Kepa te Rangihiwinui.

Sir Donald McLean, now the Native and Defence Minister, had altered the terms of Maori service from a daily rate of pay to a lump sum according to the amount of service, and this was not to the liking of the Arawa and Ngatikahungunu, who left the field to the Wanganui operating from Opotiki and the Ngatiporou from Poverty Bay. In late summer 1870, Kepa and Ropata mounted a joint operation and though some natural jealousy arose between these two great Maori leaders it went very well; Ropata was certainly angry when Kepa made peace with Eru Tamaikowha, but Tamaikowha's *hapu* of the Urewera had never joined Te Kooti, as the old-time savage was too content with his private course of being the mountain robber baron terrorising the *Pakeha*. Then on 11 April the staunch Wanganui under Kepa sailed away from the Bay of Plenty out of the war, to return to the West Coast. The unyielding Ropata, ably seconded by that splendid colonial soldier, Captain Porter, took on the prosecution of the hunt.

Ropata and Porter mounted three more expeditions into the Urewera country in May, 1870, January and June, 1871, causing a steady drain of casualties on the harried Urewera tribe, until one dramatic day, at dawn 1 September, 1871, Ropata, Henare Potae and Porter and their warriors surrounded the village of Ruahapu to where Te Kooti's ragged band had been tracked. But premature shots alerted the tense, hunted band and Te Kooti himself set off on a headlong bolt into the bush after he had burst out of his *whare* crying: 'It is Ngatiporou—save yourself!'

Te Kooti escaped again, but melted away to slink ignominiously through uncharted bush, with one surviving wife and five pathetic followers, to take refuge in the King country with Rewi Maniapoto. This daemonic man of forceful personality and astute guerrilla leadership, Te Kooti, was submerged finally in obscurity after his long trail of conflict and terror. But after Ruahapu, Ropata was not yet done.

> 'The next day the united column marched for Ruatahuna, where, as it was Ropata's policy to humble the Urewera, he built a strong *pa*. When asked why he took so much trouble, he replied: "I may have to live here for years. You say you cannot catch Te Kooti or Kereopa, so I shall have to do it." This reply horrified the Urewera, who were by no means desirous of having Ngatiporou for neighbours; and from this moment they began thinking of catching the two chief offenders.'

Consequently, Te Whiu Maraki, a young Urewera who had fought against the Government since 1866 and had now surrendered, ran down a fleeing Kereopa in the forest and handed him over to Ropata and Porter. After recovering his surprise at not being shot out of hand, the tattooed, grey-bearded villain crouched on the ground while the Ngatiporou flung themselves into a thunderous war dance about him. Kereopa later observed that he knew his luck would be bad in the end because when he swallowed the Rev Carl Volkner's eyes, one of them stuck in his throat.

CHAPTER 21
Healing the Wounds

'From shire and parish they came, from croft and hamlet, country cottage and city terrace. For 90 anxious days they trod the timber decks under creaking canvas, dashed by sea spray. And when they stepped gratefully ashore, it was to see Auckland as a raw town in a harsh frontierland. This would be their home for good or ill. Here would be born their children's children.'[1]

But in 1870, when Gilbert Mair humiliated Te Kooti at Rotorua and the end of the long war was at last in sight, not many immigrants came out to New Zealand: a mere 3,577 compared to 35,000 in 1863. The frightening reports of continued strife and terror reaching Britain could only have the obvious effect. Conversely, when Te Kooti fled into oblivion in 1872, the annual immigrant figures leapt within two years to 17,513, with another 14,530 'on the water'.

In 1870 New Zealand had a population of 256,000, of which only 46,000 were Maoris—a terrible figure when a conservative estimate in 1840 placed their numbers at 120,000. What of the Maori as the wars faded away?

'He had been decimated by disease, by inter-tribal warfare made more terrible than ever by the use of firearms, and by war against the *Pakeha*.

'Sick in body, broken in spirit by sorrow and by the confiscation of vast areas of land as punishment for rebellion, the Maori had gone back to the mat and was waiting to take the spirit trail . . . The mission schools, which since the 1830s had brought literacy

[1] 'In Our Time 1870–1970', *The Auckland Star Centennial Supplement.*

and a knowledge of European trades and agriculture to the Maori, along with Christianity, were in ruins. In many places, the Waikato in particular which had begun to blossom as farming knowledge grew, Maoris turned their backs on the missions.["]

Such a racial tragedy could only have cruel undertones. Before the confrontation over land in the 1860s the Maori was prospering materially, despite declining numbers from a high infant mortality rate through a lack of hygiene and sanitation in the *pas*, and also susceptibility to the *Pakeha*'s infectious diseases, such as measles, tuberculosis and influenza. The wheatfields of the Waikato supplied Auckland and even the savage Urewera drove pigs to Auckland market; Maori farmers also grew food for other large townships, such as Wellington and Nelson. About North Island, Maori schooners and luggers carrying their crops to market had a monopoly of the coastal trade.

'Military defeat meant an end to co-operation between *Pakeha* and Maori in many cases. And in just as many the mutual respect which had built up died.'[2]

Hone Heke's war of 1845–46 had its whiff of early nationalism with his fixation about the Maiki Hill flagstaff and its flag and also a grim hint of land troubles to come with the later phase of Te Rangihaeata's hostility over the Hutt Valley. But despite those very rough days the First Maori War was conducted on gentlemanly lines, marred only by those pieces taken from Captain Grant's body at Ohaeawai. Foes were courageously despatched on the field of battle, and women, children and missionaries were respected.

The outbreak of the Second Maori War, sparked off by Wiremu Kingi's adamant stand over Waitara in 1860, hinted at deeprooted bitterness and the danger of resistance, since land alone was concerned, to the encroachments of the *Pakeha*. The Maori King movement made for a certain unity of front and certainly its main protagonists, the Waikato and Ngatimaniapoto, came to fight for Wiremu Kingi, as did such a keen tribal enemy as the Taranaki and also the Ngatiruanui. Land was the binding

---

[1] 'In Our Time 1870–1970', *The Auckland Star Centennial Supplement.*
[2] ibid.

aka vine that drew together the divergent poles of ancient inter-tribal rivalry.

Maori defiance was broken by Duncan Cameron's regiments and artillery and overall superior organisation in the Waikato campaign: at the bloodbath of Rangiriri, the deep and deliberate penetration along the Waikato and the Waipa, and the shattering of Orakau. Only stubborn Maori intransigence and gallant bravura kept the fight going against the overwhelming powerful *Pakeha* enemy. Then the insidious and potent growth of *Pai-Marire* enveloped a defeated and desperate people and despite its overtly pious texts, heralded a reversion to barbarism: cannibalism, mutilation and the smoke-drying of heads. The conflict degenerated into savagery, with little quarter asked or given by either Hauhau or Government forces. When the Imperial Regiments departed, except for one garrison unit, and the false lull of 1867 set in while the Self-Reliant Policy took root, two brilliant leaders of bush warfare, Titokowaru and Te Kooti, then arose like evil genie on either coast to terrorise the *Pakeha* and the moderate Maori and further goad the harried Colonial Government. Though the big battalions under Cameron had crushed the hostile Maori, Kingite or Hauhau, as an organized military force, Titokowaru achieved a remarkable recovery of ground. Te Kooti, for all his *mana* and clever tactical eye for the weak point of attack, was never really more than one of 'the desperate banditti' Cardwell had warned about as a side-issue of Confiscation, but he also possessed the quality of incredible durability.

The Imperial Government behaved shabbily in its unyielding attitude to the withdrawal of the British regiments and leaving the Colony to solve its internal strife. Whether the sturdy advocation of the Self-Reliant Policy by the Weld Ministry was really involuntary or merely facing the inevitable, can only be a matter of conjecture. William Fox, in his book published (embarrassingly early) in 1866 (three years later, as Premier, having voiced his criticisms of the British soldier he was obliged to work without him) waxed very indignant that the Imperial Government was asking £40 a year maintenance per soldier from the Colony, which does seem to be a typical bureaucratic solution as seen from

Whitehall. But when it is remembered that the British soldier was paid 15 pence a day (13 pence before 1867), most of which was taken away from him in recoveries, while the Wellington Government was prepared to hire Arawa and Ngatiporou mercenaries for 3 shillings a day, with rations, the perspective is not quite as clear as Fox would have it.

'The fact remains that it fell to the lot of the hard-suffering soldier to break the power of the Maoris, and that he found them on the whole the grandest native enemy that he had ever encountered. Gurkhas and Sikhs were formidable before them, Zulus were formidable after them: but all of these had copied European discipline. The Maori had his own code of war, the essence of which was a fair fight on a day and place fixed by appointment, when the best and bravest man should win. The British soldier upset his traditions, but could not touch his proud courage nor degrade his proud honour. A Maori was capable of slaughtering wounded and prisoners and perhaps eating them afterwards, but he could also leap down into the fire of both sides to save the life of a fallen foe. The British soldier, therefore, held him in the deepest respect, not resenting his own little defeats but recognizing the noble side of the Maori and forgetting his savagery.'[1]

James Cowan, that painstaking historian of old New Zealand who unearthed so many tales of interest by his interviews with survivors of the wars and his own tours over the ground, estimates that total casualties between 1845 and 1872 were 560 European dead and 1,050 wounded, 250 friendly and 2,000 hostile Maori dead and at least the same number wounded. Fifteen Victoria Crosses* were awarded, and it is significant that the New Zealand campaign medal, starting from Hone Heke's war in 1845, stops its eligibility in 1866. In the later, wholly Colonial, phase, twenty-three of that unique decoration, the New Zealand Cross*, were won. The colonial soldier of the Militia was to set down the great traditions of the citizen soldiers of the nation's armies of 1914–18 and 1939–45, while the professional of the apologetically-named Armed Constabulary laid the foundations of the Permanent Forces with the Forest Rangers obvious forebears of the present day 1 Ranger Squadron NZSAS.

[1] *The History of the British Army*, Vol. 13, Sir John Fortescue.
* See appendices.

The Imperial soldiers, in the main, left with their Regiments, but the proportion who took their discharge in the young Colony were to be an invaluable stiffening in the initial fumbling days of Self-Reliance; their erstwhile commanders, Thomas Pratt, Duncan Cameron and Trevor Chute finished their careers in Britain laden with honours. On the colonial side a new member of the Legislative Council was Major-General Sir George Whitmore, owed much for his terrier-like tenacity in the early difficult era, while former Governor, Sir George Grey, who had returned to Kawau Island from England, became Premier during 1877–79. However, with justice, it could be said that the greatest colonial New Zealanders were the fine Mair brothers, William and Gilbert, closely followed by the determined Thomas McDonnell. From the Maori race, Tamati Waaka Nene, Kepa te Rangihiwinui and Ropata Wahawaha stand out as great personalities. These superb natural leaders were ably seconded by Roberts, Biggs, Northcroft, Porter, Preece, the tragic Hunter brothers, Gascoygne and Newland, to name a select few from many; by Ihaka Whanga, Mokena Kohere, Henare Potae, Haimona Hiroti, Hone Wiremu Hipango, Hori Kingi te Anaua, Wirihana, the fighting Winiata and faithful 'Taranaki Jim'.

In 1881 King Tawhiao, accompanied by many Waikato chiefs and warriors, laid down his weapon with impressive dignity at the feet of William Mair, then Resident Magistrate in the Upper Waikato, and Tawhiao said: 'There will be no more trouble. It means peace.' The Amnesty Act of that year even developed into a pardon for Te Kooti, who was later given a block of land by the Government at Ohiwa Harbour where he was revered as a demi-god by his devotees, though his movements were severely curtailed to protect him from the vendettas of many Maoris who hated him.

Unlike most racial conflicts the Maori Wars ultimately had a happy ending. After reaching a nadir in 1896 of 42,000, the Maori birthrate resurged dramatically through a renaissance of racial culture and pride brought about by a talented galaxy of young educated Maori leaders until now, in a total population in New Zealand of $2\frac{3}{4}$ million, the Maoris are approaching $\frac{1}{4}$ million. As early as the 1914–18 War, 2,200 Maoris left to

fight overseas at Gallipoli and in France for the grandson of
'Kuini Wikitoria', with the main enlistments in the Maori Battalion from those old friends of the *Pakeha*, the Ngapuhi, the
Arawa and Ngatiporou. In France the grandson of the young
chief of the Ngatikahungunu, Karaitiana Roto-a-Tara, who was
murdered at Whataroa in 1868 by Te Kooti's adherents, won the
Military Medal while in the North African campaign in 1943 2nd
Lieutenant Te Moana-nui-a-Kiwa Ngarimu was awarded the
highest decoration for bravery in the British Commonwealth and
Empire, the Victoria Cross. To complete the cycle, today the
great-great-granddaughter of King Tawhiao, the Maori Queen
who has descended from the stormy, war-ridden King movement of the 1850s–60s:

> 'knows that Maoris will come to her courtyard on great occasions,
> knows that Governors, Prime Ministers, diplomats, high church-
> men will pay respects at Turangawaewae.'[1]

In a world obsessed by problems of colour and race, *Pakeha*
and Maori are now beginning to appreciate each other's cultural
qualities and the contribution they can make to the development of their nation. They are all New Zealanders.

[1] 'In Our Time 1870–1970', *The Auckland Star Centennial Supplement.*

APPENDIX I

The New Zealand Cross

This decoration was instituted by an Order-in-Council by Sir George Bowen at Government House, Wellington, on 10 March, 1869, for award to members of the Militia, Volunteers and Armed Constabulary who particularly distinguished themselves by bravery in action or devotion to duty. It is clear that Colonel George Whitmore had much to do with its instigation as he writes in his book that he pressed for such a decoration to 'raise the tone' and give a 'higher inducement' to his colonial soldiers, and he mentions, as he paused before moving over the swamps of Te Ngaere in south Taranaki in 1869, of presenting the award to men he had recommended.

The New Zealand Government's initiative in setting up this decoration considerably embarrassed and nettled the Imperial Government, who had not been consulted, and so the Queen was unaware. However, faced with this colonial *fait accompli*, the Secretary of State for the Colonies could only content himself with acidly informing Sir George Bowen that he had overstepped his authority while going on to say that 'in the very exceptional circumstances, however, the Queen had been pleased to sanction the institution of the decoration'.

The New Zealand Cross consists of a silver Maltese cross with a gold star on each limb. In the centre, in a circle within a wreath of laurel in gold, are the words 'New Zealand'. The Cross is surmounted by a crown in gold which is attached by a ring and a V to a silver bar ornamented with gold laurel leaves, through which the ribbon passes. The ribbon, $1\frac{1}{2}$ inches, is crimson. As the New Zealand Cross was awarded only to twenty-three officers and men for bravery in the Maori Wars and has not been used since, it is a unique and rare decoration. On 17 December, 1969, the New Zealand Cross of Tom Adamson, complete with his New Zealand campaign medal, was sold in London for £1,700. The sturdy Tom Adamson won his award during the ambush of 7 May, 1869, when Whitmore was penetrating the Urewera mountains, and Adamson was severely wounded, among others, and Taranaki Jim killed.

Awards of the New Zealand Cross

1. Trooper Antonio Rodrigues, Taranaki Mounted Volunteers, at Poutoko on 2 October, 1863, and Kaitake, Taranaki, 11 March, 1864.

2. Lieutenant-Colonel Thomas McDonnell, New Zealand Militia, particularly for his services during the Waikato campaign, 1863–64, and later in Wanganui, the East Coast and south Taranaki.

3. Captain Francis Mace, Taranaki Militia, notably at Kaitikara River, 4 June, 1863; at Kaitake, 11 March, 1864; and Warea, 20 October, 1865.

4. Doctor Isaac Featherston, Superintendent of Wellington Province, for meritorious and intrepid services during Major-General Chute's campaign 1865–66, and especially at Otapawa *pa*, 13 January, 1866.

5. Sergeant Samuel Austin, Wanganui Volunteers, at Putahi *pa*, South, 7 January, 1866, and Keteonetea, 17 October, 1866 (at Putahi, Austin carried Thomas McDonnell, wounded in the foot, from the field, and at Keteonetea he rescued the severely-wounded William McDonnell just as he was about to be tomahawked).

6. Ensign Henry Northcroft, Patea Rangers, at Pungarehu, south Taranaki, 2 October, 1866, and Tirotiro Moana, November, 1866.

7. Cornet Harry Wrigg, Bay of Plenty Cavalry Volunteers, for carrying despatches through hostile country between Opotiki and Tauranga, East Coast, 29 June, 1867.

8. Major Kepa Te Rangihiwinui, Wanganui Native Contingent, at Moturoa, 7 November, 1868.

9. Inspector John Roberts, Armed Constabulary, at Moturoa (his previous distinguished conduct at second Te Ngutu-o-te-Manu was also recalled).

10. Constable Henare Kepa Te Ahururu, 1 Division Armed Constabulary, at Moturoa.

11. Major Ropata Wahawaha, Ngatiporou Native Contingent, for both first and second attacks on Ngapata, December, 1868.

12. Sub-Inspector George Preece, Armed Constabulary, for the first attack on Ngapata.

13. Constable Solomon Black, 1 Division Armed Constabulary, at Ngapata, January, 1869.

14. Constable Benjamin Biddle, 1 Division Armed Constabulary, at Ngapata.

15. Trooper William Lingard, Kai-Iwi Cavalry Volunteers, at Tauranga-ika, 28 December, 1868.

16. Sergeant Christopher Maling, Corps of Guides, for most valuable and efficient services as Sergeant of the Corps of Guides, but especially for daring reconnaissance after Titokowaru had left Tauranga-ika.

17. Assistant Surgeon Samuel Walker, Armed Constabulary, especially at Otautu, 13 March, 1869.

18. Sergeant Richard Shepherd, Armed Constabulary, also at Otautu.

19. Constable George Hill, 1 Division Armed Constabulary, at the siege of Mohaka *pa*, Hawke's Bay, 10 April, 1869.

20. Private Thomas Adamson, Corps of Guides, Urewera mountains ambush, 7 May, 1869.

21. Cornet Angus Smith, Bay of Plenty Cavalry Volunteers, at Opepe, 7 June, 1869.

22. Sergeant Arthur Carkeek, Armed Constabulary, for carriage of vital information through hostile country from Ohinemutu, Rotorua, to Tapapa, 8 February, 1870.

23. Captain Gilbert Mair, for his pursuit and defeat of Te Kooti in the Rotorua district, February, 1870.

APPENDIX II

Victoria Crosses awarded during the Maori Wars

1. Leading Seaman William Odgers, HMS *Niger*, at Kaipopo *pa*, Taranaki, 28 March, 1860.
2. Colour-Sergeant John Lucas, 40th Regiment, at Te Arei *pa*, Taranaki, 18 March, 1861.
3. Colour-Sergeant Edward Mackenna, 65th Regiment, near Cameron on the Waikato, 7 September, 1863.
4. Lance-Corporal John Ryan, 65th Regiment, near Cameron, 7 September, 1863.
5. Ensign John Down, 57th Regiment, at Poutoko, Taranaki, 2 October, 1863.
6 Drummer Dudley Stagpool, 57th Regiment, at Poutoko, 2 October, 1863.
7. Assistant Surgeon William Temple, Royal Artillery, at Rangiriri, Waikato, 20 November, 1863.
8. Lieutenant Arthur Pickard, C Battery 4th Brigade, Royal Artillery, at Rangiriri, 20 November, 1863.
9. Major Charles Heaphy, Auckland Militia, at Mangapiko Creek, Waikato, 11 February, 1864.
10. Lieutenant-Colonel John McNeill, 107th Bengal Infantry, near Te Awamutu, Waikato, 30 March, 1864.
11. Assistant Surgeon William Manley, Royal Artillery, at the Gate *Pa*, Tauranga, 29 April, 1864.
12. Captain of the Foretop Samuel Mitchell, HMS *Harrier*, at the Gate *Pa*, 29 April, 1864.

254

13. Captain Frederick Smith, 43rd Regiment, at Te Ranga, Tauranga, 21 June, 1864.

14. Sergeant John Murray, 68th Regiment, at Te Ranga, 21 June, 1864.

15. Captain Hugh Shaw, 18th Regiment, at Nukumaru, Wanganui, on 24 January, 1865.

APPENDIX III

British Regiments which served in the Maori Wars

Twelve Regiments of the Line saw active service in New Zealand during the Maori Wars.

1845–46

> 58th Regiment (later The Northamptonshire Regiment, now The Royal Anglian Regiment).
>
> 96th Regiment (later The 2nd Battalion, The Manchester Regiment, now The King's Regiment).
>
> 99th Regiment (later The 2nd Battalion, The Wiltshire Regiment (Duke of Edinburgh's), now The Duke of Edinburgh's Royal Regiment (Berkshire and Wiltshire)).

1860–66

> 12th Regiment (later The Suffolk Regiment, now The Royal Anglian Regiment).
>
> 14th Regiment (later The West Yorkshire Regiment (The Prince of Wales' Own), now The Prince of Wales's Own Regiment of Yorkshire).
>
> 18th Regiment (later The Royal Irish Regiment, disbanded 1922).
>
> 43rd Regiment (later The Oxfordshire and Buckinghamshire Light Infantry, now The Royal Greenjackets).
>
> 50th Regiment (later The Queen's Own (Royal West Kent Regiment), subsequently The Queen's Own Buffs (The

Royal Kent Regiment) and now The Queen's Regiment).

57th Regiment (later The Middlesex Regiment, now The Queen's Regiment).

65th Regiment* (later The York and Lancaster Regiment, disbanded 1969).

68th Regiment (later The Durham Light Infantry, now The Light Infantry).

70th Regiment (later The East Surrey Regiment, now The Queen's Regiment).

Another notable British Army participant was C Field Battery 4th Brigade Royal Artillery, now in the Regular Army as 94 (New Zealand) Medium Battery, Royal Artillery.

Sections of the ubiquitous Royal Engineers were well to the fore in the primitive communications and wild terrain of the campaigning areas and a major achievement of this versatile Corps was the setting up of a field telegraph network to link up posts in the Taranaki and Waikato. This military use of the infant telegraph was at least as early as the American Civil War, where it was proving its great possibilities.

The Military Train served as cavalry, as they did in the Indian Mutiny, and the Commissariat Staff Corps efficiently overcame the many problems of supply. Both were forerunners of the Royal Army Service Corps, now the Royal Corps of Transport.

* Also took part in the end of the 1845–46 War.

BIBLIOGRAPHY

The New Zealand Wars and the Pioneering Period, Volumes I and II, James Cowan, FRGS (Government Printer, Wellington, 1923).

New Zealand's First War, T. Lindsay Buick (Government Printer, Wellington, 1926).

Reminiscences of the War in New Zealand, Thomas W. Gudgeon (Sampson Low, Marston, Searle & Rivington, London, 1879).

The Last Maori War in New Zealand Under the Self-Reliant Policy, Major-General Sir George Whitmore, KCMG, MLC, NZ Militia (Sampson, Low, Marston & Company, London, 1902).

The War in New Zealand, William Fox (Smith, Elder and Co, London, 1866).

Bush Fighting, Major-General Sir James Alexander, KCLS, FRSE (Sampson Low, Marston, Low and Searle, London, 1873).

The Story of New Zealand, W. H. Oliver (Faber and Faber, London, 1960).

The Story of New Zealand, A. H. Reed (A. H. & A. W. Reed Ltd, Wellington, and Phoenix House Ltd, London, 1955).

United Service Magazine (Hurst and Blackett, London, 1862).

The Story of the Durham Light Infantry, S. G. P. Ward (Thomas Nelson & Sons).

Historical Records of the Forty-Third Regiment, Sir Richard Levinge, Bart. (W. Clowes & Sons, London, 1868).

History of the Manchester Regiment, Colonel H. C. Wylly, CB (Forster Groom & Co Ltd, London, 1923).

The History of the Northamptonshire Regiment 1742–1934, Lieutenant-Colonel Russell Gurney (Gale & Polden, Aldershot, 1935).

The York and Lancaster Regiment, 1758–1919, Colonel H. C. Wylly, CB (1930).

The Campaigns and History of the Royal Irish Regiment 1684–1902, Lieutenant-Colonel G. Le M. Gretton (William Blackwood and Sons, Edinburgh and London, 1911).

Historical Records of the Fifty-Seventh, 1755–1878, Lieutenant-General H. J. Warre, CB (W. Mitchell & Co, London, 1878).

The South Lancashire Regiment, Colonel B. R. Mullaly (The White Swan Press, Bristol).

Historical Records of the 14th Regiment, Captain H. O'Donnell (A. H. Swiss, Devonport, 1892).

The History of the 50th, Colonel Fyler (Chapman and Hall Ltd, London, 1895).

History of the 31st Foot and 70th Foot, Colonel Hugh W. Pearse, DSO (Spottiswoode, Ballantyne & Co Ltd, London, 1916).

History of the 12th (The Suffolk) Regiment 1685–1913, Lieutenant-Colonel E. A. H. Webb (Spottiswoode & Co Ltd, London, 1914).

The Strangest War, Edgar Holt (Putnam & Company Ltd, London, 1962).

History of the British Army, Vol. 13, Sir John Fortescue.

The Wiltshire Regiment, Tom Gibson (Leo Cooper Ltd, London, 1969).

In Our Time 1870–1970, The Auckland Star Centennial Supplement.

The Story of the Bands of the British Imperial Forces in New Zealand 1845–70, Stanley P. Newcomb.

New Zealand, Harold Miller (Hutchinson's University Library, 1950).

Racial Conflict in New Zealand 1814–1865, Harold Miller (Blackwood and Paul, Sydney, 1966).

INDEX

Maori names have been listed under the first letter of the first name, eg, Wiremu Kingi is under 'W'; Te Rauparaha is under 'T'.